Discourse in Late Modernity

Discourse in Late Modernity

Rethinking Critical Discourse Analysis

Lilie Chouliaraki and Norman Fairclough

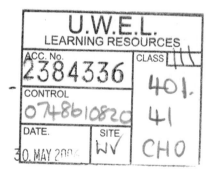
Edinburgh University Press

© Lilie Chouliaraki and Norman Fairclough, 1999

Edinburgh University Press
22 George Square, Edinburgh

Reprinted 2001, 2002, 2004, 2005

Typeset in Garamond
by Norman Tilley Graphics, Northampton,
and printed and bound in Great Britain
by Antony Rowe Ltd, Chippenham, Wiltshire

A CIP record for this book is available from
the British Library

ISBN 0 7486 1082 0 (paperback)

The right of Lilie Chouliaraki and Norman Fairclough
to be identified as authors of this work
has been asserted in accordance with
the Copyright, Designs and Patents Act 1988.

Contents

Acknowledgements

We are grateful to the following people for reading and commenting on parts of the book at various stages: Erzsébet Barát, Basil Bernstein, Staf Callewaert, Bessie Dendrinos, Frans Gregersen, Ruqaiya Hasan, John Haywood, Marianne Winther Jorgensen, Louise Phillips, Joan Pujolar, Andrew Sayer and Ruth Wodak. Lilie acknowledges the financial support of the Danish Research Agency for the Humanities, and thanks the Institute for Dialectology, Copenhagen University, for hosting her research. She would like to thank Jon for his invaluable support throughout the writing of this book, and Daphne and Amanda for always reminding her of the wonderful continuities between theory and practical life.

COPYRIGHT ACKNOWLEDGEMENTS

Series Preface

Critical Discourse Analysis (henceforth CDA) starts from the perception of discourse (language but also other forms of semiosis, such as visual images) as an element of social practices, which constitutes other elements as well as being shaped by them. Social questions are therefore in part questions about discourse – for instance, the question of power in social class, gender and race relations is partly a question of discourse. And careful linguistic and semiotic analysis of texts (e.g. newspaper articles or advertisements) and interactions (e.g. conversations or interviews) therefore has a part to play in social analysis.

CDA has attracted a great deal of interest in the past twenty years or so, not only amongst specialists in linguistics and language studies but also within other social science disciplines. Just to give one example: the Department of Urban Studies at Glasgow University held well-attended and successful conferences on discourse in relation to aspects of urban policy in 1998 and 1999, where many of the presentations drew upon CDA. The current interest in CDA reflects, I believe, an upsurge in critique of language within contemporary society. There is widespread cynicism about the rhetoric of advertising and the simulated personalness ('have a nice day') of people working in impersonal commercial organisations, and a developing consciousness of linguistic forms of racism and sexism.

Why this enhanced critical consciousness about language? Language (and more generally, semiosis) has become an increasingly salient element of contemporary social practices. For instance, language has become more important economically. With the shift to 'knowledge-based' economies, many of the 'goods' that are produced have a linguistic or partly linguistic character – the language used by service workers is part of the service they provide, and the products of the advertising industry are semiotic products. Moreover, key areas of social life (such as politics) have become increasingly centred upon the mass media, and those involved in these areas have consequently become increasingly self-conscious about the language they use. These changes have led to an increase in conscious interventions to shape linguistic and semiotic elements of social practices in accordance with economic, organisational and political objectives. Language has become subject to the wider contemporary preoccupation with design, it has become 'technologised' in the sense that it is increasingly seen as another material to which social technologies can be applied in the search for greater profit or better performance. Enhanced critical consciousness of language is at least in part a response to these colonisations of language.

It is clear that these tendencies are growing. A critical perspective on discourse is therefore a socially and politically important element in contemporary social and language study. The 'Critical Discourse Analysis' series launched by Edinburgh University Press is on one level a recognition of this need. It also aims to contribute to the development and consolidation of CDA as a field of study. In the latter regard, the series is intended to address a number of themes and needs. First, the development of CDA has raised a number of theoretical problems, some of which need more sustained attention than they have so far received – for instance the theorisation of discourse as an element of social practice, or the relationship between discourse and ideology. More generally, a debate is needed about the relationship between CDA and critical and post-structuralist social theory. Second, the series is intended to reflect the considerable range of social issues and problems where CDA has a contribution to make – in the media, politics, law, the workplace and so forth. Third, we hope the series will encourage authors to explore the exciting possibilities for working across disciplines, as well as the problems of interdisciplinarity. The series encourages books written by two or more authors based in different disciplines, as well as books co-authored by discourse analysts and practitioners in the domain in focus, e.g. journalists, lawyers or doctors. Fourth, a number of relatively distinct positions and approaches have been developed within CDA, and the series aims to reflect that range and explore relationships between them. Fifth, the series is international in scope, bringing together work by scholars who are developing and using CDA in various parts of the world.

Norman Fairclough
Series Editor

Chapter 1

Discourse in late modernity

Critical discourse analysis (henceforth CDA[1]) has established itself internationally over the past twenty years or so as a field of cross-disciplinary teaching and research which has been widely drawn upon in the social sciences and the humanities (for example, in sociology, geography, history and media studies), and has inspired critical language teaching at various levels and in various domains. But the theories it rests upon and the methods it uses have not been as explicitly and systematically spelt out as they might have been.[2] Our main aim in this book is to contribute to remedying this by 'grounding' CDA, establishing its theoretical bases, in two directions.

First, we locate it within a version of critical social science, and specify the onto-logical and epistemological claims it is based upon (i.e., its assumptions about what social life is, and how we come to know about it). This is centrally the role of Chapter 2, which sets out a view of social life as 'social practices', and of discourse as one of a number of elements of social practices which are in a dialectical relationship. Part of the argument here is that the opposition between 'interpretivist' and 'structuralist' social science needs to be transcended in favour of what Bourdieu alternately calls 'constructivist structuralism' or 'structuralist constructivism' (Bourdieu and Wacquant 1992: 11) – a way of seeing and researching social life as both constrained by social structures, and an active process of production which transforms social structures.

In Chapters 3 and 4 we continue with the theme of combining interpretivist and structuralist orientations, but now with specific attention to discourse. We present a dialectical view of discourse and framework for critical analysis of discourse, and illustrate its use in research on late modernity through a reanalysis of texts previously analysed by the feminist sociologist Dorothy Smith (Smith 1990). Readers should note that while we set out a version of CDA especially in Chapter 4, this book is not an introduction to CDA; such introductions exist elsewhere (Fairclough 1989, 1992a, 1995a).

Second, we locate CDA within critical research on social change in contemporary (we follow for example Giddens 1990 in calling it 'late modern') society, and specify its particular contribution to this research. In Chapter 5 we discuss different 'narra-tives' or general accounts of late modernity within critical research (for example, the narrative of late modernity as the restructuring of capital on a global basis), with particular attention to what they say or imply about the role of language in contemporary social change. On this basis we suggest a research agenda for CDA – language issues arising from research on late modernity, which CDA can take further than this research has.

Chapter 6 draws upon the work of Bourdieu and Bernstein to localise the view of language in late modernity set out in Chapter 5 within specific social fields (for example, education) and relationships between fields. We show with respect to these theories how CDA can figure within properly 'transdisciplinary' (as opposed to merely 'interdisciplinary') research, involving a dialogue (or 'conversation') between theories in which the logic of one theory is 'put to work' within another without the latter being reduced to the former.

The emphasis in the theories discussed in Chapter 6 is on the structural constraint of social life, whereas in Chapter 7 the emphasis shifts to the 'openness' (creativity, contingency) of social life. Our main theoretical reference point here is the 'post-Marxism' theory of discourse of Laclau and Mouffe (1985), but we differ from them in arguing that people stand in more or less open relationships to discourse, and relationships which are open in different ways, depending on their social positioning. We discuss the postmodern focusing of difference and the contingency of the social as a response to a 'totalitarian' late modern 'closing of the universe of discourse' (Marcuse 1964; Lyotard 1984), and argue that rather than just asserting difference, critical social research and CDA need a focus on working across and dialoguing across difference.

The final chapter of the book discusses the grounding of CDA in a different direction – that of linguistics. The chapter focuses on systemic functional linguistics (SFL – Halliday 1978, 1994a; Hasan 1996; Davies and Ravelli 1992) as the major linguistic theory which is closest to the perspectives of critical social research. In addition to a discussion of how CDA can strengthen its analysis of language, we hope to initiate a dialogue with SFL in this chapter, arguing that CDA and SFL can be seen as complementary to each other.

Our aim in this opening chapter is threefold. Firstly, to establish the need for critical analysis of late modern society, and the place of CDA within such critical analysis. We also discuss the institutional conditions for such a critique in terms of the status of universities as a public sphere. Secondly, to give a preliminary sense of the agenda for CDA within the critique of late modernity by analysing an example of advertising discourse. We have chosen advertising because we see it as a key cultural practice of late modernity which condenses many themes relevant to our agenda. Thirdly, to specify the social scientific status of CDA: is it a theory, a method, or both?

LATE MODERNITY: THE CASE FOR CDA

Critical research on language is certainly not new – for instance, Volosinov's (1973) influential Marxist theory of language dates from the 1920s – but it has emerged as a distinct and reasonably substantial position, especially in Western Europe (though also for instance in Latin America) since the 1970s. Those who worked within 'critical linguistics' (Fowler et al. 1979; Hodge and Kress 1993) and other groups at that time were very much driven by a sense of the social and political importance of a critical perspective on language in contemporary society. The social changes of the past twenty years or so have arguably if anything increased the need for this. Of course there are many accounts of these changes, and there is no single account which we can take as authoritative. In Chapter 4 we shall refer to several such accounts (or 'narratives'), and argue that CDA should be seen as contributing to a field of critical research on late modernity, not a particular theory or narrative. But for present purposes we have put together one narrative which incorporates a number of prominent themes in this field of research.

The past two decades or so have been a period of profound economic and social transformation on a global scale. Economically, there has been a relative shift from 'Fordist' mass production and consumption of goods to 'flexible accumulation'. 'Flexibility' has become a key concept and practice which covers both intensive technological innovation in the diversification of production, and the 'flexibility' of labour where short-term and part-time working are increasingly the pattern (Harvey 1990). At the same time, units of production are increasingly transnational. Politically, 'neo-liberalism' has established itself internationally. These deep economic changes have been described as introducing a new 'post-industrial' era in the organisation of modern capitalism (Bell 1978). The cultural transformations that are widely referred to as 'postmodernism' are, according to some social theorists, the cultural facet of these economic changes (Beck, Giddens and Lash 1994; Giddens 1991; Harvey 1990, 1996; Jameson 1991; Lash and Urry 1993). Advances in information technology, mainly communications media, underlie both economic and cultural transformations, opening up new forms of experience and knowledge and new possibilities of relationships with faraway others via television or the internet. Postmodernist theory has fixed upon the consequential economic and cultural centrality of signs detached from specific material locations and circulating across boundaries of space and time. According to Baudrillard, for instance, reality has been displaced by the 'simulacra' constituted by these circulating signs: 'whereas representation tries to absorb simulation by interpreting it as false representation, simulation envelops the whole edifice of representation as itself a simulacrum' (Baudrillard 1983). We refer to this new phase of social life as 'late modernity' (Jameson 1991; Giddens 1990, 1991, 1994a).

These social changes create new possibilities and opportunities for many people. They also cause considerable disruption and suffering for societies, communities and individuals – in destroying long-established industries (such as coal-mining in Britain), in forcing millions of people to migrate, and so forth. They have also profoundly affected our sense of self and of place, causing considerable confusion and what has been widely referred to as a loss of meaning (Baudrillard 1983, 1993; Featherstone 1995). Whether beneficial or detrimental, they are widely perceived as inevitable. The global scale and sheer complexity of contemporary economic and social processes increase the sense of helplessness and incomprehension. A pervasive postmodernist claim is that there is little that practical action can do to change this condition (Baudrillard 1983, 1988; Lyotard 1984, 1990). Yet these changes are at least in part the outcome of particular strategies pursued by particular people for particular interests within a particular system – all of which might be different. Social forms that are produced by people and can be changed by people are being seen as if they were part of nature. There is a compelling need for a critical theorisation and analysis of late modernity which can not only illuminate the new world that is emerging but also show what unrealised alternative directions exist – how aspects of this new world which enhance human life can be accentuated, how aspects which are detrimental to it can be changed or mitigated.

Thus the basic motivation for critical social science is to contribute to an awareness of what is, how it has come to be, and what it might become, on the basis of which people may be able to make and remake their lives (Calhoun 1995). And this is also the motivation for CDA. One interesting feature of social scientific theorisations and analyses of the transformations of late modernity, from various theoretical perspectives, is that they emphasise that these transformations are to a significant degree (though certainly not exclusively) transformations in language and discourse (Habermas 1984, 1987a; Giddens 1990, 1991; Harvey 1996; Thrift 1996). These theories create a space for critical analysis of discourse as a fundamental element in the critical theorisation and analysis of late modernity, but since they are not specifically oriented to language they do not properly fill that space. This is where CDA has a contribution to make.

It is an important characteristic of the economic, social and cultural changes of late modernity that they exist as *discourses* as well as processes that are taking place outside discourse, and that the processes that are taking place outside discourse are substantively shaped by these discourses. For example, 'flexible accumulation' as a new economic form has been 'talked into being' in the substantial literature on the new capitalism – including the works of management 'gurus' which fill the shelves of airport and railway bookshops internationally – as well as being put into practice through practical changes in organisations. Harvey (1990) disputes the claim that 'flexibility' is just a discourse – and an ideology. But although, as he argues, flexibility is an organisational reality, and so the discourse of the new capitalism is in that sense extra-discursively grounded, nevertheless the discourse shapes and reshapes the organisational reality and is thus socially constitutive (as Harvey 1996 recognises). Bourdieu (1998b) explains this process: a 'flexible' global capitalism is already partly a reality, but it is also backed by social forces (for example, the banks) which aim to make it more of a reality, and the discourse of flexibility is one of the resources they have (specifically, a symbolic resource) for achieving this. It follows that a critical analysis of the discourse of flexibility (and other economic discourses) is a quite fundamental part of – though only a part of – a critical analysis of late modern economic change. Such an analysis would have to attend to questions of power. Because of the potency of economic discourses in shaping economic realities, there are considerable economic interests at stake in achieving the hegemony of this discourse (and so the marginalisation of others) within the economic discursive field.

The discourse of flexibility is just one discourse among many economic discourses with no inherent privilege in representing economic realities (which does not mean that all these discourses are equally good – see Chapter 7); achieving hegemony for this discourse means achieving a misperception of its arbitrariness (in that sense) so that it comes to be seen as transparently reflecting economic realities rather than constructing them in a particular way. This is a mystifying effect of unequal relations of power on language – it is discourse working ideologically.

But what we have just referred to as the 'organisational reality' is itself also partly made up of changes in the social use of language in work. Language is relevant not only in the discursive construction of the changing practices of late modernity – what is changing in these practices is in part also language. For example, 'flexibility' in the practices of the workplace is partly a matter of the increasing prominence of 'team work', and 'team work' is partly constituted by new forms of dialogue which for instance transcend old divisions between shopfloor and management.[3] So flexibility *is* in part new ways of using language, and critical analysis of new economic forms needs to be in part critical analysis of language. Again there are questions of power. There are powerful economic interests at stake in getting workers to change their language practices, and the increasingly large category of 'face' workers for instance (such as shop assistants or receptionists) have little choice in the routinised simulation of conversational spontaneity (even to the point in some cases of having to talk to each customer as if he or she were a close friend), and little opportunity to express an opinion on whether this colonisation of the communicative arts of everyday life (to put the point contentiously) might have damaging consequences for the latter – perhaps in undermining trust and creating a heightened suspicion about motives. Thrift (1996, ch. 6) discusses the example of the contemporary international financial system as an intersection of power, money and communicative practices partly geared to engineering interpersonal relationships which minimise risk and maximise trust between participants.

The plurality and fragmentation of late modern social life has been highlighted in the literature on postmodernity with its emphasis on social difference. The processes involved here are again substantively linguistic in nature: fragmentation and differentiation are partly constituted in a proliferation of languages (using that term in a loose sense to include genres, discourses, and also 'languages proper'). For instance, whereas analyses of the public sphere – the social space where issues of social and political concern are openly and freely addressed by groups of citizens outside the structures of the state – in earlier modern society identified a single, unitary public sphere (Habermas 1989), recent analyses of late modern society (particularly feminist ones – see for example Fraser 1989, 1992; Flax 1990) suggest that there are many different public spheres, centred for example on social movements like feminism and ecologism. The crucial insight, however, in Habermas's analysis of the bourgeois public sphere was that a public sphere is constituted as a particular way of using language in public, and the proliferation of public spheres (as a 'sphere of publics' – Calhoun 1995) is a proliferation of ways of using language in public. This brings us to the heart of the contemporary political problem of democracy. In a world which is increasingly dominated by forces which are global or international in scale and outside existing democratic structures, and which is a pluralistic world where the recognition of difference is imperative, effective political intervention by citizens depends upon dialogue across difference on local, national and international (global) levels. If one central plank of democracy in late modernity needs to be the recognition of difference and different public spheres, another needs to be a commitment to dialogue across difference (Benhabib 1992; Giddens 1994a, 'Introduction'; Fraser 1989, 1992, 1997; Calhoun 1992). In order to act together, people need to talk together. But we should stress that the concept of dialogue does not presuppose consensus: dialogue involves both space for voicing difference (including polemically) and a search without guarantees for alliances across difference – for a voice that does not suppress difference in the name of essential identities (be they gender, ethnic or class identities) but emerges as a voice in common on specific issues. Critical analysis of discourse, both in the sense of critique of what is and discernment of what could be, is again quite central.

It is important to recognise the social import of discourse without reducing social life to discourse – a reductionism characteristic of postmodern views of the social world that is a constant risk and temptation for discourse analysts. CDA has set out a dialectical view of the relationship between discourse and other, extra-discursive, facets of the social world (for example, in Fairclough 1992a). Along similar lines, Harvey (1996) proposes a dialectical view of the social process in which discourse is one 'moment' among six: discourse/language; power; social relations; material practices; institutions/rituals; and beliefs/values/desires. Each moment internalises all of the others – so that discourse is a form of power, a mode of formation of beliefs/values/desires, an institution, a mode of social relating, a material practice. Conversely, power, social relations, material practices, institutions, beliefs, etc. are in part discourse. The heterogeneity within each moment – including discourse – reflects its simultaneous determination ('overdetermination') by all of the other moments. The question of how flows – 'translations' – occur across moments becomes crucial and is a central concern for CDA, as well as for any critical social analysis. We shall return to this framework in Chapter 2.

THE NEED FOR A CRITICAL DISCOURSE ANALYSIS

CDA belongs to a tradition of language critique which can be traced back to classical antiquity and which is present in many modern academic disciplines (Stubbs 1997; Toolan 1997). What is distinctive about CDA within this tradition however is that it brings critical social science and linguistics (specifically, Systemic Functional Linguistics – see Chapter 7) together within a single theoretical and analytical framework, setting up a dialogue between them. Having said that, the contemporary field of critical analysis of discourse is itself quite diverse (Jørgensen and Phillips 1999). One might reasonably include within it Said's analysis of the discourse of orientalism (Said 1978) which is based upon Foucault's theory of discourse but which, unlike Foucault, also includes, as Stubbs (1996, 1997) points out, some analysis of texts, though without drawing on any linguistic theory. One might also include other post-structuralist and postmodernist critiques of discourse (see Simons and Billig 1994). Even within approaches which call themselves 'critical discourse analysis' there is a considerable diversity of positions (Fairclough and Wodak 1997; Fowler 1996; Gouveia 1997; Toolan 1997). In this book we focus upon a version of CDA which sets up a particular form of dialogue between critical social theory and linguistics, focusing, except for Chapter 8, upon the former. We offer this as a contribution to CDA and to the broader contemporary field of critique of discourse.

There are other approaches to discourse analysis which are critical of CDA, the most influential of which is conversation analysis; we refer specifically to a recent critique of CDA by Schegloff (1997 – see Wetherell 1998 for a reply). Schegloff argues that 'serious critical analysis of discourse presupposes serious formal analysis (of discourse), and is addressed to its product', and that furthermore 'formal' analysis of discourse (i.e., conversation analysis) should resort only to those social categories in its analysis which are manifestly oriented to by the participants in their discourse. For instance, in analysis of a conversation between a woman and a man, the category of gender should be used only if it is manifestly oriented to in the conversation. Schegloff is suggesting that CDA often applies sociological categories to discourse when formal analysis does not justify doing so, and thereby imposes its own pre-occupations on the discourse in a 'kind of theoretical imperialism' which rides roughshod over the preoccupations of the participants in the discourse.

We want to make two observations in response to this. First, that all analysts are operating in theoretical practices whose concerns are different from the practical concerns of people as participants, and all analysis brings the analysts' theoretical preoccupations – and categories – to bear on the discourse. In the case of conversation analysis, the theoretical preoccupation is with showing that conversation makes sense in its own terms – Schegloff admits to holding that view (1997: 171) – and the categories include categories like 'preference organisation' and 'adjacency pair'. Second, that the analyst's theoretical preoccupations determine not only what data is selected for analysis but also how it is perceived. This includes how it is historically framed – for instance, Schegloff in his analysis of an example in his paper (a telephone conversation between separated parents) does not go beyond the historical framing of the segment he focuses on in the telephone conversation it occurs within; he resists a framing in a general history of gender relations on the grounds that it does not fit with 'the relevancies to which the participants show themselves to be oriented' in their talk, and does not for instance consider a framing in terms of the particular history of relations between these people; it further includes how this historical framing determines what the analyst sees in the discourse – even Schegloff's fine-grained analysis fails to mention certain details which might lead to a different understanding of the talk within a different historical framing.[4] What we are contesting is the idea that a formal analysis which excludes theoretical pre-occupations of the analyst is possible. Any discourse is open to no end of formal analysis, and all forms of formal analysis are theoretically informed. This is not an argument that 'anything goes' – on the contrary, we shall argue that CDA should be answerable to text in a significant sense, but Schegloff's version of this is indefensible.

The critical project has come under attack from postmodernists on the grounds that it rests upon unsustainable meta-narratives or 'grand narratives' about social life such as Marxism, and assigns to (social) scientific discourses of the social a privilege over other discourses which is ungrounded and indeed elitist. Any claim to such a status for science is to be regarded as a bid for power – science is, in Lyotard's terms, just one language game amongst others, even if it attempts to rhetorically disclaim its particularity, and language games are 'incommensurable' and therefore not open to dialogue or translation (Lyotard 1984, 1990). The implication is that social agents are enclosed within particular language games, and Rorty argues along similar lines that intellectuals are confined within their own private space and properly excluded from public space (Rorty 1985). Rorty's intellectual is a poet capable of radical thought for playful 'redescriptions' of the social world – the conceptual and political are subordinated to the aesthetic (Fraser 1989). Postmodernists certainly do critique discourse, but many take an extreme relativist and reflexivist position which treats all discourse as equally suspect, including the discourse of critique (Simons and Billig 1994). The key debate here is realism versus relativism (Parker 1998). We argue in Chapter 6 that although epistemic relativism must be accepted – that all discourses are socially constructed relative to the social positions people are in – this does not entail accepting judgemental relativism – that all discourses are equally good (Bhaskar 1979).

INSTITUTIONAL CONDITIONS FOR CRITICAL SOCIAL RESEARCH

Our own primary field of activity is in universities in Britain and Denmark. We believe that the academic critique of late modernity including language critique depends upon the universities functioning as a public sphere. Yet universities these days are under increasing pressure to operate as a market that is shaped by its service relation to other markets – more in Britain than in Denmark, but increasingly in the latter too. The tradition of the universities as a public sphere still survives, though in an embattled form (Giroux 1997) – but then, it always has been. We do not deny that universities have certain responsibilities towards the economic sphere in their research and their teaching, but we reject the current attempt to reduce them to a role of servicing what those who control the economy, aided and abetted by those in government, see as its needs (in the case of Britain, see The National Committee of Inquiry into Higher Education 1997). A battle is on to preserve universities as a public sphere, and to preserve and develop critical voices. It is a significant part of the battle for democracy within late modernity referred to above. The enemy in this battle is a form of philistinism in which the prestige and survival of academic institutions, the professional advancement of individuals, and the servicing of the demands of those who hold the purse strings become the driving force. We are conscious of using a military metaphor here, but we feel that an open and polemical stand is much needed and long overdue – but that polemic needs to be framed within a dialogue oriented to building an alliance for change. It needs to be an international dialogue, because the shackling of universities to economies is happening on an international scale – though as Mouzelis (1998) points out with respect to Greece, in some countries universities are as much or more shackled to the state as to the economy.

But effective critique depends not only upon the vitality of the universities as a public sphere but also upon an open and dynamic relationship between the universities and other public spheres. Contemporary pressures on universities again create obstacles in tying universities ever more tightly into relationships with the economic system and the state in a way which makes it difficult for them to sustain relationships with social groups, movements and struggles outside these systems (in the 'lifeworld', in Habermas's terms – see Chapter 5). Claims that social critique carried out by academics is elitist have substance in so far as universities are cut off from other public spheres, but the solution to that problem is not the disastrous abandonment of critique which some of those who make this criticism seem to seek (see the discussion above of postmodern critiques of critique); it is the admittedly difficult but not impossible task of opening up channels (critiques of the insulation of the academic field from wider society are legion within the Marxist tradition, and more recently within feminism – see Cameron 1995; Fraser 1989). This involves recognising that critique (including critique of language) is not just academic but a part of social life and social struggles, that critical social science is informed by and indebted to social movements and struggles, and that it can in turn contribute to them providing there is a real dialogue across public spheres. CDA, like other critical social sciences, therefore needs to be reflexive and self-critical about its own institutional position and all that goes with it: how it conducts research, how it envisages the objectives and outcomes of research, what relationships researchers have to the people whose social lives they are analysing, even what sort of language books and papers are written in. The relationship of CDA to other public spheres outside the university (as well as to other social sciences within it) can be seen as one aspect of a strategy of alliances – we agree with Fraser and Nicholson (1990) that political practice is becoming increasingly 'a matter of alliances rather than one of unity around a universally shared interest or identity'.

We referred above to the contribution CDA can make to the contemporary problem of democracy – to finding effective forms of public space, effective forms of dialogue across difference. But CDA is relevant not only to the forms of democratic dialogue but also to its themes, its contents: CDA is a matter of democracy in the sense that its aim is to bring into democratic control aspects of the contemporary social use of language which are currently outside democratic control (including the effects of unequal power relations referred to above), to thematise language not only in the public space of the universities but also within the dialogue across public spaces referred to above. Part of its project has been advocating a critical awareness of language as a fundamental element in a language education for a democratic society – fundamental because language is so central to contemporary social life, and to the calculations of and struggles over power, so that no one these days can develop the grasp of their social circumstances which is essential if they are to have any control over them, without a critical awareness of how language figures within them (Clark et al. 1990, 1991; Fairclough 1992b, forthcoming a; Ivanic 1990).

CRITICAL ANALYSIS OF LATE MODERN DISCOURSE: AN EXAMPLE

We now work though a single sample of contemporary public discourse as a way of introducing some significant characteristics of discourse in late modernity which need to be prominent in CDA's research programme. Taking a single example will inevitably give only a partial picture of CDA's agenda; we address it more systematically in Chapter 5.

The example is an advertisement for *The Big Issue in the North* (Fig. 1.1), the North of England edition of *The Big Issue* which 'was set up in 1991 to give homeless people the chance to make an income. It campaigns on behalf of homeless people and highlights the major social issues of the day.' We shall present our analysis in the form of a series of points about the advertisement.

1. Advertisements advertise commodities, but they are also themselves commodities – the commodities produced in the advertising industry. Both the commodity advertised – a magazine, and its Christmas Appeal – and the advertisement itself are very odd sorts of commodity from the perspective of classical analyses of earlier capitalism (compared with a car or a tube of toothpaste), but they represent an important and growing category of commodities in contemporary capitalism – what we might call cultural commodities.
2. Cultural commodities consist of signs – they are semiotic. What is produced, circulated and consumed in the case of cultural commodities is words and images (a magazine consists of words and images, so does an advertisement). This is not to say that more conventional commodities such as cars do not have a semiotic aspect – material objects as commodities are precisely semioticised, so that for instance the name given to a model of car is calculated as carefully as the technical specifications of its engine. And conversely, magazines are still material objects. What is different about cultural commodities, in terms of Harvey's dialectical view of the social process, is the specific mode of internalisation of the moment of discourse within the material practices of commodity production and exchange – the increased salience of discourse within them (see further Chapter 2).
3. Within this shift language becomes increasingly commodified – it comes to be treated, worked, according to the logic of commodities (Lyotard 1984; Jameson 1991; Fairclough 1992a, 1995b). The concept of 'design' which is pervasively applied to contemporary commodities also applies to semiosis and language – texts like this one are carefully designed to sell (in two senses in the case of advertisements: to sell the goods advertised, and to sell themselves). You might object that (at least some) texts have always been carefully designed, and

Figure 1.1 The Big Issue Christmas Appeal

that is so. What is different is that even socially and politically engaged texts like this one are now specifically subject to *aesthetic* design to make them sell. For example, the heading (*Homeless this Christmas. But not for life.*) seems to us to be structured to catch the reader's attention through two syntactically parallel phrases (the second is an elliptical reduction of *not homeless for life*) conjoined with a contrastive conjunction (*but*) and also contrastive as positive versus negative. The linguistically structured contrast carries a contrast between different discourses: the first phrase is a descriptor of a condition, whereas the second is a declaration or undertaking; the first belongs to a discourse of charitable appeals, the second to a discourse of political mobilisation. The commodification of language in late modernity entails a pervasive primacy for the aesthetic. This is one factor in the mixing of different semiotic modalities (photographs, drawings, diagrams, music, sound effects) that is characteristic of late modern 'texts' (Kress and van Leeuwen 1996) and is illustrated here.

4. The commodification of language is also a primary instance of the 'instrumental' rationality which is predominant in the systems (the economy, the state) which dominate modern society (Habermas 1987a). Instrumental rationality means making everything subservient to maximising the effectivity of institutional systems, whether it is a matter of maximally effective ways of producing or selling commodities, or maximally effective ways of organising or educating people.

5. *The Big Issue in the North* could in principle have avoided advertising altogether, and therefore the pressure it entails to commodify, aestheticise language. Twenty years ago it might have produced a letter for street circulation which made the appeal on the basis of political argument. That is the way such campaigns operated then, but it is not a realistic option now. Advertising raises money, xeroxed letters do not. There are alternatives available now, but within the range of modern forms of publicity (for example, using the internet). Social and political campaigns and movements are being drawn into the orbit of advertising and the commodified language of the market – as also are social and public services, the professions and the arts. There is a process of extending the market economy and the language of the market economy, of social and linguistic normalisation.

6. Some of the language of the text however is a language of social engagement, which suggests a refusal to compromise too far with the logic of commodities. Two sentences stand out in particular:

> The Big Issue exists to challenge stereotypes and to help homeless people reclaim their sense of self-worth and dignity by earning a living – all year round.

> But we are committed to providing homeless people with the resources they need to break out from the damaging culture of long term homelessness and find homes, jobs and better futures.

This is the sort of language professional politicians use. It draws on a mixture of vocabulary from academic social science (*challenge stereotypes, sense of self-worth, resources, culture of long-term homelessness*) and from everyday language (*earning a living, find homes, jobs*). Notice the density of 'nominalisations' in the former – expressions like *homelessness* and *self-worth* which abstract from the experiences and relationships of real life by the grammatical device of turning processes and relations involving particular people (for example, *I don't have a home*; *homeless people often don't think much of themselves*) into abstract nouns. Although homeless people are socially marginalised, the text does not attempt to incorporate the voices or experiences of marginalisation, rather it uses a mainstream political language. (In contrast, *The Big Issue* magazine itself has a section with 'views of the streets' in which the voices of homeless people are directly included.) Like advertising, mainstream political language is perhaps another orbit that campaigns are drawn into as a condition for having an impact – more normalisation and homogenisation.

7. We have suggested that submitting oneself to normalised professional political discourse is a way of distancing oneself from the normalised, commodified discourse of advertising. This gives us an indication of how in general terms particular collectivities and particular individuals can assert their particularity and individuality and establish distinctive identities for themselves in the face of language practices which are increasingly homogenised and increasingly unavoidable. These general, anonymous practices (in certain circumstances – not independently of circumstances) can be treated as resources which can be creatively articulated together in new ways to project particular identities and differences, in hybrid texts like this one. In this case, there is a mixture of standard advertising discourse (for example, the heading), mainstream political discourse, what we might call the 'director's notes' of the characterisation of the 'guilt-tripping' style of advertisement which is rejected (shorthand, abbreviated, verbal specifications for a film or video – a mix of visual and verbal semiosis), and the discourse of charitable appeal (for example, *Please support our Christmas Appeal and help us help vendors leave the streets for good*). Hybridity is not a matter of moving from 'pure' to hybrid practices – people are always working with practices which are already hybrid (like the mixture of academic and everyday language in political discourse which we mentioned in 6.). So what is at issue is rearticulation, articulatory change (Laclau and Mouffe 1985). Hybridity as such is inherent in all social uses of language. But particular social circumstances create particular degrees of stability and durability for particular articulations, and particular potentials for articulating practices together in new ways (Laclau and Mouffe 1985; Bernstein 1990, 1996).

In late modernity, boundaries between social fields and therefore between language practices have been pervasively weakened and redrawn, so that the potential seems to be immense, and indeed hybridity has been widely seen as a characteristic of the 'postmodern'. But there are still social constraints on rearticulation which need to be established for different domains of social life

(Bourdieu 1984, 1990; Bernstein 1990, especially ch. 5). How the potential for articulatory change within a particular social field is taken up depends on how social subjets act within the field (see Chapter 6). The concept of 'subject' is felicitously ambiguous between passivity (being subjected) and activity (as in 'the subject of history'). The capacity of a person to be active and creative depends upon the resources ('habitus' in Bourdieu's terms – see Chapter 6) which he or she has, and people vary in their habitus according to social circumstances. We might say that people are active – agents – to the extent that they are capable of pursuing collective or individual strategies in their discourse. But whether articulatory shifts in discourse constitute substantive shifts in identity or resistance to domination depends, in terms of Harvey's view of the dialectic of discourse (see above), on how the moment of discourse is inserted within the social process overall – whether and how articulatory change in discourse maps onto articulatory change in other moments. So, to socially interpret the *Big Issue* advertisement, we would need to look at it within the social process it is a part of.

8. Hybridity, as we have argued, is a potential in all discourse which however takes particular forms in particular social circumstances. It is also open to various uses. In 7. we have discussed hybridity as a strategy for resistance, but it can equally be a strategy for domination, for instance in struggles to establish new hegemonies in the political domain. There is an analysis of the discourse of Thatcherism in Britain in the 1980s in these terms in Fairclough (1989). Hybridity is also a resource for dialogue. One might see effective public sphere dialogue in terms of the particular quality of articulations between the voices of participants, where how I internalise the voice of the other – how I 'give voice' to it in articulating it with my own voice – is a moral issue. The potential for hybridity is part of specific social power of the semiotic, and part of the openness of social life – it is a potential which can be effectively limited, but never entirely controlled. It gives a semiotic explanation for all the processes above – resistance, (restructuring) hegemony, and non-repressive dialogue (Barát 1998).

9. Advertisements are forms within mass communication. A print advertisement like this one has a potential readership of thousands or even millions. Recent scholarship on mass communication has focused upon the reception of broadcasting and the press by audiences and readers, and shown that a single text or programme is open to diverse interpretations. People also establish their identities and their differences through the diverse ways in which they interpret texts, and more generally incorporate them into their own practices. This can also be approached in terms of hybridity: different interpretations entail bringing different discourses to the interpretation of a text, creating in a sense a new, hybrid text which combines the text interpreted with the discourses that are brought to it in the process of reading. The social fragmentation of late modern society makes it difficult to sustain the characteristic earlier modern view that meaning resides in texts – meaning seems rather too

variably produced in interpretations of texts. So the homogenisation of the spread of advertising goes along with a heterogenisation of meaning. But interpretations do not vary without limit, and overstating heterogenisation is as misleading as overstating homogenisation.

10. This text is actually reflexive about the commodification of language in advertising – it refers dismissively to one style of advertising as 'guilt-tripping', and gives a characterisation of it. This again shows that the homogenised practices of late modernity are not an iron cage – it is possible to take positions in relation to them, and to constitute one's identity and one's difference in that way. Moreover, a heightened reflexivity – a heightened capacity to use knowledge about social life to transform it – seems to be a characteristic of late modern society, which has actually been referred to as 'reflexive modernity' (Beck et al. 1994). Agency entails reflexivity. As we saw in 7., agents can pursue strategies in discourse. These include strategies with respect to discourse – they can consciously intervene to apply their knowledge of language practices to changing language practices, as part of wider strategies of change. Such agency with respect to discourse seems to be increasing sharply in late modernity – for instance, managements consciously intervene to change language practices in work as part of a strategy to transform workplaces (see the example of workplace discourse discussed in Chapter 7, and Fairclough 1996a on 'technologisation of discourse').

11. In acting strategically, one nevertheless has to work with these normalised practices. The text remains an advertisement – it does not evade commodified language, it opts within it. Thus both the heading and the appealing picture of the vendor, Carl, are aesthetically designed to sell. Moreover, strategies that people develop in trying to use these homogenised practices for their own identificational purposes are themselves likely to be assimilated into these practices. Thus rejecting (one way of) advertising has become a recognisable and rather common advertising device in the 'anti-advertisement' – which is still an advertisment.[5] It has been suggested that late modernity (postmodernity) is characterised by this ability to appropriate and incorporate resistance to itself (Billig 1994; Featherstone 1991; Jameson 1991). This makes the prospects for contesting the system look dismal to some, but systems cannot assimilate resistance without limit – in favourable circumstances, resistance can topple systems.

Let us sum up. The picture that emerges from this example is a contradictory one. On the one hand, it exemplifies the commodification of language, and the spread through contemporary societies of homogenised discourses which are very difficult to evade. But on the other hand, it also exemplifies that these discourses can be resources for creativity and differentiation – they can be hybridised in many different ways, they can be variously interpreted (also a matter of various hybridisations), people can self-reflexively distance themselves from them. Yet these ways of 'turning' the powerful discourses of late modern social systems seem to be all too easily appropriated and assimilated by them. In broad terms, the picture that emerges is of a tension, a dialectic, between structure and agency – between homogenisation of discourses and what we referred to earlier as the 'proliferation of languages' which has been seen as feature of the postmodern. This of course is an extremely partial picture emerging from one example, but we shall suggest that this dialectic is in fact a general and fundamental feature of discourse in late modernity (see Chapter 4).

Finally, some reflexion on what we have been doing in making these comments on the advertisements, especially in the light of our discussion above of institutional conditions for critical social research. One limitation is that although we have re-ferred to the social process the advertisement is a part of, we have only analysed the advertisement, making assumptions about the wider social process in doing so. As we argue in Chapter 2, CDA is best seen as one contributory element in research on social practices – in this sense, it should be seen as working in combination with other methods in social scientific research (see for example Chouliaraki 1995, 1996, and Pujolar 1997, for a combination of CDA with ethnography). Furthermore, our analysis is an academic one, located within a theoretical practice of social (discourse) analysis which we have not attempted to explicitly connect with the practical practice of campaigning on the question of homelessness – we have not made the link between these two public spheres which we recommended above. However, the analysis does in various ways link theoretical and practical perspectives on the basis of assumptions about the latter – for instance, in 5. and 6., in suggesting that prac-tical pressures manifest themselves in a tense relationship to advertising discourse (it is used, yet it is distanced) and the mixing of advertising with political discourse.

CDA – THEORY OR METHOD?

We see CDA as both theory and method: as a method for analysing social practices with particular regard to their discourse moments within the linking of the theor-etical and practical concerns and public spheres just alluded to, where the ways of analysing 'operationalise' – make practical – theoretical constructions of discourse in (late modern) social life, and the analyses contribute to the development and elaboration of these theoretical constructions. We therefore agree with Wacquant (Bourdieu and Wacquant 1992: 26–35) that it is necessary to avoid both theor-eticism – 'theory for its own sake' – and methodologism – seeing method as a theory-free means of achieving results. Our comments on Schegloff above and in note 4. can be taken as a critique of his methodologism. We see CDA as bringing a variety of theories into dialogue, especially social theories on the one hand and linguistic theories on the other, so that its theory is a shifting synthesis of other theories, though what it itself theorises in particular is the mediation between the social and the linguistic – the 'order of discourse', the social structuring of semiotic hybridity (interdiscursivity). The theoretical constructions of discourse which CDA tries to operationalise can come from various disciplines, and the concept of 'operation-alisation' entails working in a transdisciplinary way where the logic of one discipline (for example, sociology) can be 'put to work' in the development of another (for example, linguistics). Given our emphasis on the mutually informing development of theory and method, we do not support calls for stabilising a method for CDA (Fowler 1996; Toolan 1997). While such a stabilisation would have institutional and especially pedagogical advantages, it would compromise the developing capacity of CDA to shed light on the dialectic of the semiotic and the social in a wide variety of social practices by bringing to bear shifting sets of theoretical resources and shifting operationalisations of them.

HOW WE WROTE

We very much see this as our book – not Chouliaraki's, not Fairclough's, but the result of extensive dialogue and reworking. We began by dividing the chapters between us in terms of main responsibility, but quickly abandoned that in favour of working together on each chapter. One of us would produce a plan, the other would turn it into a first draft, this would be extensively reworked and rewritten by the planner, and the other would then produce a new version. We have been conscious in writing of contradictory pressures on the one hand towards greater theoretical elaboration and coherence – for although we see the project of CDA as bringing together theory and practice, this particular book is a theoretical one – and on the other hand towards being accessible to as wide a readership as possible. We have done our best to write clearly, and used examples where we could, without compromising our theoretical aims. Readers will judge whether we have succeeded.

This is a theoretical book directed at an academic readership. Some readers may see this as inconsistent with the aim in critical research (alluded to above, but developed in Chapter 2) to set up an open relationship between the theoretical practice of the academy and the practical practices of non-academic life – and between different public spheres. We do not see this as inconsistent at all – this objective of critical research should not be interpreted as a populist retreat from theory, which is what some contributions to a recent debate in the journal *Discourse and Society* (van Dijk 1995a, 1995b) on 'esoteric discourse analysis' seem to call for. Theoretical practice has its own logic and its own preoccupations, and needs its own literature – seeking for an open relationship with practical life does not negate that. Moreover, we suspect that what appears as democratic anti-elitism may be part of the colonising incursion of the market into universities which we discussed above, and which is evident in the first question publishers tend to ask academic authors: 'is it useable as a course book?'.

NOTES

1. See for example van Dijk 1987, 1991, 1993; Fairclough 1989, 1992a, 1995b; Fairclough and Wodak 1997; Fowler et al. 1979; Hodge and Kress 1993; Kress 1985; Lemke 1995; Thibault 1991; Wodak et al. 1990; Wodak 1996.
2. For critiques of CDA, see for instance Hammersley 1996; Pennycook 1994; Schegloff 1997; Stubbs 1997; Toolan 1997; Widdowson 1995, 1996; Fairclough 1996b is a reply to Widdowson.
3. We are grateful to Lesley Farrell of Monash University for this example, based on her current research into changes in literacy and identity in an Australian workplace.

4. The segment which Schegloff focuses on is:
       35   Tony: W't's 'e g'nna do go down en pick it up later? er
       36   somethin like (   ) [well that's aw]:ful
       37   Marsha: [H i s friend]
       38   Marsha: Yeh h[is friend Stee   ]
       39   Tony: [That really makes me] ma:d,
       40   (0.2)
       41   Marsha: hhh Oh it's disgusti[ng ez a matter a'f]act.
       42   Tony: [P o o r J o e y,]
       43   Marsha: I- I, I told my ki:ds. who do this: down et the Drug
       44   Coalition ah want th'to:p back

   Schegloff notices that the overlapping talk in 36 and 37 starts simultaneously so there is no interruption, but he does not notice that Tony's talk in 39 does interrupt Marsha, nor the short pause in 40. There is also an odd observation that 'although the transcript reads, and the tape sounds, as if Marsha is saying "Oh it's disgusting as a matter of fact" (in 41), there are substantial grounds for parsing this differently, namely, "Oh it's disgusting. As a matter of fact I told my kids ...".' Schegloff unfortunately does not have the time to go through the argument here, but it appears that there is at least ambivalence about the parsing – the way it sounds on the tape supports the first parsing, which again would entail Tony interrupting Marsha. Schegloff would presumably explain Tony's first interruption of Marsha by appeal to the common conversational practice of upgrading second assessments in response to weak agreements (like Marsha's *yeh* in 38) in first assessments (Tony's first assessment in 36 is *that's awful*). But there is a further question which an appeal to this common practice cannot itself answer: is there any social pattern to who uses the practice to override an also common injunction against interruption? Is there for instance a social pattern based on gender difference? We do not know the answer to this – we want to make the point that Schegloff's theoretical preoccupation leads him not to ask a question which ours does lead us to ask. Furthermore, might not the brief pause in 40 register a problem on Marsha's part with Tony's interruption in 39?

5. Mixing genres in a self-conscious way and playfully bringing together images, discourses and practices is one feature of the postmodern tendency to experiment with aesthetic experience – in architecture (Harvey 1990, ch. 4) but also in forms of pop art from fashion to video clips. Past forms are reworked in contemporary art, with a mixture of nostalgia and ironic subversion of the past. For some, irony and subversion are the only forms of resistance available in the postmodern condition (Rorty 1989; Lyotard 1984; Featherstone 1991; Simons and Billig 1994), though they may rather be seen as resigned acceptance.

Chapter 2

Social life and critical social science

Our objective in Chapters 2, 3 and 4 is to show how CDA is located within a tradition of critical social scientific theory and analysis. Chapter 2 develops a view of social life and the the study of social life which accords with critical theory – that is, a critical ontology, and critical epistemology. Chapters 3 and 4 focus upon language and the concept of discourse, setting out a view of language in social life (3) and of critical analysis of language (4). This is the first stage in our attempt to 'ground' CDA in this book – that is, to provide a coherent rationale for its particular ways of theorising and analysing language.[1] The second stage is to locate CDA within a specific research endeavour of contemporary critical social science – its attempt to provide a coherent critical account of late modern society and its transformations. We shall do this by showing that CDA's particular orientation to the social use of language in late modern society is informed by that wider endeavour, but also constitutes a distinct contribution to it. This will be the concern of Chapters 5–7.

LIFE AS AN OPEN SYSTEM

Life (natural and social) is an 'open system', in which any event is governed by simultaneously operative 'mechanisms' (or 'generative powers'). This is a view that has recently been developed within 'critical realism' (Collier 1994; Bhaskar 1986). The various dimensions and levels of life – including physical, chemical, biological, economic, social, psychological, semiological (and linguistic) – have their own distinctive structures, which have distinctive generative effects on events via their particular mechanisms. Because the operation of any mechanism is always mediated by the operation of others, no mechanism has determinate effects on events, so that events are complex and not predictable in any simple way as effects of mechanism. (Bhaskar's term 'mechanism' can be misleading – as this indicates, its normal mechanistic and deterministic connotations do not apply in this theory.) Life therefore cannot be conceived as a closed system – it is an open system, which is indeed determined by mechanisms (and therefore structures), but in complex ways.

The relationships between mechanisms are stratified: one mechanism presupposes many others, but it is rooted in and emergent out of maybe just one or a small number of other mechanisms. For instance, the semiological (linguistic) mechanism presupposes physical and chemical mechanisms, but it is hardly rooted in them (Volosinov 1973: 46). We might say it is rooted on the one hand in biological mechanisms, and on the other hand in social mechanisms, i.e., that there are both biological and social bases to semiosis (Luria 1981; Vygotsky 1962; Wertsch 1991). It therefore makes sense to see language in terms of an intersection of the biological and the social (Halliday 1995; Hasan 1992a; Scollon and Scollon 1981). Semiosis (including language) is emergent from biological and social mechanisms – which means that we can 'explain' its own properties as a mechanism by reference to biological and social mechanisms without being able to 'explain them away'; the concept of 'emergence' entails that a mechanism has distinctive properties which are not reducible to other mechanisms. Of course, the particular relationships between mechanisms are contentious and a focus for theoretical debate. So for instance, should we not say that semiosis is also rooted in psychology? And is it not the case that the social and the psychological are also in some sense emergent from semiosis, so that emergence can be a two-way relation?

Because the effect of individual mechanisms on events is always mediated by others, there are no straightforward ways for science to establish the nature of individual mechanisms by analysing events. This is why experiment is an essential part of science: experiments are ways of intervening in events to isolate the effects of individual mechanisms (Collier 1994). Identifying the properties of individual mechanisms (such as the semiological) is particularly problematic in the social sciences, where experiment is rarely feasible. Social scientists have to resort to other devices (see further below).

The object of study in social science is social life, and a major issue, particularly in critical social science, is the relationship between spheres of social life and activity, the economic, the political and the cultural. Marxism has given rise to forms of economic determinism which in the extreme case treat other dimensions of society as merely epiphenomenal – superstructural reflections of the economic base (Barrett 1991; Larrain 1994). Marxism has also generated dialectical theories of the relationship which in some cases abandon economic determinism altogether (for example, Laclau and Mouffe 1985), and in others claim the determinism of the economic 'in the last instance' while attributing considerable autonomy and determining effects of their own to other dimensions of society (Althusser and Balibar 1970; Althusser 1971; Poulantzas 1978). The issue can be seen in terms of relations between mechanisms. It is possible to identify ways in which other dimensions of society are rooted in and emergent from the economy (and in that sense 'determined by' it) , without reducing them to the economy. The issue is also an empirical issue: the precise relationship between economic and other mechanisms needs to be empirically established for particular times and places. Having said that, we see contemporary capitalist societies as heavily determined by (though certainly nor reducible to) their economic mechanisms.

SOCIAL LIFE AS PRACTICES

With respect to social life, we begin from the assumption (shared within a considerable body of contemporary social theory[2]) that it is made up of *practices*. By practices we mean habitualised ways, tied to particular times and places, in which people apply resources (material or symbolic) to act together in the world. Practices are constituted throughout social life – in the specialised domains of the economy and politics, for instance, but also in the domain of culture, including everyday life (Mouzelis 1990). The advantage of focusing upon practices is that they constitute a point of connection between abstract structures and their mechanisms, and concrete events – between 'society' and people living their lives.

All practices involve configurations of diverse elements of life and therefore diverse mechanisms. We assume that social science investigates the interaction between different mechanisms as it is specifically instantiated in particular social practices. A particular practice brings together different elements of life in specific, local forms and relationships – particular types of activity, linked in particular ways to particular materials and spatial and temporal locations; particular persons with particular experiences, knowledges and dispositions in particular social relations; particular semiotic resources and ways of using language; and so forth. In so far as these diverse elements of life are brought together into a specific practice, we can call them 'moments' of that practice, and in Harvey's terminology (1996) see each moment as 'internalising' the others without being reducible to them[3] – the local dialectical relationship corresponding to the general relationship between mechanisms discussed above. In other words, a general account of the relationship between elements of life and their mechanisms is not enough: we need specific accounts of the form which their dialectical relationship takes in particular practices, a form which is constantly open to change.

The concept of 'articulation', which we take from Laclau and Mouffe (1985), is helpful in describing the bringing together of elements of the social as moments of a practice, and the relations of internalisation between them. Articulation implies the view of elements of the social as first, in shifting relationships with each other, though capable of being stabilised into more or less relative permanences as they are articulated together as moments within practices; and as second, transformed in the process of being brought into new combinations with each other. The concept of articulation can also be extended down into the internal structure of each particular moment to specify the particular, local form it takes in a particular practice. Thus the discourse moment of any practice is a shifting articulation of symbolic/discursive resources (such as genres, discourses, voices) which themselves come to be articulated into relative permanences as moments of (the moment of) discourse, and transformed in that process.[4] The particular form taken by the articulation of resources within a moment in a practice is shaped by its relation to other moments – that is, the effect of its internalisation of other moments.

The word 'practice' is ambiguous in a way which is helpful in the present context. A practice can be understood both as a social action, what is done in a particular time and place, and as what has hardened into a relative permanency – a practice in the sense of a habitual way of acting. This ambiguity is helpful in that it points to the intermediate positioning of practices between structures and events, structure and agency – practices have partly the character of both. We take a dialectical view of practice, rejecting both a determinism which puts all the emphasis on stabilised structures (which Althusser has been accused of – see Barrett 1991; Larrain 1994) and a voluntarism which puts all the emphasis on concrete activity (which Laclau and Mouffe have been accused of – see Mouzelis 1990; Best and Kellner 1991). We see social action as depending upon and constrained by relative permanencies which it ongoingly reproduces however (as both 'things' and 'flows' in the terminology of Harvey's account of dialectics: 1996, ch. 2) – by which we mean partly sustains, partly transforms, though the balance between the two varies according to social circumstances. The relative permanence of practices can be theorised in terms of specific institutions or institution complexes (Bourdieu's 'fields' – see Chapter 6). The institutional dimension of practice is important in critical social science because institutions have internal logics that can be reduced neither to abstract structures nor to clusters of events (Cohen 1989; see also Thrift 1996 on 'regions' and 'locales').

We also find it helpful to focus on 'conjunctures', in contrast with both structures and events. Structures are long-term background conditions for social life which are indeed also transformed by it, but slowly. Events are the individual, immediate happenings and occasions of social life. Conjunctures are relatively durable assemblies of people, materials, technologies and therefore practices (in their aspect as relative permanencies) around specific social projects in the widest sense of the term. Conjunctures cut across and bring together different institutions. The durability and scale will vary considerably – from the establishment of an industry to the enlargement of a hospital, from campaigns for universal suffrage to protests over the building of a road, and so forth. The advantage of focusing upon conjunctures is that it allows us to trace through time the effect not just of individual events but of conjuncturally linked series of events in both sustaining and transforming (re-articulating) practices.

We take practices to have three main characteristics. First, they are forms of production of social life, not only economic production but also production in for instance the cultural and political domains. Second, each practice is located within a network of relationships to other practices, and these 'external' relationships determine its 'internal' constitution. Third, practices always have a reflexive dimension: people always generate representations of what they do as part of what they do.

Although any practice can be characterised in terms of these three aspects, practices vary substantially in their nature and complexity. Modern societies have developed practices which are highly complex in their forms and social relations of production, in the networks of practices they enter into, and which draw upon specialised theories (themselves the outcome of particular forms of practice) in their reflexivity. These modern practices are often organised across great distances of time and space – for example, globalised contemporary economic practices. They operate through sophisticated technologies of mediation, including contemporary information technology. Relatively simple practices based on the co-presence of people in particular places and times still exist in everyday life, but it is a feature of modernity that they are increasingly tied in with and dependent upon more complex practices.

PRACTICES OF PRODUCTION

In seeing all practices as practices of production, the aim is not to reduce the whole of social life to economic production or something analogous to economic production, but on the contrary to overcome the misleading idea that production is purely economic by insisting that people produce their social world in all their practices (Collier 1994). So 'production' has to be understood in a very broad sense. Any practice of production involves particular people in particular relationships using particular resources – applying 'technologies' to 'materials' within particular social relations of production. 'Technology' also is used in a broad sense to refer to any apparatus applied to materials within a practice of production to achieve particular social (economic, political, cultural) effects. For instance, in modern societies political technologies include technologies of administration and coercion which regulate state–citizen relations, as discussed by Mouzelis (1990) and the processes of surveillance, as discussed by Foucault in his analysis of disciplinary technologies of power (Foucault 1977).

Both the technologies and materials of production range from physical resources ('raw materials' like plants, minerals) to symbolic resources – like photographs and, more abstractly, socially organised semiotic practices, i.e., discourses and genres. (Notice the potential terminological problem here – not all 'materials' are 'material' in the sense of physical.) All practices of production combine physical and symbolic resources, in varying degrees, and discourse is always a significant moment because all practices are, as we have said, reflexive – constructions of a practice constitute part of a practice. Symbolic, including discursive, elements of practices are just as real as physical elements, in that they have effects upon and within practices (including their non-symbolic elements). One might call them 'material' on the basis of these 'material' effects, but this can be misleading given the more normal sense of 'material', so we call them 'real' (Bhaskar 1979, ch. 3). Yet words can be 'mere' words and 'empty' words, and changes in discourse which appear to constitute changes in social practices can be no such thing. The only way of determining whether this is so is to analyse the relationship between discourse and other moments of social practices (see further below).

RELATIONS BETWEEN PRACTICES

Each practice is located within a network of practices which determine 'from the outside' its 'internal' properties. The concepts (articulation, internalisation) we have drawn upon above for the 'internal' analysis of practices and their individual moments can be extended to analysing relations between practices. Practices are shiftingly articulated together to constitute networks of which they themselves become moments in ways which transform them. Here articulation refers to the relationship of 'overdetermination' (Althusser 1969; Althusser and Balibar 1970) between practices within such a network, not only in the sense that each practice is simultaneously determined by others without being reducible to any of them, but crucially also in the sense that each practice can simultaneously articulate together with many others from multiple social positions and with diverse social effects. This moves us away from the monist base-superstructure determination of classical Marxism (Hall 1996a: 14).

Networks of practices are held in place by social relations of power, and shifting articulations of practices within and across networks are linked to the shifting dynamics of power and struggles over power. In this sense, the 'permanences' we referred to above are an effect of power over networks of practice, and the tensions within events between permanences (boundaries) and flows are struggles over power. These relations of power at the level of networks are relations of domination and include not only capitalist relations between social classes but also partriarchal gender relations as well as racial and colonial relations, which are diffused across the diverse practices of a society. This is power as what Hall (1996a: 11) calls 'structure in dominance'.

But power in the sense of domination also figures at the level of the particular practice, where subjects are positioned in relation to others such that some are able to incorporate the agency of others into their own actions and so reduce the autonomous agentive capacity of the latter (Giddens 1984; Bourdieu 1977, 1991). These 'internal' power relations are an effect of the 'external' power relations within networks of practices – so for instance what gives power to a new elite of specialist managers in public-service institutions such as universities at present is a shift in relations between practices which (further) subordinates public services to the economy. These systemic imbalances are expressed and contested in social struggles over both the constitution of particular practices and relations between practices.

In this sense, we agree with the post-structuralist view that all social practice is embedded in networks of power relations, and potentially subordinates the social subjects that engage in it, even those with 'internal' power. At the same time, we believe that the view of modern power as invisible, self-regulating and inevitably subjecting ('bio-power', Foucault 1977) needs to be complemented with a view of power as domination, i.e., a view of power that acknowledges the overdetermination between 'internal' and 'external' practices, and establishes causal links between institutional social practices and the positions of subjects in the wider social field. Otherwise, it can collapse into structural determinism and anti-humanism which leaves no space for agency in social practices (Fraser 1989; Bourdieu and Wacquant 1992: 47–8, 167; Fowler 1997 on Bourdieu and Foucault; Bernstein 1990: 134).

Gramsci's concept of 'hegemony' is helpful in analysing relations of power as domination. Hegemony is relations of domination based upon consent rather than coercion, involving the naturalisation of practices and their social relations as well as relations between practices, as matters of common sense – hence the concept of hegemony emphasises the importance of ideology in achieving and maintaining relations of domination (Forgacs 1988; Thompson 1984; Fairclough 1992a; Larrain

1994). The concept of articulation as the mode of relating between elements (moments) of the social is used by Laclau and Mouffe (1985) to conceptualise power: hegemony is seen in terms of the relative permanency of articulations of social elements. This conceptualisation also highlights the inherent possibility of de-articulation and rearticulation. Hegemony is a bid for closure of practices and net-works of practices which is destined to fail to a greater or lesser extent because the social is by its nature open – the simultaneous operation of diverse mechanisms within any practice, and the fact that any practice is overdetermined (simultaneously determined by others), mean that outcomes are never entirely predictable, and that resources for resistance are always likely to be generated (though Laclau and Mouffe overrate the openness of the social – see Best and Kellner 1991, and Chapter 7).

Consider for instance the positioning of social subjects within a practice as an effect of the 'outside' on the 'inside' – an effect of the network of practices on a particular practice within it. We referred above to contemporary practices of education in Britain in their shifting relation to economic practices. Subjects are positioned and related in contradictory ways as, for instance, teachers and students but also simultaneously as producers and consumers of educational products. These contradictory positionings constitute antagonisms both between different subjects and within individual subjects (Laclau and Mouffe 1985). The claim of antagonisms within a subject implies that identity is heterogeneously constituted as an effect of the diverse positionings of a subject (Jenkins 1996). From the perspective of relative permanences of practices in their relation to social systems, we might see these antagonisms as structural imbalances and describe them as contradictions; from the perspective of social action, we can see these as played out in social struggles. Notice that 'subject' has a felicitous ambiguity parallel to that we noted for 'practice' – subjects are subjected (in Althusser's terminology, 'interpellated' – Althusser 1971), but subjects also act (as agents) constrained by these positions yet in ways which transform them. This view rejects both a structuralism which construes social life as an effect of structures and eliminates agency, and a rationalism which views social life as entirely produced through the rational activity of agents (Bourdieu 1990; Collier 1994: 151–60).

With respect to the interplay between this and the other two characteristics of practices that we are differentiating (that they are practices of production, and that they are reflexive), the relations of power and the positioning of subjects that we are discussing here are 'externally' produced effects upon the practices of production discussed above – defining the social relations and subjects of production – while subjectivity is inherently reflexive – the individual and collective identities of subjects are partly constituted by the way they represent themselves and are represented by others (Jenkins 1996).

REFLEXIVITY OF PRACTICES

Practices also include a reflexive element (Bourdieu 1977, 1990; Giddens 1991, 1993; Mouzelis 1990): people constantly generate representations of what they do as a part of what they do. This suggests that there is no simple opposition between practice and theory but rather a close and practical relation between them, because people's reflexive representations of what they do are in a sense already theories ('proto-theories' – Collier 1994) of their practices, which are a normal part of their practices. This applies also to linguistic aspects of practices: they too are reflexively 'theorised'. In modern and especially late modern societies, reflexivity becomes an increasingly important feature of social life, i.e., knowledge about practices becomes an increasingly significant part of engagement in practices – a relationship which Giddens has referred to as a 'double hermeneutic': 'sociology … deals with a pre-interpreted world, in which the meanings developed by active subjects actually enter into the actual constitution or production of that world' (1993: 170). This tendency within modernity is institutionally realised in the separation out of practices which are specialised in the production of knowledge about practices – 'theoretical practices' (see Althusser 1971; Bourdieu 1977; Castoriades 1987; Larrain 1983). Other practices (be they economic, political or cultural) are increasingly shaped by their relations with theoretical practices. The element of reflexivity, which we have characterised as an inherent aspect of any practice, therefore changes in nature in that it becomes increasingly informed 'from the outside' by theoretical practices. Theoretical practices have the same general characteristics as any other sort of practices (they are practices of production, locked into networks with other practices, and reflexive), as well as distinctive features – to do with the fact that their 'raw material' is other practices – which we discuss below.

There are two other important aspects of reflexivity. First, reflexivity is caught up in social struggle. Reflexively applied knowledges about a practice are positioned knowledges, knowledges generated from particular positions within a practice or outside it (within theoretical practices), and they are both resources for and stakes in struggle. Second, as we have already indicated, the reflexivity of practice entails that all practices have an irreducible discursive aspect, not only in the sense that all practices involve use of language to some degree (though in varying degrees – compare sheep farming with teaching philosophy), but also in the sense that discursive constructions of practices are themselves parts of practices – that is what reflexivity means.

Practices may depend upon these reflexive self-constructions for sustaining relations of domination. In so far as reflexive self-constructions function in this way, we shall call them ideologies (Thompson 1984: 130–1; Larrain 1979). Ideologies are constructions of practices from particular perspectives (and in that sense 'one-sided') which 'iron out' the contradictions, dilemmas and antagonisms of practices in ways which accord with the interests and projects of domination. The effect of ideologies in 'ironing out' (i.e., suppressing) aspects of practices is what links ideologies to 'mystification' (Barrett 1991: 167) and 'misrecognition' (Althusser 1971; Bourdieu 1991). Ideologies are discursive constructions, so the question of ideology is part of the question of how discourse relates to other moments of social practices. But the concept of ideology has emerged in modern societies and is tied to relations within modern networks of practices, specifically relations between discursive practices (i.e., between the discourse moments of different practices). We may say that the discourse of one practice colonises that of another, or that the latter appropriates the former, depending on how power relations are expressed as relations between practices and discourses. So ideologies are domination-related constructions of a practice which are determined by specifically discursive relations between that practice and other practices. For instance, to refer again to the example of contemporary changes affecting education, managerial ideologies in education are discursive constructions of education which draw upon discourses which come from other practices that are closely tied in with contemporary practices of education – specifically, from economic practices. Notice that ideology conceived in terms of relations between practices 'refers to a function or mechanism but is not tied to any particular content, nor to any particular agent or interest' (Barrett 1991: 167; see also Zizec 1994; Hall 1996a). The advantage of this view of ideology is that it retains its focus on forms of domination (as opposed to 'neutral' definitions of ideology which cut the concept off from domination – see van Dijk 1998; Larrain 1994) while ceasing to be exclusively tied to social class domination.

Modern social practices are, as we have suggested, networked in increasingly complex ways with theoretical practices, and theoretical practices are always involved in the relations between practices which determine ideologies, either directly in that theoretical discourses come to work ideologically within a practice, or indirectly in that the mode of appropriation of discourses from other (non-theoretical) practices is theoretically mediated – the practice concerned is 'theoretically informed' in that sense. The question of the relationship between theory and ideology has in fact to be raised on two interconnected levels. First, since theory is itself a practice, there is the question of ideological knowledges within the reflexive self-representations of a theory, which is, as we have seen, linked to the question of how the particular theoretical practice is networked with other practices. Second, there is the question just raised of the ideological effects of a theory on the social practices it theorises. The two are interconnected, in the sense that the capacity of a theory to resist ideological appropriation within social practices depends on its capacity to resist ideological reflexive self-representations – but without guarantees in that no theory can be made 100 per cent ideology-proof at either level.

To minimise misrecognised ideological effects within theory, theoretical practices can and should be reflexive in the sense of seeking to illuminate their own conditions of possibility, including their own location within networks of practices and the internal (including ideological) effects of these external relations (Bourdieu and Wacquant 1992). A critical theoretical practice aims to unpick the relations which constitute social practices and so identify the mechanisms which produce antagonisms and struggles, also making explicit its own position in these struggles. Critical theoretical practice has a particular 'knowledge interest' (Habermas 1972) in the social practices it theorises, an interest in knowledges which show up and so problematise relations of domination and the means for surpassing them, which positions critical theoretical practice within the struggles of the social practices it theorises: 'by uncovering the social mechanisms which ensure the maintainance of the established order and whose properly symbolic efficacy rests on the misrecognition of their logic and effects, social science necessarily takes sides in political struggles' (Bourdieu and Wacquant 1992: 51). None of this excludes theory coming to work ideologically, but it makes its ideological appropriation more problematic.

THE MOMENT OF DISCOURSE

Post-structuralist theory, and especially the theory of Foucault (1972, 1977, 1981), has firmly established the category of 'discourse' in the humanities and social sciences. The extent of its uptake indicates a recognition that modern social theory, including critical social theory, has neglected language and the semiotic. One might see this as part of its more general neglect of the cultural aspect of social life. It is right and important that critical theory in particular should correct this omission. However, discourse theory has its dangers. Many of those who have worked with the concept of discourse have ended up seeing the social as nothing but discourse, i.e., in a 'discourse idealism', similar to traditional philosophical idealism except that rather than seeing social life as produced in thought, they see it as produced in discourse. This is true of many advocates of 'social constructivism', for instance in contemporary social psychology (Shotter 1993). It is also true of the 'post-Marxism' of Laclau and Mouffe (1985) which we discuss in some detail in Chapter 7 (see Best and Kellner 1991; Geras 1987; Mouzelis 1990 for critical responses).

We believe that it is important for critical social science to incorporate discourse in its theorising, but to do so in a non-idealistic way which does not reduce social life to discourse. We have already referred to Harvey's (1996) attempt to do this (see also Hennessy 1993), which draws upon Volosinov (1973) and Williams (1977). Harvey recognises the social import of discourse ('discourse internalizes in some sense everything that occurs in other moments' of social practices) both as part of action and in the reflexive construction ('signification') of social life, and the socially transformative work of discourse ('counter-hegemonic and dissident discourses ... erupt to challenge hegemonic forms and it is out of such contestation that social change may flow'). He also recognises that this process involves the rearticulation of discourses ('discourses are always porous with respect to each other'), and 'intertextuality'. His position here is very close to the version of CDA we are working with, though he does not 'operationalise' the theory as an analytical framework. He insists however that discourse is just one moment of the social, and that its relation to other moments is a matter for analysis and evaluation (given that discourse can 'obfuscate, hide, and misrepresent relations to other moments'). He identifies the following other moments: social relations, power, material practices, beliefs/values/desires, and institutions/rituals. His concept of 'internalisation' is useful here – each moment 'internalises' the others without being reducible to any of them. For instance, if we recognise that words can be 'mere' or 'empty' words (as we think they can), we can see this in terms of an absence of internalisation – a divorce for instance between the ways in which people act and the ways in which they discursively construct their actions, the former not internalising the latter. However, we prefer to use the concept of 'practices' in a different way from Harvey: rather than treating 'material practices' as one moment of the the 'social process' as Harvey does, we see the social process as constituted by 'social practices', and we refer to 'material activity' as one moment of a social practice. The terminology is important here: Harvey's materialism takes the form of privileging the moment of 'material practices' in his account of social dialectics, so that 'empty words' is discourse which has no effects on material practices. By contrast, we do not privilege any one moment of social practice but say rather that 'empty words' is a matter of discourse not being integrated into the practice, i.e., an absence of relations of internalisation between discourse and other moments. This is a different form of materialism, which privileges practices as such, while arguing (as we said above, following Bhaskar) that all moments of a practice (and not just material activity) are 'real'.

CRITICAL RESEARCH IN THEORETICAL PRACTICE

As we have already said, theory is itself a practice. It is important to grasp the specificity of theory which sets it apart from other practices, but without falling into the common trap of 'forgetting' that theory is itself a practice which, like other practices, is caught up in networks of relations with economic, political and cultural practices which determine its internal constitution and can have ideological effects within it. So theoretical practitioners should reflect on the social location of their theoretical practice and the consequences that flow from this. This responsibility applies to critical theorists and critical discourse analysts as well as others, and one particular concern for them is the consequences of their social and political 'commitment' in terms of for instance how their theoretical practice intersects with and is shaped by practical practices and struggles. However, this responsibility applies to all social and language researchers – it is misleading if not disingenuous to see it as peculiarly a problem for critical researchers (Widdowson 1995). There is a tension between 'rationality and commitment' (Toolan 1997) for all researchers, though the nature of the 'commitment' is somewhat different in critical research.

Theoretical practice is distinctive in taking other social practices as its 'raw materials'. In Habermas's earlier work on epistemology, the link between theoretical practices and other social practices is formulated in terms of 'knowledge interests'. We may say that theoretical practice has a variety of 'knowledge interests' in other practices, and that what distinguishes critical social science is an emancipatory knowledge interest – an interest in emancipation from 'ideologically-frozen relations of dependence that can in principle be transformed' (Habermas 1972). This is in contrast with a 'technical' interest in manipulation and control in the empirico-analytical sciences, and a 'practical' interest in intersubjective understanding in the historico-hermeneutical sciences.

The emancipatory knowledge interest of critical social science entails a dialectical social theory. We can explain this in terms of the different forms of theoretical knowledge discussed by Bourdieu (1977: 1–3). Phenomenological (including 'ethnomethodological') knowledge sets out to make explicit the primary, practical experience of the world that people have as part of their engagement in social practices. Objectivist (including 'structuralist') knowledge breaks with the perspective of the participant in social practice in order to identify objective relations which structure practices and the practical experience of practices described by phenomenologists. However, it does so at the cost of positioning itself outside the practice, thereby cutting itself off from the generative principle of a practice, which can only be grasped from within. Dialectical knowledge in turn breaks with the perspective of objectivism by reflexively exploring the conditions of possibility of the objectivist knowledge which constructs practices from the outside as a fait accompli; that is, it looks at theory itself as a practice, its own materials and technologies of production, the location of a theoretical practice within networks of practices and relations of power, the 'internal' effects of that location, the effects of a theoretical practice on other practices, and so forth. Exploring the conditions of possibility of objectivism, (based on its technical knowledge interest) is the basis for exposing its limits – in the sense that objectivism tends to obliterate the distinction between the practical logic of engagement within a social practice and its own theoretical logic, substituting the latter for the former. Drawing creatively on both phenomonology and objectivism, critical theoretical practice recognises that social science has a hermeneutic basis (it needs to ground itself in the symbolic practices of the world) but cannot be limited to that (it also needs to be a 'depth science' of the generative mechanisms that make these practices possible – see Bhaskar's 'Afterword' to Shotter 1993). In this sense, critical social science constructs as the object of scientific research the dialectical relationship between objective relations and structures on the one hand, and the practical dispositions of subjects engaged in practices on the other.

However, we believe the success of critical social science in sustaining this dialectical focus depends on how discourse is envisaged as an element of social practice. For example, Bourdieu acknowledges the power of discourse to constitute the social only as a power of certain social groups in certain circumstances. In not recognising that discourse is inherently constitutive of social life, Bourdieu slips into an objectivist ontology which posits a dimension of the social that is outside the ongoing process signification and constitution (Collins 1993). CDA by contrast develops a theoretical practice which is simultaneously oriented to the analysis of communicative events (a hermeneutic task of interpretation) and the analysis of their structural conditions of possibility and structural effects. Any discursive event demands the conjoint operationalisation of these two perspectives. (See Chapter 6 on Bourdieu and Chapter 4 on CDA.)

CRITICAL EPISTEMOLOGY: CRITICAL RESEARCH AND SOCIAL PRACTICES

Theoretical practice is largely (though not exclusively) located in the upper reaches of the educational system, where research and other critical functions of universities, research institutes, etc. take place, within the educational 'field of production' – though systematically recontextualised within the 'field of reproduction' where knowledges are adapted for the purposes of teaching and learning (Bernstein 1990, 1996). This institutional location of theoretical practice draws a line between what is 'thinkable' and what is 'unthinkable' (Bernstein's 'distributive rules') which limits how other social practices can be recognised ('thought of') and taken in. A theoretical practice recontextualises the social practices it theorises: that is, it delocates them from their original contexts and inevitably in so doing dislocates them, 'breaks off' certain aspects of them from the rest; and it relocates them, bringing different social practices into a new relation which is dictated by the internal logic of the theoretical practice itself, and the 'languages of description' it employs to make sense of social practices (Bernstein 1996). As Bernstein puts it, 'pedagogic discourse' (which includes what we are calling theoretical practice) 'is constituted by ... a recontextualizing grammar' (1990: 188), and it is the nature of this grammar that gives theoretical practice its distinctiveness in its ways of relating to other social practices.

The possibilities for a specifically critical theoretical practice depend upon the location of theoretical practice within a network of practices – including its degree of autonomy from the state and the economy. What is specific about critical theoretical practice is that (a) it maintains a weak boundary between theoretical practice and the social practices it theorises, and (b) it applies a relational/dialectical analytical logic to the practices it theorises. With respect to the first of these features, critical social research is 'involved' in the social practices it theorises in that it positions itself in relation to the struggles within them, given its emancipatory knowledge interest. It also produces knowledges with an eye to their potential as resources within these struggles. In these respects it is in contrast with objectivist research, which maintains a strong boundary between theoretical practice and the social practices theorised, in order to make objective truth claims about them; and with hermeneutic research, which also maintains a weak boundary but is indifferent to emancipatory struggles, neither positioning itself in relation to them nor orienting its results towards them (this is the difference between hermeneutic 'understanding' and critical 'explanation' – Outhwaite 1987).

Critical social research is initiated and terminated in flows between theoretical practice and the other practice(s) it is researching. An ideal form of such flows is perhaps critical action research, where the researcher is a participant in the practice researched and the research arises out of and feeds back into emancipatory struggles (Morrow and Brown 1994). In the field of language policy, one example of critical research is the work of Phillipson (1992) and Skutnab-Kangas (for example, 1990) in which theoretical practice is informed by and informs social struggles on linguistic rights of ethnic and racial minorities, as part of human rights struggles at local, national and global (world organisation) levels. However, the relationship between critical theoretical practice and researched practices can only exceptionally be so close. More often (as in for instance media research), the critical researcher is more distanced from the researched practice, and the import of knowledges produced about a practice for the practice itself is less than obvious. In some cases the results of critical research may have a longer-term but indirect impact, for instance in the case of media research through critical media education in the school system.

We now turn to the dialectical logic of critical social research. The recontextualisation of social practices with a critical theoretical practice entails applying to them both a relational logic, and a dialectical logic. The relational logic reflects the 'revolutionary' contribution of structuralism to social analysis, in shifting the focus away from entities and their substance to relations between them, so that the social field can be seen as a system of relations of selection and combination (Bourdieu 1990). Applying a relational logic to a social practice means showing how it is embedded within networks of practices whose relative stabilisation underpins the relative stability and permanence of the practice itself as a set of options for selection and combination (a 'space of compossibles' – Harvey 1996; Bourdieu 1990). Our own account of practice as articulation, and of networks of practices as overdetermination, above, are drawing on post-structuralist contributions to the specification of relational logic – we see ourselves as working within a post-structuralist perspective, but without adopting either post-structuralist reductions of the whole of social life to discourse, or post-structuralist judgemental relativism. (See Chapter 6 for discussion.) A relational logic is able to identify structured relations which underpin practices and their antagonisms but which are not focused in practical logics (and indeed are defocused by ideologies). It is here that the claim of critical theoretical practice to be social science is partly located – in its capacity to apply its technologies to explicate structural relations which are not apparent to practical logic.

But a relational logic in itself is not critical – it is shared with objectivist social science (Morrow 1994). Critical social research projects a relational logic into a dialectical logic through its analysis of stabilisation as an effect of power and a factor in reproducing relations of power, and its focus on the dialectical tension between structural permanences and the practical activity of people engaged in social practices – the former constitute both the conditions of possibility and the limitations of possibilities for the latter; the latter both depend upon and contest/transform the former. Critical theoretical practice needs to transcend the unproductive divide between structure and action by developing an epistemology which is a 'constructivist structuralism' (Bourdieu 1990; see also Morrow and Brown 1994), though with due emphasis on the constitutive function of discourse (recall our critique of Bourdieu in this respect). It is structuralist in that it is oriented to relational systems which constitute relative permanences within practices; it is constructivist in that it is concerned to explicate how those systems are produced and transformed in social action. Social systems are both the precondition of social action and the products of social action. Every moment in the structure/action dialectic is a moment in the power struggle over whether the social world is to be maintained as it is or changed.

Following Bhaskar (Collier 1994), we see critical social science as having a 'transitive' as well as an 'intransitive' object. Its intransitive object is the actual practices it is analysing. Its transitive object is the proto-theories which are produced as a part of those practices – the reflexive element of practices. In terms of its transitive object, critical theory sets out to transform proto-theories into scientific theories through applying the dialectical logic we have sketched out above. In so far as proto-theories are shown through critical analysis to be working ideologically – to be helping the practices sustain relations of domination – critical social science may subvert the practices it analyses, by showing proto-theories to be miscognitions, and producing scientific theories which may be taken up within (and enter struggles within) the practices.

We see CDA as a form of what Bhaskar (1986) calls 'explanatory critique', and we shall sketch out such a view of CDA in Chapter 4. 'Explanatory critique' takes the general form of showing (a) a problem, which may be either cognitive, for example, a misrepresentation, or an unmet need (the former is transitive critique, the latter intransitive critique); (b) what obstacles there are to it being tackled; in some cases (c) what the function (including ideological function) of the misrepresentation or unmet need is in sustaining existing social arrangments; and (d) possible ways of removing the obstacles. The two types of problem point to two aspects of CDA: one a form of transitive critique of discursive constructions of practices (their reflexive element); the other an intransitive critique of discursive dimensions of practices in terms of whether they meet or fail to meet the communicative aspects of the needs of people engaged in the practices.

CRITIQUE AND POSTMODERN RELATIVISM: SOME ISSUES

Each variant of explanatory critique presupposes grounded judgements: in the case of cognitive critique, judgements of whether constructions of practices are true or false, adequate or inadequate; in the case of needs-based critique, judgements about what people need. The former depend upon claims that the relational logic of social science yields truths about social practices which are not accessible within the practical logic of those operating within those practices. We realise that such claims are contentious not so much for implying that social practices are opaque to people – this assumption is shared by much postmodernist theorising (Larrain 1994) – but rather for assuming privileged scientific access to 'the truth'. The main criticism is directed towards objectivist theory, including earlier structuralist versions of critical theory (Barrett 1991; Morrow and Brown 1994). Yet scepticism towards the possibility of objective truth has today grown into scepticism towards the enlightenment project and towards science in general, putting into question the use of scientific reason for reconceptualising the practical world (Norris 1994). This is a position best illustrated in the work of Lyotard (1984, 1990), for whom the relationship of science to the social world is cast in terms of self-justificatory narratives, particularly science's promise to liberate humanity, a promise not only futile and imaginary but also undesirable: in an ironic reversal, this illusory promise has been responsible for totalising and terroristic (in the sense of suppressing difference) modes of thinking and acting. Science should therefore be cut down to size, as one 'language game' among many.

We accept that scientific claims to privileged knowledge have in some cases worked in terroristic ways (see Chapter 7 for further discussion), but we do not accept that the solution is to give up the very possibility of truth claims. We agree with Norris (1994: 12) that such arguments typically confuse the issue by ignoring ... the crucial difference between 'truth' as a matter of privileged access, vouchsafed to some religious or secular elite already (so to speak) 'in the know', and truth as arrived at through reasoned enquiry in the public sphere of open participant debate

– a debate which postmodernists themselves contribute to (Norris 1994: 11). We have three points to make here, with particular regard to social science. First, that social science applies a logic to gaining knowledge of social practices (a dialectical logic in the case of critical social science) that yields types of knowledge not generally achievable within those practices, on the basis of which reflexive self-constructions within those practices can be assessed. Second, that social science produces competing accounts of any given social practice, which can be assessed against each other as truth claims through argumentation in the public sphere – the efficacy of science depends on this. Third, the truth claims of science are also assessed against each other in the course of the social practice concerned, not only through argumentation within the practice (in its reflexive aspect) but also through practical testing of truth claims in action (Collier 1998). Truth claims are not assigned or denied the status of absolute truth in this process, but judged in terms of 'epistemic gain', the 'movement from a problematic position to a more adequate one within a field of available alternatives' (Calhoun 1995; see also Taylor 1989).

Claims about what people need in explanatory critique are just as problematic: even assuming that there are certain general human needs we could all agree upon, needs-based critique will more often than not be oriented to needs which are socially and culturally specific and in many cases hotly contested (Sayer 1997). Sayer (1997) argues that explanatory critique must at this point be tied to a communicative or discourse ethics such as Habermas has proposed (Habermas 1984, 1990; Benhabib 1992): needs (like the value of claims to truth) have to be democratically determined in open and equal dialogue. We see this in terms of a crucial link between critical social science, and the contemporary struggle for democracy and an effective public sphere. Such a link is urgently required in the context of the erosion of representative democratic forms by the new global capitalism (Fairclough forthcoming b), as well as in the context of contemporary epistemological arguments for weakening the connection between theory and social practices (Rorty 1985, 1989).

Lyotard's postmodernism and Rorty's pragmatism both assume an 'untranslatability' between science and other social practices (Jameson, 'Foreward' to Lyotard 1984). Rorty views academics as romantic intellectuals, 'poets' capable of radical thoughts and playful 'redescriptions' of the social world which have no relevance in public life. We argue in contrast that what critical social science most needs is effective public spheres both to ground its critique and to put into place the open relationship between theory and social practice that it calls for. Epistemic gains, more adequate understandings of the social in the service of emancipation, can arise from that process. This is especially significant in the late modern context of increasing social fragmentation and complexity: tracing unsuspected structural connections and systematicities across practices can provide alternative conceptualisations of social life which may become the basis for new political alliances and forms of action. That is, the relational logic can contribute to emancipation through redrawing maps of the social (Hartsock 1990; Calhoun 1995; Harvey 1996). This entails opening up the reflexive element of practices to open and equal dialogue which can first, establish inputs for critical social science by debating and defining needs, second, draw outputs from critical social science into dialogue on social practices, and third, feed into and transform social practices. In this process neither CDA nor other forms of critical social science are in the business of 'prescribing' alternative practices (Toolan 1997), but rather helping to clear the ground for those engaged within a social practice to seek the changes they want, by clarifying obstacles to change and possibilities for change. So, an appropriate metaphor for the role of contemporary intellectuals is that of 'interpreters' (rather than 'legislators' – see Bauman 1987) – 'translating' between language games establishes links between practices and helps clarify problems and potentials for change.

CONCLUSION

We conclude with a summary of main features of 'critical' social science (including CDA).

1. A critical engagement with the contemporary world recognising that the existing state of affairs does not exhaust what is possible.
2. An emancipatory knowledge interest initiated and terminated in flows between theoretical practice and non-theoretical social practices, and anchored in the public sphere.
3. An engagement in explanatory critique directed at both intransitive and transitive objects (i.e., both practices themselves and theories of them), applying a dialectical logic.
4. A recognition of discourse as one moment in the dialectics of social practice, and of changes in discourse as capable of opening up new social possibilities.
5. A 'modest' yet non-relativistic understanding of scientific truth as epistemic gain, where what counts is relative explanatory power and contribution to meeting needs.
6. A reflexive understanding of the historical and social positioning of the researcher's own activity.

NOTES

1. Hammersley (1996) criticises CDA for having failed in the past to attend to the theoretical foundations of its critique. He reviews several theoretical rationales for critical social research in general and CDA in particular, all of which he finds wanting. The basic issue is whether one can ground the move from 'is' to 'ought' in critical social science. The 'critical realism' of Bhaskar on which we base this chapter offers a different approach to this question from those reviewed by Hammersley.
2. Bourdieu 1977; Giddens 1993; Habermas 1984, 1987a; Castoriades 1987; Bhaskar 1986 are all inspired by the Marxist 'philosophy of praxis' (Arendt 1958; Gramsci 1971). In a different epistemological frame, the ontological primacy of practice also underlies Wittgenstein's 'linguistic philosophy'

and diverse traditions in phenomenology (Husserl, Schultz) and hermeneutics (Heiddeger, Gadamer), up to post-structuralist theory (Foucault; Laclau and Mouffe – see below).

3. In terms of Althusser's concept of 'overdetermination', each moment is overdetermined, i.e., simultaneously determined by others. The concept comes from Freud, who used it for the condensation of a number of dream-thoughts in a single image, or the displacement of psychic energy from a particularly potent thought to an apparently trivial image. See Althusser and Balibar 1970: 315; Laclau and Mouffe 1985; Hall 1996a.

4. We find the concept of articulation a rich one used in conjunction with Harvey's dialectical view of the internalisation of moments of the social, but that does not mean that we accept the theory within which Laclau and Mouffe developed the concept, which equates the social with discourse (see Barrett 1991: 79 for a view of their work as deconstructionism re-engaging with Marxism).

Chapter 3

Discourse

Chapters 3 and 4 are together organised in a similar way to Chapter 2, moving from questions about the nature of discourse (Chapter 3) to a discussion of critical discourse analysis (Chapter 4). We begin this chapter with a discussion of discourse as 'joint action' (Shotter 1993) – that is, as a particular form and facet of the productive activity of social practices – dialectically related to discursive and linguistic structures. We then discuss specific characteristics of the way that dialectic works in (late) modern society, in terms of Smith's (1990) view of the 'textually mediated' nature of contemporary social life, and move from that to a discussion of the category of 'text'. We argue that the dialectical character of discourse calls for dialectical (constructivist–structuralist) theories of language and other semiotic systems, as opposed to the one-sidedly structuralist or interpretivist theorising which has dominated in linguistics and other areas of language and semiotic theory. We discuss Volosinov's (1973) formulation of a dialectical theory of language and discourse, and more recent moves towards such a theory within systemic functional linguistics.

DISCOURSE IN SOCIAL PRACTICE

We begin with a summary of what we said in Chapter 2 about social life as practice, with a focus on discourse. We argued that any practice articulates together diverse elements of life (as its 'moments'), and therefore diverse mechanisms. Discourse is one such element, with its own mechanism. The moments of a practice are articulated within a dialectic – each internalises the others without being reducible to them. Practices themselves are articulated together within networks of practices, and their 'internal' features are determined by these 'external' relations. Any practice is a practice of production – people in particular social relations applying technologies to materials. Also, any practice has a reflexive element – representations of a practice are generated as part of the practice. Discourse therefore figures in two ways within practices: practices are partly discursive (talking, writing, etc. is one way of acting), but they are also discursively represented. In so far as such representations help sustain relations of domination within the practice, they are ideological. Networks of practices and particular practices within networks constitute particular relations which can be conceptualised in terms of the concept of hegemony – as struggles for closure which can never totally succeed, which always give rise to resistance. Focusing on social life as practices is a way of mediating between abstract structures and concrete events, combining the perspectives of structure and agency. We suggested that analysis of 'conjunctures' – cross-institutional assemblies of practices around specific projects – might be a productive way of operationalising such a focus.

We shall use the term 'discourse' to refer to semiotic elements of social practices. Discourse therefore includes language (written and spoken and in combination with other semiotics, for example, with music in singing), nonverbal communication (facial expressions, body movements, gestures, etc.) and visual images (for instance, photographs, film). The concept of discourse can be understood as a particular perspective on these various forms of semiosis – it sees them as moments of social practices in their articulation with other non-discursive moments.

Social practices are always ways of socially interacting – ways for people to act practically together in the production of social life, in work, in play, in their homes, in the street, and so forth. It is easy for a critical social science oriented to the abstract structures and social relations of societies and the ways in which they are reproduced or transformed to miss the richness and complexity of social interaction. And yet it is of crucial importance for any dialectically conceived critical theory to grasp the complex qualities of social interaction. For not only is any social structure dependent upon its ongoing instantiation in social interaction, and not only is it in social interaction that structures are problematised and contested, but social interaction is also the nursery for new social forms and themes of all sorts (Volosinov 1973) out of which the materials are forged for new social relations, new social identities and new social structures. So the generative, emergent qualities of social interaction are crucial. Not all interaction is discursive – people can interact for instance by tidying a house together – but most interaction substantively and centrally involves discourse, and the generative, creative properties of interaction are very largely to do with properties of discourse. So it makes sense to focus on discourse to gain insights into social interaction.

To illustrate the emergent nature of interaction in the form of concrete text, we begin with a short extract from a conversation which took place during an evening meal involving five members of the same family, Richard W., Derek and Brenda K., and Susan and Derek G. (Watts 1992: 25–6). There is nothing at all special about this example – it was picked rather at random as the first example of casual conversation we came across in preparing this chapter. But it illustrates that interactive discourse is 'joint action' (Shotter 1993), co-production; this property of discourse is at the heart of the creative potential of social interaction.

```
1   DG: But (.) I've always been in the belief that it was being
2        (.) (.) it was always being negotiated. But (0.8) I
3   DK:  What?
4   R:              mm
5        slowly came the conclusion that I was sort of
```

```
 6       fighting a losing battle as far as the :erm(.): - -
 7  B:                                Yes.
 8  R:                                          Well
 9       you were the only one in fact who was in dispute,
10  DG:                           Yeah.
11       and so they were just hoping that it would die down
12       and sooner or later you would accept what/th- their
13  DG: Yeah.
14  DG:                            That's right.
15  DG:                                          Yeah.
16  R:   conditions that they would wear you down presumably
17  DG:            mm
18  B:                                          But –
19  S:                                          They don't
20       know us.
```

In the comments that follow we are partly drawing upon and partly extending Watts's analysis to try to give an 'insider's view' of what is going in this short episode – Watts was a participant in the interaction (R), so his commentary is in that sense 'from the inside'.

This is 'joint action' in the sense that the account of DG's problems at work is jointly developed by DG and R, though their contributions to it are rather different: DG's is a 'personal assessment of the situation' (Watts 1992: 26), R's an 'explanatory position'. This is the ideational aspect of the interaction – its representation of the way (this bit of) the world is. But it is not at all a simple matter of subjects depicting an objectively given world. For one thing, language is being used 'indexically' (Garfinkel 1967; Heritage 1984) in the sense that the expressions that are used to describe the way the world is are only vague and general pointers which co-participants routinely fill out by drawing upon their shared knowledge and experience – their 'common sense'. A case in point is DG representing himself having come to the conclusion that he was 'sort of fighting a losing battle'. The hedging expression 'sort of' is indicative of the implications of the indexicality of language for speakers: representing the way of the world is an uncertain process of adequation in which the limited categories available linguistically are adequated to massively variable social experiences in ways which are no more than 'adequate for practical purposes' (Garfinkel 1967).

This case also illustrates how co-participants are not only ongoingly interpreting each other's indexical expressions but practically doing the interpretative work in the contributions they themselves make – so R in lines 9–16 fills out DG's representation of what was going on with representations of his own which, amongst other things, demonstrate an interpretation of what was meant but left unsaid when DG represented himself as 'fighting a losing battle'. Notice that there are six different formulations of what was going on, two offered by DG (*I've always been in the belief that* …) *it was always being negotiated, I was sort of fighting a losing battle*), the others by R (*you were the only one who was in fact in dispute, they were just hoping that it would die down, (they were just hoping that) sooner or later you would accept their conditions, (they were hoping) that they would wear you down*). Three of these use metaphors which are part of the language of ordinary life (*fighting a losing battle, die down, wear you down*), whereas the other three use vocabulary which belongs to the public discourse of workplace relations (*negotiated, in dispute, accept ... conditions*).

Whereas DG only represents what was going on in the language of ordinary life, R also represents it in terms of public discourse. And whereas DG's formulations of what was going on are subjectively framed as his belief and conclusion, R's are statements of fact (notice *in fact* in line 9; by contrast there is a modal hedge in line 16 – *presumably* – but it loses part of its force by being positioned after the proposition it hedges). DG's supportive feedback seems to endorse R's contributions as part of an interpretative elaboration of what he meant in saying he came to the conclusion that he was 'sort of fighting a losing battle', as well as the cause–effect relations R is proposing between these propositions. This joint accumulation of formulations of what was going on and the causal ordering of them is an active collaborative process of constructing the world through an articulation of the language of ordinary life with the discourse of the economic system. The joint action and articulation of discourses is in this case rather mundane, but it is a resource which can be put to more creative uses.

This joint construction of the world is carried out within and as part of the social relations of the interaction. Notice that R's turn begins during DG's voiced pause (lines 6–8) and might therefore be interpreted as a face-threatening interruption, and that it is not ostensibly supportive of DG so its relevance as a contribution to a joint account is not apparent. Watts suggests that in prefacing his turn with *well* (line 8), R can be seen as 'highlighting the possible perception of lack of relevance and thus ... minimising a face threat' (1991: 27). Notice also how much supportive feedback DG gives to R (lines 10–17). Watts suggests that maybe DG wishes to signal that R's intervention in line 8 has not been seen as an interruption. Feedback is an inherent part of communicative interaction which makes the contributions of all participants continuously subject to the evaluation of their communicative and social partners. This evaluative process is an important part of the social relations of communicative interaction which gives it a moral quality in constantly subjecting actions to the measure of 'common sense', and it is crucial to participants having a sense of belonging and shared identity. DG's supportive feedback in this case can be seen as intensified positive evaluation of R's contribution, signalling community and shared identity in the response to a possible disturbance.

Generalising, we may say that in addition to ongoingly interpreting and helping to elaborate what was meant about the world in what was said in contributing to the interaction, participants are ongoingly interpreting what was done with respect to their social relations with co-participants in what was said, and practically designing their contributions to act upon these social relations in this light. Moreover, in so doing they are actively constructing identities for themselves and each other – the intensity of DG's supportive feedback also constructs him as a cooperative and amenable person, as well as constructing R as a person of good intentions. Identities are also joint productions. These orientations to the world, to each other and to oneself are difficult to pull apart. Notice for instance that DG's supportive feedback in reassuring R contributes to a joint construction of what was going on – or, in contributing to a joint construction of what was going on, it reassures R. The general point is that in communicative interaction people do not represent the world abstractly but in the course of and for the purposes of their social relations with others and their construction of social identities.

But the simultaneous representational, relational and identificational processes identified in the example above are not carried out for their own sake. They are part of a practical engagement with the world Watts identifies in the way he frames the extract: 'DG has tabled as a topic the problem he has been having at his place of work and what sort of action he should take either with or without the help of his trade union.' The discourse is on the one hand a reflexive construction of the social prac-tice of the workplace and as such may perhaps lead to future action within that practice. But on the other hand it is a part of the social practice of family life, whose social relational and affective moments are here internalised in the talk, which works to create family solidarity with and around DG. In articulating together workplace and family discourses, the interaction connects the two social practices, constructing a continuity between family solidarity and workplace solidarity. In the terms of Chapter 2, the discourse is one moment in a social practice which is dialectically linked to others, with an orientation to a practical intervention aimed at changing (this bit of) the world.

Moreover, this is effected through an appropriation of structural resources in joint action. Joint action depends on relatively permanent social resources (structures) including in this case both a particular language system and a particular order of discourse (network of discursive practices). While these resources are on the one hand appropriated and rearticulated – for instance, into new articulations of dis-courses – for local purposes such as the creation of solidarity, on the other hand they constrain what can be done in interaction. For instance, the workplace discourse drawn upon here is appropriated as a resource for the purpose at hand, but in being drawn upon it nevertheless constitutes a colonisation of one social practice (the family) by another (the workplace). Analysis has to be constantly attentive to both structure and action – what the structural preconditions (resources) for action are and what the structural effects of action are (for example, in terms of colonisation), but also how structural resources are locally appropriated and worked. This structure–action dialectic (including a colonisation/appropriation dialectic) must be kept constantly in view.

TEXTUALLY MEDIATED SOCIAL LIFE

In Chapter 2 we claimed that modern societies have developed practices which are highly complex in their forms and social relations of production, and in the networks of practices they enter into, and which draw increasingly upon specialised theories in their reflexivity. They are often organised across great distances of time and space – 'globalised' – and depend upon sophisticated technologies of mediation. Ordinary face-to-face practices are increasingly dependent upon (we might say 'colonised by') these complex modern practices, as well as appropriating them. The extract discussed above is a case in point. In short, modernity has involved a radical change in the nature of social practices and in the relations between social practices.

The social functioning of discourse has been transformed as part of these changes. The ways in which the moment of discourse is articulated with other moments in social practices are radically changed – for instance, the ways in which relations of power are discoursally inflected (i.e., how power internalises discourse) and in which discourse is invested with power (i.e., how discourse internalises power) have been transformed. There has always been a dialectic between discourse and power; what has changed are its forms. There have also been radical changes in relations between different types of discourse, and in how discursive constructions of practices (their reflexive elements) figure as parts of practices.

The development of writing and print literacy are a part of modernity. There are fundamental differences between face-to-face discourse and written discourse (say, an exchange of letters). First, writing is a spatialisation of spoken discourse which transforms the unfolding of interaction in time: the 'middle' or 'end' of a conversation is a point in time, the 'middle' or 'end' of a letter is a position in space. With writing, the category of 'text' enters discourse. Second, texts such as an exchange of letters can be kept as a permanent record, whereas in pre-electronic times there was no way of preserving a conversation. Third, writing (and reading) requires special skills which are difficult to acquire, producing a division between those who are literate and those who are not. Fourth, writing makes possible an increase in time–space distantiation – it allows communicative interaction to take place at a temporal and spatial distance.

Written discourse is mediated discourse, in the sense that a technical medium is used to increase time–space distantiation. Other forms of mediated discourse are telephone and email conversations, which bring enhanced spatial distantiation without the time gap (or costs) associated with writing: letters need to be physically transported from their context of production to their context of reception. A splitting of contexts is a characteristic of mediated discourse: whereas people in face-to-face discourse are in a shared context, the context of for instance the writer of a letter is different from the context of the reader. There is correspondingly a reduction in shared knowledge and a narrowing of the range of symbolic resources available for making and interpreting meaning – in face-to-face communication these include intonation and non-verbal communication (facial expression, gesture, etc.). Mediated discourse has to compensate in various ways for these absences. This splitting of contexts is also an articulation of forms of discourse. In the practical activities of everyday life, a telephone conversation, for example, is embedded in face-to-face conversations, so there might be separate conversations going on at either end of the line, both of which the telephone conversation is in a sense a part of.

But the intersection goes deeper than this. Different forms of discourse come to shape and transform each other in ways which fundamentally transform modern social life. According to Thompson (1995), one salient feature of modernity is the rise of mediated quasi-interaction. This is communicative interaction in mass communication – books, newspapers, radio, television – where the co-involvement of large numbers of spatially and temporally dispersed people is added to the time–space distantiation of mediated interaction. Whereas mediated interaction is still (like face-to-face interaction) dialogue between specific persons, mediated quasi-interaction entails a division between an individual producer or relatively small production team and a body of receivers that is indeterminate in size and member-ship. It is monological in character, hence only quasi-interaction.

The contexts which are separated out and articulated together through mediated quasi-interaction are on the one side the institutional and organisational contexts of the modern social systems of the economy and the state, and on the other hand the contexts in which people live their ordinary lives. The relations between different forms of discourse entailed here (mediated, conversational) are part of relations between different social practices. So, what has changed is not simply the range of forms of discourse but also the relationships between them, how they are articulated together within social practices. In the terms of one influential social theory, mediated quasi-interaction links 'system' to 'lifeworld' (the world of everyday experience). Indeed, the emergence of mass communication and mediated quasi-interaction has been an important factor in facilitating the separation out of systems from the lifeworld within modern societies (the 'uncoupling' of lifeworld and systems – Habermas 1984, 1987a). One aspect of this separation is the specialisation out from conversation of forms of face-to-face discourse for systemic purposes (for example, all the many types of interview) which results in an ongoing dialectic between conversation and face-to-face discourse in systems (this specialisation-out is a focus of concern in conversation analysis, though in a unidirectional way which misses the dialectic – see for instance Zimmerman and Boden 1991). Systems sustain a necess-ary anchorage in the lifeworld through the intersection of mediated quasi-interaction with conversational discourse. The social relations of this intersection are contra-dictory and are relations of struggle. On the one hand, books, newspapers, pam-phlets, radio and television allow systems to penetrate the wide and indeterminate variety of local contexts of the lifeworld, and to reproduce their order throughout social life (Smith 1990). On the other hand, the intersection gives people unprece-dented access to immense resources with which they can enrich their lives.

These changes in the forms of discourse and relationships between them con-stitute part of changes in social practices and relationships between social practices, changes in the form of the social dialectic. They are a part of the modernisation process, which can be conceived as increasing time–space distantiation which allows social activity to take place and power to be exercised across differences in space and time through technical advances in forms of mediation (see Chapter 5 for this view of modernisation). One part of this process is the emergence of modern social systems. For example, take the case of the connection between writing and social relations of power, which we have already referred to. With the emergence of writing, new forms of social activity became possible: for instance, people could keep records, and with the gain in time–space distantiation this meant that people could cooperate over larger geographical areas and longer time spans. But the economic, political and cultural possibilities opened up by writing were not equally available to all: on the contrary, they became resources through which relations of domination could be elaborated. On the one hand, the fact that writing and reading require special skills and that access to these skills could in various ways be controlled facilitated this appropriation of their potential. On the other hand, writing as a mode of record-keeping facilitated the development and refinement of processes of record-keeping, classification and surveillance and became an important technique of disciplinary power (Foucault 1977). But the communicative relations of written discourse have probably always been contested – they certainly have in more recent history: access to the possibilities opened up by writing as well as the particular uses of modes of mediated communication have been an ongoing focus of social struggle – access to and the uses of the internet is now becoming one.

However, never before has the struggle over forms of and access to mediated and quasi-communication assumed such importance as today, when late modern societies are increasingly seen as information and communication societies. As advanced technologies that process and reproduce information are integrated with technologies that move information through space in practically no time, new patterns of communication emerge that deeply affect social experience and radically transform social relationships (see for example Poster 1990; Thrift 1996; and also Chapter 5), to the point where some theorists have argued that traditional social structures are now replaced by information and communication structures and that social identities are defined in terms of positions in and access to the mode of information rather than the mode of production (Lash 1994).

The deep impact of the changes in forms of and relationships between discursive practices is evident in recent debates about what the economic and social changes of late modernity mean for individuals. It has been argued that late modernity is a 'post-traditional' social form in which individuals have to undertake the 'project' of constructing their own lifestyles and identities (Giddens 1991). They have access via mediated quasi-interaction to a huge resource of knowledge, practices, ways of being, and so forth, which they can draw upon. But this resource is shaped elsewhere, it comes to them from systems they have no control over. So the unprecedented autonomy of individuals goes with an unprecedented dependence upon mass mediated symbolic resources. As Smith puts it, social consciousness has become 'externalised' in late modern societies: people have to turn to specialised systems and the experts who organise them for information, know-how, ways of reasoning, etc. which they need in order to handle even the most personal and intimate aspects of their being – such as their sexuality. They do so by entering forms of mediated quasi-interaction – reading magazines or 'lifestyle' books, watching television shows, etc. In doing so they are drawn into the social relations of capitalism: not only are the magazines etc. commodities which they consume, the lifestyles on offer are generally dependent upon all sorts of other commodities.

But people are not simply subjected within these mediated quasi-interactions, for they intersect with conversational discourse. We may say they are 'recontextualised' within conversation (Bernstein 1990), and this implies that they can be appropriated and transformed in diverse and unpredictable ways, and undesirable ways from the perspective of those who are selling the commodities. It also implies of course at least a certain colonisation of conversation by mediated quasi-interaction (and of life-world by systems). The extract discussed in the previous section exemplified this colonisation/appropriation dialectic in the way it articulated the discourse of the workplace with the discourse of family life. Whether the appropriation is more salient than the colonisation or vice-versa – whether therefore the creative, emergent potentials of discourse in social interaction discussed earlier can be realised – depends upon how the moment of discourse is dialectically connected to other moments in a particular social practice. But there is always a dialectic of colonisation/ appropriation.

Through researching this dialectic, the analysis of discourse can contribute a focus on relations between different types of discourse to the analysis of relations between different social practices. One example of such research is discussed by Cicourel (1992) concerning the appropriation of elements from lectures and written lecture notes in professional conversation between doctors in a hospital. Scollon's recent work on media for example focuses on people's face-to-face interactions that draw on quasi-mediated discourse (news), appropriating it as a 'site of engagement' upon which other ongoing social practices and contestations of identity may be con-structed. Discourse analysis here works together with ethnographic research that locates discourse as a part of a wider set of social practices in the familial local context (Scollon 1998). Media research can also combine a critical discourse analysis of TV news with audience interview analysis, as in Chouliaraki (1998b, 2000), which demonstrates that audiences draw upon diverse expert discourses to reflexively rework media discourse in a context of 'life-politics', so that the news text is appro-priated in both reproductive and transformative ways. Finally, Thrift (1996) provides a rich research agenda for the communicative practices of the international financial system, arguing that the global network of market forces opens up a huge number of dispersed, local discursive communities that reflexively appropriate and rework the global financial discourses and practices. Here, CDA can usefully be combined both with qualitative methodologies, such as ethnographies of banking organisations (Thrift's own research was in the City of London), as well as quantitative ones based on questionnaires and statistics. With its focus on interdiscursivity, i.e., the shifting articulation of different discourses, genres and voices in interactions and texts, CDA is well placed to research these issues.

TEXTS

The category of 'text' arises with mediated interaction. We understand a text to be a contribution to communicative interaction which is designed for travel, so to speak – which is designed in one context with a view to its uptake in others. So the category of text is linked to the category of mediation. In this sense, texts are generated in mediated interaction and in mediated quasi-interaction, but not in face-to-face interaction, though face-to-face interaction may be transformed into text for specific purposes, i.e., redesigned for uptake in other contexts – as when linguists transcribe and analyse conversations.

The first texts were of course written, but the texts of contemporary mediated interaction and quasi-interaction are also spoken (radio), televisual (so combinations of speech and image and sound effect), or electronic (for example, email). Even 'written' texts are increasingly multisemiotic, not only combining written language with visual images (photographs, diagrams, etc.) but also treating the written language itself as a visual surface which is often intricately worked. The term 'text' is not ideal for this diverse set of forms because it still powerfully suggests written language, but we shall use it nevertheless in the absence of any better alternative.

Smith (1990) develops a compelling analysis of how the 'relations of ruling' of contemporary societies are 'textually mediated': for instance, people in negotiating their sexuality draw upon texts from TV or magazines which tie them in to the social relations of commodity production and consumption. It is important not to lose this focus on the concrete text; nevertheless, as I have suggested above, the mediation often abstracts away from specific texts and becomes mediation by discourses. But an important implication of Smith's analysis for critical discourse analysis is that texts work within interactions. A great deal of critical discourse analysis – including some of Fairclough's own work – has been analysis of texts in abstraction from interactions. Let us quote Smith on what is needed and what needs to be avoided:

> Texts are not seen as inert extra-temporal blobs of meaning, the fixity of which enables the reader to forget the actual back and forth work on the piece or pieces of paper in front of her that constitute the text as a body of meaning outside time and all at once ... The text is analysed for its characteristically textual form of participation in social relations. The interest is in the social organisation of those relations and in penetrating them, discovering them, opening them up from within, through the text. The text enters the laboratory, so to speak, carrying the threads and shreds of the relations it is organised by and organises.
>
> (Smith 1990: 4)

This understanding of 'text' is however in tension with a different though equally coherent understanding coming from systemic functional linguistics, which we explain in the next section.

DIALECTICAL THEORY OF LANGUAGE

We have described discursive interaction as an active, reflexive, interpretative and collaborative process of representing the world while simultaneously negotiating social relations with others and one's own identity, as one moment in a social practice. It is an open process in which new representations, social relations and social identities may emerge, and in which outcomes are unintended and unpredictable –

but only to an extent. There is a dialectic between action and its structural resources (discursive 'permanences' – see Chapter 2), so that resources are produced and transformed in communicative interaction as well as constituting its condition of possibility. A dialectical theory of language and other semiotic systems is needed to come to grips with these properties of discourse. Yet most theorisation of language takes either the structural or the actional facet of the dialectic of discourse as its object, as if the two were alternatives. Consequently, structuralist and interactionist perspectives in language study tend to be seen as irreconcilable opposites.

Structuralism in linguistics has been the model for structuralism in other social sciences and humanities (Levi-Strauss 1963; Althusser 1971). Mainstream twentieth-century linguistics in the tradition of de Saussure (1974) has been based in a distinction between (in his terms) *langue* (the language system) and *parole* (the social act of language use), and the view of linguistics as the study of *langue* but not *parole*. The Saussurean view of the language system underlies the relational principle and relational logic which is fundamental to contemporary social science (recall our discussion of it in Chapter 2). Language is seen as a system of signs in which the value of any sign derives from its relation to other signs – its being equivalent to or different from other signs. Value, and 'meaning' in one (limited) sense, are not determined from outside the system but from inside the system. In so far as discourse and texts figure here, it is in terms of the significance of the systemic possibilities they include and exclude. There have been different conceptualisations of language system, incuding notably its conceptualisation as a set of generative rules in the work of Chomsky (1957, 1965), but these have not changed the Saussurean view of linguistics as the study of the language system as a closed system. Structuralism has certain widely discussed and in general negatively evaluated consequences which also apply to theories of langue – including a tendency to construct social subjects as 'effects' of structures which leaves no space for agency, a related inability to give a coherent account of change, and a failure to recognise that *parole* is a domain not just of individual performance unamenable to scientific analysis but of socially structured variation. Sociolinguistics has developed the latter critique, though generally in a way which has one-sidedly construed variation in language use as an effect of social difference, rather than seeing the relationship dialectically.[1]

It is important to emphasise that this brief sketch appertains only to one strand, if a dominant one, in twentieth-century linguistics. There have always been those who have problematised a one-sided commitment to structuralism in linguistics – including for instance Firth in Britain (Firth 1957). Resources for a focus on the interactional, 'joint action' side of language have come from various directions – Schutz's phenomenology, symbolic interactionism, Garfinkel's ethnomethodology, Wittgenstein's linguistic philosophy and Gadamer's hermeneutics (Habermas 1988; Giddens 1993, 1995; Outhwaite 1987) – which share an interest in interaction and the interpretation of action. Wittgenstein's (1972) conceptualisation of language as 'language games' which constitute social life turned this interest in interpretation towards language, grounding linguistic philosophy and eventually linguistic pragmatics (Austin 1962; Searle 1969). Ethnomethodology has given rise to conversation analysis (Heritage 1984), which focuses everyday interaction as a practical accomplishment of its participants. The different traditions of interpretivism converge on the assumption that language in interaction is constitutive of the social world and of the self ('constructivism'). Recent theories of discourse centre upon this constitutive or constructive character of language in interaction, for instance in psychology (Parker 1998; Shotter 1993), but it is generally seen as an alternative to a focus on linguistic and social structures (though see Parker 1992). One consequence is that the creativity of interaction can be somewhat romanticised (a tendency in Shotter 1993, for instance) by overlooking what we might call its 'scarcity' – to what degree and for whom interaction can be substantively creative depends on social structures.

Structuralism and constructivism are not real alternatives, in social science generally (see Chapter 2) or in the theorisation of discourse and language. Our view of discourse as a moment in social practices and as a form of social production ('joint action') in practices entails a constructivist focus on social life as produced in discourse, as well as a structuralist focus on the semiotic (including linguistic) and non-semiotic structures, which are both conditions of possibility of discourse and products of social (including discursive) production. The basis for such a dialectical view of discourse and language was laid in a remarkable book by Volosinov written in the 1920s (Volosinov 1973).

Volosinov highlighted the importance of a focus on discourse in analysis of social practices by pointing to the 'social ubiquity' of 'the word' (i.e., discourse – it is 'implicated in literally each and every act and contact between people ... countless ideological threads running through all areas of social intercourse register effect in the word'), and claiming that it is 'the most sensitive index of social changes, and what is more, of changes still in the process of growth, still without definitive shape and not as yet accommodated into already regularized and fully defined ideological systems' – the reference to 'ideological systems' here pointing to a distinction Volosinov drew between them (social systems such as education, science, law, government) and what he called 'behavioural ideology', the everyday social activity and communicative interaction which lies outside (or 'between') such systems. Volosinov argued for a dialectical view of such discourse as both shaped in its forms and contents ('genres' and 'themes') both by 'production relations and the socio-political order', and yet also by ongoing activity and struggle in which these genres and themes are transformed in a way that registers transformations in other elements of the social (Volosinov 1973: 19–21). In terms of the framework we have been using, this amounts to a strong claim that analysis of the discourse moment of a social practice can give insights into its dynamism which are not available from other moments.

In terms of theorisations of language as such, Volosinov contrasted two main tendencies in language theory, structuralism (what he called 'abstract objectivism') and 'individualistic subjectivism', a highly psychologised version of interactionism which saw language as individual creativity. Volosinov argued that neither produced an adequate theory of language, and he attempted to dialectically transcend the unproductive opposition between the two tendencies. His own theory included a recognition of 'language as a stable system' as 'productive only in connection with certain practical and theoretical goals', and while focusing the 'continuous generative process' of discourse, saw this as a social rather than a psychological process.

Volosinov was clearly closely associated with Bakhtin, and indeed for some scholars the former was just a pseudonym for the latter. Bakhtin's theory of language is crucial for a move towards a dialectical theory because of the insight it gives into the nature of the process through which discourse is both shaped by language structures yet works them and ultimately transforms them as well as reproducing them. Bakhtin emphasised the dialogicality of language, not only in the sense that even apparently non-dialogical discourse such as written texts is in fact always caught up in a dialogical chain – always responding, always anticipating and eliciting responses – but also in the sense that discourse is so to speak internally dialogical, it is 'polyphonic', 'double-voiced', 'double-languaged' (Bakhtin 1981). His analyses showed diverse forms of dialogicality in for instance the language of carnival, i.e., of times of licensed breaking-down of barriers and inhibitions (Bakhtin 1968), and in the novels of Dostoevsky (Bakhtin 1984), but internal dialogicality (or to employ Kristeva's (1986) widely used term 'intertextuality') can be seen as a general property of discourse capable of being manifest in many forms (Fairclough 1992c). In the most general terms, intertextuality is the combination in my discourse of my voice and the voice of another. Bakhtin applied his commitment to dialogicality to the theorising of genre not as a literary category but as a general category of discourse. A genre for Bakhtin is the language used in a particular form of activity, and it is characterised by a particular thematic content, a particular style and a particular compositional structure (Bakhtin 1986). Although discourse is constrained by genres, it is possible for genres to be mixed together in discourse. Intertextuality can therefore be understood at two levels: on one level it is the presence in my discourse of the specific words of the other mixed with my words, as for instance in reported speech; on another level it is the combination in discourse of different genres – or, we might add, different discourses (see Chapter 4 for definitions of these terms). We use the term 'interdiscursivity' (Fairclough 1992a) for the latter. The particular importance of Bakhtin in the present context is that his work suggests that a dialectical theory of language has to focus interdiscursivity.

We shall take up this argument in Chapter 8 in a dialogue with one of the major contemporary linguistic theories, systemic functional linguistics (SFL), but for the moment we want to indicate briefly how SFL has contributed to the task of formulating a theory of language incorporating both the dialectic between the semiotic (including the linguistic) and the non-semiotic social, and the dialectic between structure and action. According to Hasan (in press a), 'there is perhaps one way that a dialogical relation between distinct areas of human existence can be viably theorized – and this is to model the other universe(s) of human experience into the modelling of your primary object of study.' Elsewhere (Hasan in press b), Hasan writes of theorising language in ways which grasp the co-evolution of the 'semologic' and the 'sociologic', the logic of the semiotic and the logic of the social, which we take to be semiotic and sociological 'mechanisms' in the terms of critical realism (see

Chapter 2). First, SFL conceptualises language functionally, arguing that the grammar of a language is a network of systems corresponding to the major social functions of language – which we can interpret as the logic of the semiotic internalising the logic of the sociologic, i.e., language is socially structured at its core. Second, the SFL view of language as a 'social semiotic' includes a conceptual and analytical apparatus for showing language as systematically 'realising' social processes and relations (the 'context of situation', and through that the 'context of culture'), through its account of the social import of variation in language. Third, SFL sees language as text as well as system, and it is focused on the dialectic of text and system, including processes of 'semogenesis' – the production and change of language (the semiotic) – which unfold in texts within the co-evolution of the semologic and the sociologic. We do however have reservations about how successful SFL has been in developing a dialectical theory of language which centres precisely on its treatment of interdiscursivity (see Chapter 8, where we argue that a theory of discourse is needed in addition to a theory of language).

We referred earlier to a tension between the understanding of 'texts' as particular, mediated forms of discourse whose character is tied to properties of late modernity as a time–space regime, and the understanding of 'texts' in SFL. The functional conceptualisation of language in SFL includes the claim that three major types of process are always simultaneously going on in language: the construction of reality, the enactment and negotiation of social relations and identities, and the construction of text. These are respectively the 'ideational', 'interpersonal' and 'textual' functions of language. The claim is that you cannot semiotically construct (represent) reality without simultaneously identifying yourself and relating to other people in particular ways, and vice versa; but also that you cannot do either without simultaneously engaging in the semiotic activity of making text. We might say that text-making is the specifically semiotic facet of the production of social life in social practices, and that people can only engage with reality and each other semiotically through text-making. This concept of 'text' differs from the one above in that it applies to all discourse – it captures the 'textured' nature of all discourse. But the two senses are linked – the mediated texts of late modernity constitute a particular technological appropriation of discourse which depends on its specifically semiotic mode of materiality – its texture, the textual process, the fact that discourse unfolds in time. We believe that it is fruitful to keep in play both the latter language-theoretical conception of text and the former discourse-theoretical conception.

LANGUAGE AND OTHER SEMIOTIC SYSTEMS

The text-system dialectic has to be understood as involving other semiotic systems as well as language – bodily semiotics (gesture, touch, proximity), visual semiotics (static and moving image), and the semiotics of sound and music. Late modernity has arguably involved an 'iconic turn', a shift in the economy of semiotic systems which has led to a questioning of the pre-eminence of language that has been generally taken for granted (Kress and van Leeuwen 1996; Lash 1988, 1993; Poster

1990). Kress (1998) has recently argued that if we can distance ourselves from the presumption of the primacy of language in looking at the interplay between different semiotic systems, in for instance a contemporary science classroom, what we find is that language figures in the discourse as just one system co-equal with others.

There are complex equivalences and movements between language, other semiotic systems, and non-semiotic moments of social practices. Sex is a good example. Particular things can be done either discoursally or as material actions (or both), and if discoursally, either in language or in other semiotic forms. For instance, if I want to express my love and desire, I can caress (material activity, non-semiotic), I can smile (discoursal, non-verbal), or I can say something – or I can combine them. I can even say something in a laughing or caressing way – suggesting that discourse internalises the moment of material activity, i.e., discourse can be a material activity with somatic as well as semiotic aspects (Scollon and Scollon 1981). Conversely, the moment of discourse is internalised within material activity, so that a caress can be more or less semioticised – people develop their own codes of holding, stroking, etc. Each moment and each semiotic system has its own logic and mechanisms, and 'translation' between them is a complex process in which a great deal is 'lost' – a loving word is not a simple equivalent of a caress, or a smile. In these relationships, we might see non-linguistic forms of semiosis (for example, smiling) as lying between language and material activity, partly having the character of both.

A good example of SFL-based research that highlights the interplay of different semiotic systems in discourse, construes discourse as one moment in social practice and also takes a specific social conjuncture as its object of analysis (as we suggested in Chapter 2) is Iedema's (1997) discourse-oriented study of the building of an extension to a mental hospital. The object of research here was a conjuncture: a temporally extended process of planning, consultation and implementation, for the purposes of which a particular array of people, resources and practices was assembled. This bounded set of connected practices allowed him to trace how 'translation' within and between different moments of the social activity and between different semiotic systems took place at particular points in time – from dialogue to written documents to architectural drawings and back, from discourse to material action including the actual building work and back. It also allowed him to treat the moment of discourse as temporally extended so that processes of 'logogenesis', creativity in discourse, could also be traced in time – how for instance a polyphony of different voices and different constructions of the world may be gradually monologised over time in the course of the planning process, within interactions between bureaucracies and other parts of the population. This suggests a concrete way of pursuing the SFL interest in questions of semiogenesis. Also, in terms of CDA, analysis of 'intertextual chains' becomes possible (Fairclough 1992a) – of systematic ways in which one type of discourse is transformed into another (for example, the discourse of meetings into the discourse of minutes). The specific effect of the mechanism of discourse within the social practice, and how its potential as social interaction is realised in relation to other moments, can be shown better within such a temporally extended process (conjuncture) than in a single event such as a meeting.

CONCLUSION

Our discussion of the discourse moment of social practices continues in Chapter 4, where we turn to the critical analysis of discourse.

NOTE

1. Radical post-structuralist interpretations of the relational principle (notably Derrida's (1978)) have taken it to imply an unlimited 'play' of difference which entails that systems can never be closed, with structures correspondingly understood as only relatively permanent articulations of elements as attempted hegemonic closures (Laclau and Mouffe 1985). But see Fraser (1997: 151–70) on the need for a discourse theory in feminist politics similar to what we propose here.

Chapter 4

The critical analysis of discourse

In the previous chapter our focus was on the social ontology of discourse, and we now turn to the analysis of discourse. We begin with a reanalysis of texts previously analysed by Smith (1990) which exemplify her thesis of the textually mediated nature of contemporary social life. Our objective here is to illustrate how CDA can contribute to social (in this case, sociological) research on late modernity by showing that CDA can enhance Smith's analysis of the textual mediation of social life in this case. We then sketch out a framework for critical discourse analysis based upon the view of critical theory developed in Chapter 2 and the view of discourse in Chapter 3.

THE 'ACTIVE TEXT' AND THE HYBRID TEXT

In a paper entitled 'The active text' Smith sets out to show how texts are active in organising the social relations that they mediate – in this case the relations of 'public opinion' or 'mass communications' (Smith 1990). The conjuncture Smith's texts belong to is a dispute over the behaviour of police at a political demonstration in California in the 1960s – the texts are part of a public dialogue between a university professor and the Mayor of a city on the arrest of a young man in the course of a demonstration. The example is on the edge between mediated interaction and mediated quasi-interaction. The Professor witnesses police behaving violently towards people at a political demonstration and writes a letter to the Chief of Police with a copy to the Mayor (mediated interaction). He also 'as an afterthought' sends a copy to the local 'underground' press who publish it (mediated quasi-interaction). In response the Mayor distributes a statement which includes an extract from the Professor's letter and his own reply to the Professor. The Professor's letter (which we focus on) is reproduced as an appendix to this chapter. Smith's analysis centres upon how the Mayor's reply revises the Professor's account of the events he witnessed so as to construct everything that happened as in accordance with what Smith calls a 'mandated course of action', hence legitimate policing. The 'mandated course of action' is a sequence of steps which define proper police procedure: there is (the suspicion of) an offence; the police take action to make an arrest; if they are successful, the individual is charged; the individual is taken to court and, if found guilty, convicted.

The use of force by the police is legitimate provided it is tied to the mandated course of action. The Mayor's reply 'rewrites' the Professor's account so that this appears to be the case in each incident. For instance, the incident described as follows in the Professor's letter:

> I was standing just below the corner of Haste and Telegraph opposite Cody's and I saw a boy, 16 or 17 years old, walking up Haste and past two policeman.
>
> Suddenly a young policeman in his early twenties, with a cigar he had just lit in his mouth, grabbed this young man, rudely spun him around, pinned him against his patrol car, tore at his clothes and pockets as though searching for something, without so much as saying one word of explanation. Then he pushed him roughly up the street yelling at him to get moving.

is rewritten in the Mayor's reply as:

> You referred to four incidents which you were able to at least partially observe. The first concerned a young man who was frisked and who appeared to be then released. In fact this man was a juvenile who was arrested and charged with being a minor in possession of alcoholic beverages. He pleaded guilty and the court suspended judgement.

There are a number of interesting contrasts, which we discuss mainly in terms of the categories of SFL (Halliday 1994a; Fairclough 1992a). The modality of the Professor's account is categorical: it is a series of unqualified statements. The modality of the statements in the Mayor's reply which refer to the 'incident' is more complex. A contrast is set up with what 'appeared' to happen and what 'in fact' happened. And referring to the 'incidents' the Professor described in terms of his 'ability' to ('partially') observe them implies his 'inability' to observe other 'parts'.

The Professor's account is full of actions ('material' processes) in which the policeman is the agent and the 'boy' the patient, whereas actions are in the 'agentless' passive voice in the Mayor's reply (for example, *a young man who was frisked*) and no policeman figures as an agent. In contrast to the Professor's action-based account, the Mayor's is partly about classifications, about the (official) category the 'young man' belonged to, using attributes together with 'relational' processes: *this man was a juvenile … charged with being a minor*. Finally, the vocabulary of the Mayor's letter serves to reclassify what happened as part of normal police procedure – identifying what happened in an official way as an 'incident', reclassifying the 'boy' (a term which resonates with the Professor's construction of a case of wanton violence) as a 'young man' who is moreover in official terms a 'juvenile' and 'minor', and introducing an institutional vocabulary of action which assimilates the event to the mandated course of action (including 'stages' from it which do not figure in the Professor's account): *frisked, released, arrested, charged, pleaded (guilty)*. As Smith points out, reducing the Professor's detailed account of what the policeman did to *frisked* not only loses the detail through summary but also turns the policeman's actions into a stage in a series – frisking comes after an offence and before an arrest – and suggests that the Professor's account is based on partial observation. Summing up then, these features of the rewriting (only some of which are noticed by Smith) cumulatively establish behaviour according with the mandated course of action.

Smith's argument is that the mandated course of action involves a particular mode of interpretation, what Garfinkel called the 'documentary method interpretation': 'treating actual appearances as "the document of," as "pointing to," as "standing on behalf of" a presupposed underlying pattern' (Garfinkel 1967: 78), which remains inexplicit in the process of reading: the mandated course of action as part of an official discourse of policing is taken for granted – actually in both letters, as Smith argues – as an interpretative principle but not made textually explicit:

> Not only is the underlying pattern derived from its individual documentary evidences, but the individual documentary evidences, in their turn, are interpreted on the basis of 'what is known' about the underlying pattern. Each is used to elaborate the other.
>
> (Garfinkel 1967: 78)

There is a general point here: one way in which interactions may be shaped by system discourses is through implicit interpretative principles which shape how people contribute and interpret the contributions of others.

Smith's analysis effectively shows the textually mediated character of social life in this instance, but we want to suggest that the analysis can be developed and enhanced by drawing upon CDA. We approach this argument by looking at a rather striking feature of the Professor's letter which Smith's analysis does not refer to: its hybridity.

The extract from the Professor's letter reproduced above consists of two paragraphs. The first of them is linguistically similar to the paragraph which preceded it in the letter (lines 007–011 – see appendix). There is alternation between actional processes and mental processes. The subject ('experiencer') in the mental processes is 'I' (the Professor), while the subjects of the actional processes are in some cases 'I' but also 'the boy' and 'people'. The police do not explicitly figure as agents – in one case where they might have, an agentless passive is used (*two men ... were being dragged*). This is an observational language which foregrounds the Professor's perception of events and the vantage points from which he was able to observe, which depicts events 'objectively' (notice the precision of the specifications of place and the amount of numerical detail: *several (three, I believe), four men in each, two men, many people, 16 or 17 years old*), avoids attributing responsibility (the agentless passive) and ostentatiously avoids explanation (*for whatever reason*).

The language of the second paragraph is different. The Professor as observer has gone, and the description of events is no longer grounded in him being in a position to see what was going on. The processes are actions, the agent is an individual policeman, the patient (victim) is the 'boy'. The two paragraphs differ in the sort of detail they focus: in the first it is place, position, number; in the second it is the manner in which actions were performed. This is specified here through adverbials (*rudely, roughly*) and through an actional vocabulary which represents both the nature of the action and the manner of its performance (*grabbed, spun, pinned, tore at, pushed, yelling* – for example, *grabbed* = laid hold of in a rough way). The focus is on the individual performance and what it tells us about the personality of the policeman, and this is enhanced by the detail ('irrelevant' in terms of what happened) that he had a just lit cigar in his mouth. The contribution of 'just lit' is to draw the reader into the drama of the event, to position the reader as vicariously sharing the awful experience rather than (as in the previous paragraph) a citizen attending to evidence. The arbitrariness of the policeman's actions, and so their lack of legitimacy in precisely not falling within the mandated course of action, is conveyed by the adverbial *suddenly* which moreover is the marked theme of the first sentence and of the paragraph (and so colours the whole paragraph).

The hybridity of the Professor's letter is illustrated by the different things that are going on in these paragraphs. We need a way of talking about this hybridity which can bring together the detailed linguistic differences we have pointed out. Let us say that these linguistic differences 'realise' different 'genres' (a genre is a type of language used in the performance of a particular social practice). We might call the first paragraph an example of the genre of witness accounts. The label we use is not so important (there is no closed 'list' of genres or discourses, and there are relatively few that have stable names either for analysts or for participants); the important point is that is recognisable as the type of language used in domains like the law for giving 'objective', 'factual' accounts of first-hand experiences which can be taken as evidence. The second paragraph, by contrast, is an example of what we might call the genre of story-telling. It is story-telling with a roughly 'literary' quality which comes from the manifest ways in which it is worked up as a story, the effort that has manifestly been put into the texture of the text to make it work as a story. So one contrast here is between a broadly 'factual' discourse in paragraph 1 and a broadly 'fictional' discourse in paragraph 2.

Let us now bring the immediately following paragraph into the picture:

> I shall never forget the face of that policeman, his eyes bulging out, his face distorted by a vile sneer, his whole countenance exuding hatred, his cigar arrogantly sticking out of that obscene mouth. It was a frightening sight, especially to someone uninitiated to police tactics such as I was.

The Professor as observer is explicitly back again along with mental processes, but the mental processes here are not perceptions (as they were in paragraph 1) but cognition (*forget*) and effect (*frightening*). There is a change in tense too: the first verb is now future tense, so the Professor has shifted from an account of past events to a framing of them in terms of effects, which allows the description of this particular policeman to be taken symbolically as a picture of arrogant and callous power. Most of the processes are actional, but the agents are body parts (*eyes, face, countenance*) or attributes (*cigar*): the detail observed has shifted from object events, via the manner of performance of actions, to the person of the actor (the policeman) – though the manner of performance of actions by the agentified body parts and attributes is still focused through an adverbial (*arrogantly*), an adverbial transformed into an adjective as part of the nominalisation of an action (*a vile sneer*), and actional vocabulary which denotes nature + manner of action (*bulging out, sneer,* and perhaps *exude*). The demonstrative determiner 'that' (*that obscene mouth*) draws the reader into the event by constructing him or her as one who was there and could see for him- or herself. The vocabulary includes words which belong to what is stereotypically constructed as a 'literary' vocabulary (*exude, countenance, vile, obscene*), and indeed this whole collection of features is deployed here to produce a 'literary' portrait of the policeman. So we can say that the first sentence of the third paragraph continues the genre of literary narrative of the previous paragraph, but shifts more specifically into what we might call a 'sub-genre' of 'characterisation'.

Where is this analysis leading? What we are trying to establish is that the Professor's letter is considerably more hybrid than Smith's analysis suggests, and that indeed his strategy in writing the letter seems to be to assemble and combine a substantial variety of different genres and discourses. In short, that the active text is also a hybrid text, and that understanding its hybridity is the key to understanding its activeness. At some points the frequent shifts of discourse and the shifts in the Professor's voice (the capacity in which and perspective from which he is writing) which go along with them are particularly striking, for instance the construction of policemen and their actions in the next three paragraphs (lines 025–044). Policemen are referred to as: *policemen, uniformed thugs, cop, a huge strong man, uniformed hoods, 'pigs', perpetrators* (*of such bestiality*). 'Pigs' is used by others but not the professor, so it should be set aside. Otherwise the Professor moves through five different discourses in these few lines: an official one (*policeman*), a lifeworld one (*cop, hoods*), a political opposition one (the collocation of *uniformed + thugs/hoods*), a 'literary' one (*perpetrators*), and perhaps a feminist one (*a huge, strong man*). There is a similar instability in how actions are represented, ranging from a lifeworld term for violent attack (*beat up*) through broadly 'literary' representations which nominalise and metaphorise the action (*such bestiality*), and dramatise the action by making its instrument the agent (*a cop's club repeatedly descending on her*), to a legal term or nominalisation (*acts of violence*).

The analysis is not complete, but it is complete enough for the argument we are pursuing here, which is that attending to the hybridity of the letter indicates that we need to go beyond Smith's analysis, and especially the way in which she proposes to connect social interaction with the social structuring of the semiotic. As we have seen, she sees this connection in terms of a version of the documentary method of interpretation – treating (in this case) a letter as the 'document' of a presupposed underlying pattern. This actually works well in accounting for what the Mayor does in interpreting and rewriting the Professor's letter, where the underlying pattern is the mandated course of action. But what underlying pattern is the Professor's letter the document of? We have shown that it shifts across different genres and discourses, and we might say that these are themselves so many underlying patterns, and that therefore the letter is a document of several different underlying patterns. But this misses the point that it works a particular relationship between these genres and discourses – for instance, between a witness account and a literary narrative – for which there is also an underlying pattern: there is a social structuring of semiotic diversity, such that for instance legal, political and literary discourses are related (separated, connected) in ways that have acquired a certain permanence. We shall call this social structuring of semiotic diversity the 'order of discourse'. So are we to say that the letter is a document of the order of discourse? Perhaps. In so far as it is, then the implicitly dialectical wording at the end of Garfinkel's gloss on the documentary method of interpretation ('each' (i.e., both the letter and the underlying pattern) 'is used to elaborate the other') would seem to apply: the letter is a specific, locally motivated reworking of the order of discourse. But in fact the order of discourse seems more analogous to the language system than to a specific underlying pattern – it is a potential which any discourse only selectively draws upon, and dialectically reworks.

What we are arguing is that just as in sociological analysis it is necessary to envisage a 'middle-range' level of social structuring between the overall structure of a society and social action which applies to specific social 'fields' and their inter-connections (Bourdieu 1984; and see Chapter 6), so in semiotic analysis it is necessary to recognise a social structuring of the semiotic into what we call (adapting Foucault's term – Foucault 1971) orders of discourse and their interconnections. An order of discourse is the socially ordered set of genres and discourses associated with a particular social field, characterised in terms of the shifting boundaries and flows between them. This is a structuring of the semiotic that is different from semiotic systems (including the language system), which are specifications of the potential of the different semiotics without reference to the social division and limitation of that potential. Smith's account of the 'web of texts' that connect everyday processes with market relations in contemporary capitalist societies undertheorises the social structuring of the semiotic. In terms of the framework we set out in Chapter 2, we envisage a network of practices of production ordered in terms of social fields whose discourse moments constitute a network ordered in terms of orders of discourse. In this case there is a conjuncture at the intersection of the political and legal fields which includes an encounter between the practices of what is on the one hand ambivalently an even-handed exercise of citizenship and the conduct of oppositional politics, and on the other hand official reaction to public protest. The Professor's letter purports to be the letter of a concerned citizen to relevant authorities which appeared in the press as an 'afterthought', but the hybridity we have identified is more consistent with it being part of a political campaign taking on the appearance of a gesture of civic concern. The hybridity of the letter shows that the network of orders of discourse is not a simple positioning device but a resource in interaction which can be drawn upon more or less creatively in ways which themselves depend on positioning within that network – this example shows for instance that letters to the press give more space for creative rearticulation of the resource than letters from officials. It is a characteristic of the latter to reduce the generic and discursive diversity and dialogicality of the former by 'translating' it into a monological official discourse (what Smith identifies as the mandated course of action), a form of pre-dictable logogenesis which belongs to the order of discourse (which does not mean that the actual forms it takes in real cases are predictable). Having said that, official discourse in contemporary society has its own particular hybridising tendencies which we have referred to in earlier work as 'conversationalisation' (Fairclough 1994), the institutional appropriation of conversational discourse. (Networks of) orders of discourse are conceived dynamically with a focus on such shifting boundaries and flows within and between them.

Analysis of any discourse in contemporary societies with their complex intersections of different forms and types of discourse should include an 'interdiscursive' analysis of how different discursive types are mixed together (Fairclough 1992a). The claim is that such hybridity is an irreducible characteristic of complex modern discourse, and that the concepts of 'order of discourse' and 'interdiscursivity' constitute a powerful resource for researching what Smith calls the textually mediated character of contemporary social life (recall the discussion of Volosinov and Bakhtin in Chapter 3). Moreover, analysis of all forms and types of discourse should include a 'structural' dimension as well as an interactional dimension – the irreducible hybridity of modern communicative interaction is a matter of it being inevitably and always framed by and oriented to (structured by, but capable of structuring) the social structuring of the semiotic as a network of orders of discourse. The structural dimension attends to how interaction is constrained by the network of orders of discourse, while the interactional dimension attends to how that network is interactionally worked and potentially restructured through a rearticulation of resources (and so the interactional dimension feeds back into the structural dimension).

CRITICAL DISCOURSE ANALYSIS: A FRAMEWORK

Our aim in this section is to sketch out a framework for critical discourse analysis based upon the views of social life, critique and discourse we have developed in Chapters 2 and 3, and incorporating the focus on orders of discourse and interdiscursivity we have stressed in our reanalysis of Smith's texts. This framework gives a view of what is involved in actually doing a critical discourse analysis. The main headings can be seen as stages in CDA, though they are not necessarily all carried out in the order in which they are listed. There have been various previous versions of this form of CDA (for example, Fairclough 1989, 1992a, 1995b). Offering a new version of the analytical framework at this juncture accords with the view we expressed in Chapter 1 that CDA as a method should be seen as constantly evolving as its application to new areas of social life is extended and its theorisation of discourse correspondingly develops. The framework is rather a complex one, and for certain purposes analysts might focus on some parts of it rather than others, but we believe that the complexity is necessary to 'operationalise' the theoretical position we have set out in Chapters 2 and 3. We differ from Toolan (1997) in believing that the complexity of the framework should not be evaluated in terms of whether all the apparatus 'to demonstrate racism, sexism and so on' in particular case is needed – it probably is not, and the framework can be slimmed down in various ways for various purposes (for example, pedagogical purposes, in relation to 'critical language awareness' in education – see Fairclough 1992b); it should be evaluated rather in terms of its capacity to produce theoretically grounded analyses in a wide range of cases.

The framework we have summarised below is modelled on Bhaskar's 'explanatory critique' which we discussed in Chapter 2.

1. A problem (activity, reflexivity).
2. Obstacles to its being tackled:
   (a) analysis of the conjuncture;
   (b) analysis of the practice re its discourse moment:
      (i) relevant practice(s)?
      (ii) relation of discourse to other moments?
         – discourse as part of the activity
         – discourse and reflexivity;
   (c) analysis of the discourse:
      (i) structural analysis: the order of discourse
      (ii) interactional analysis
         – interdiscursive analysis
         – linguistic and semiotic analysis.
3. Function of the problem in the practice.
4. Possible ways past the obstacles.
5. Reflection on the analysis.

We briefly comment on each stage in turn.

Problem

CDA begins from some perception of a discourse-related problem in some part of social life. Problems may be in the activities of a social practice – in the social practice per se, so to speak – or in the reflexive construction of a social practice. The former may involve (in the terms of SFL) the ideational, interpersonal and/or textual functions of discourse, whereas the latter are ideational problems, problems of representations and miscognition. The former are needs-based – they relate to discursive facets of unmet needs of one sort or another. Illustrations of the two types of problem in the Smith example might be first, the failure of this sort of encounter as a public sphere, i.e., its typical failure to achieve real dialogue between the participants, and second, the tendency in official circles to represent everything officials (for example, police) do as in line with proper procedures. Although these problems are stated in a general way, they can be addressed with reference to detailed features of the discourse. (See Chapter 2 on the desirability of grounding problem-claims in public spheres.)

Obstacles to its being tackled

We comment first on the three sorts of analysis subsumed under this heading, and then come back to a discussion of how they can jointly specify the obstacles to a problem being tackled. The first type of analysis here is *analysis of the conjuncture* – i.e., a specification of the configuration of practices which the discourse in focus is located within. The focus here is on the configuration of practices associated with specific occasioned social goings-on. Such a conjuncture represents a particular path through the network of social practices which constitutes the social structure. Conjunctures can be more or less complex in terms of the number and range of practices they link together, more or less extended in time and in social space. Smith does not contextualise the texts enough to give a full picture of the conjuncture, but one would think that the more immediate conjuncture the texts are located within is the public contention over police behaviour. As this implies, conjunctures can be identified at different levels of specificity – for instance, we might say that the contention over police behaviour is located within the more extended conjuncture of political protest in the 1960s – and there is no clear cut-off between conjuncture and structure. These are not matters for discourse analysts to decide – the point here is to have at least a broad sense of the overall frame of social practice which the discourse in focus is located within. One aspect of the analysis of more immediate conjunctures is to locate the discourse in focus in real time in a way which links it to its circumstances and processes of production and its circumstances and processes of consumption, which brings the question of how the discourse is interpreted (and the diversity of interpretations) into the analysis.

The second type of analysis here is *analysis of the particular practice or practices* which the discourse in focus is a moment of, with particular regard to the dialectic between discourse and other moments. What is at issue may be either discourse as part of the activity, or discourse in the reflexive construction of the practice, or both. We can identify four main moments of a social practice: material activity (specifically non-semiotic, in that semiosis also has a material aspect, for example, voice or marks on paper); social relations and processes (social relations, power, institutions); mental phenomena[1] (beliefs, values, desires); and discourse. We have arrived at just four moments by combining three of those distinguished by Harvey (1996) under 'social relations and processes' (Harvey's categories are listed in the brackets). The objective here is to specify relationships between discourse and these other moments – how much of a part and what sort of a part discourse plays in the practice (for instance, some practices, for example in education, consist of little but discourse, while in others, for example some parts of industry, discourse may be relatively marginal), and what relations of internalisation there are between moments. In the case of the exchange of letters analysed by Smith for example, one wants to know what went on 'behind' the letters, how they came to be written, who was involved, what else was done on either side – the example illustrates how difficult it can sometimes be to 'reconstruct' the practice some discourse is located within and to get a proper sense of how the discourse figures in the practice, if all one has is (in this case) the letters.

This is why discourse analytical research should be seen as only one aspect of research into social practices working together with other social scientific methods, particularly ethnography (see also Chapter 1). The combination can be useful for both. Ethnography requires the systematic presence of the researcher in the context of the practice under study, usually for an extended period of time (fieldwork), and can therefore establish precisely the sort of knowledge that CDA often extrapolates from text, that is, knowledge about the different moments of a social practice: its material aspects (for example, locational arrangements in space), its social relationships and processes, as well as the beliefs, values and desires of its participants. Depending on the research design and its methods (field notes, video and audio recordings, interviews, document selection, archive research, etc.), ethnography can illuminate multiple aspects of a practice, both synchronically (at the time of the fieldwork) and historically. It also provides an invaluable context for assessing the articulatory process in the practice and the specific function of discourse in it (see Bourne 1992; Chouliaraki 1995; Wodak 1996; Iedema 1997; Scollon 1997; Pujolar 1998). Ethnography can benefit from CDA in the direction of reflexivity: data material should not be regarded as faithful descriptions of the external world but as themselves discursive formations that are assembled together to construct a particular perspective on the social world; neither do participants' accounts transparently reflect the social process in which they are embedded. In other words, there is a need to critically reflect upon and analyse both the ethnographer's and the informant's discursive practices (Clifford 1986).

But the general objective here is to have as clear a sense as possible of how the discourse works in relation to 'other things'. In terms of internalisation, it is noteworthy that people quite normally 'read off' other moments of social practice – social relations, power, beliefs, values, etc. – from written texts like letters (given that these may be all they have to go on). One issue with respect to the dialectics of discourse which we raised in Chapter 2 is the question of 'empty words': a concern in this part of the analysis in specifying relations of internalisation between discourse and other moments is to identify cases where internalisation is absent – where the discourse remains external to other moments. Discourse has social force and effect not inherently, but to the extent that it comes to be integrated within practices.

Problem-oriented explanatory critique inevitably raises questions about power. This is partly a matter of specifying relations between the social and discourse moments of the social practice. In the case of the Smith texts for instance, the monological official discourse of the Mayor's letter is a discourse which has internalised the power relations between officials and citizens, rulers and ruled, and whose internal features are shaped by these power relations. In a reasonable sense discourse is power in this case – writing this letter is enacting power. Looking at such relations of domination historically, we can say that power has tended on balance to migrate from material activity to discourse – it is still internalised in both, but its internalisation in discourse has become more pervasive. One consequence is that discourse more pervasively gives rise to questions of power (as well as other questions, such as questions of belief or desire). The Professor's letter reminds us that power relations are relations of struggle – that power is not simply exercised, it is also fought over, and fought over in discourse, and that the interdiscursive articulation of different genres and discourses is (amongst other things) a strategy of power struggle – a way in which power struggle is internalised in discourse (it is quite differently internalised in material activities). Power and power struggle also arise in the analysis of the conjuncture, for the question of which practices are to be brought together, and how, is itself a potential focus of power struggle. Questions of power link with questions of ideology, which, as we argued in Chapter 2, are best treated in terms of relations between the discourse moments of different practices and different orders of discourse. For instance, what Smith calls the 'mandated course of action' is a discourse that constructs the practice of policing, which is generated within practices of police work but extended, as the example illustrates, into other practices where it functions ideologically.

The *analysis of discourse* proper is simultaneously oriented to structure and to interaction – to the social resource (orders of discourse) which enables and constrains interaction, and to the way that resource is interactively worked, i.e., to interdiscourse, and its realisation in language and other semiotics. (For a detailed explanation of analysis of discourse, see Fairclough 1992a, 1995b.) Realisation itself involves the same double orientation – to semiotic systems, and to how selections from the potential of semiotic systems are worked in textual processes (see Chapter 8 for more detail). From the structural perspective, the first concern is to locate the discourse in its relation to the network of orders of discourse, to specify how the discourse draws selectively upon the potential of that network, i.e., which genres, discourses and voices, from which orders of discourse, it articulates together. (We use the term 'genre' for the sort of language (and other semiosis) tied to a particular social activity, such as interview; 'discourse' for the sort of language used to construct some aspect of reality from a particular perspective, for example the liberal discourse of politics; and 'voice' for the sort of language used by a particular category of people and closely linked to their identity, for example the medical voice, i.e., the voice of doctors and other medical professionals.) The assumption here is that the relationship between the discourse and the social network of orders of discourse depends upon the nature of the social practice and conjuncture of social practices it is located within, and on how it figures within them. A primary division here is between a broadly reproductive relation to the network of orders of discourse and a broadly transformative relation, though this is a matter of relative weighting since discourse is generally both reproductive and transformative of orders of discourse in some degree. From the perspective of interaction, the concern is with how the discourse works the resource – how the genres and discourses which are drawn upon are worked together in the textual process of the discourse, and what articulatory work is done in the text. Here the focus on genres and discourses quickly shifts to a focus on the linguistic and other semiotic details of texts which realise them.

The comments above on the exchange of letters give a partial illustration of how we envisage the analysis of discourse. From the structural perspective, we showed that the Professor's letter articulates together a wide range of genres and discourses which are actually from different orders of discourse (including legal, political and literary orders of discourse), and we argued that the Mayor's letter by contrast depends heavily upon an official, bureaucratic discourse – and, we might add, is located within a single order of discourse, (local) government. Our analysis was by no means complete – there is much more to say about the genres and discourses the letters draw upon. From the interactional point of view, we discussed to some extent some of the detail of how the Professor's letter works – articulates together – the genres and discourses it draws upon, noting for instance that there are sequential shifts in genre between the paragraphs, but the analysis does not fully show what we refer to above as the textual process. We return to this issue, and the example, in Chapter 8. We also discussed the realisation of the different genres in features of the grammar and vocabulary of the letter. We should stress however that, given the broad scope of the book, our aim throughout is to illustrate through examples, and our analyses are partial and incomplete.

How then do these three types of analysis specify the obstacles to a problem being tackled? Let us take as an example the failure of this exchange of letters (and of such exchanges of letters) as a public sphere. The objective here is to understand structural obstacles to change, so at this point we are looking at the particular example as 'typical'. That of course would need to be established – in a real project using CDA, the analysis should be based on a substantial body of material which can be seen as representing a particular domain of practice (Wodak 1996; and see the criticisms in Stubbs 1997). What constitutes a successful public sphere? The issue is a complex one, but for present purposes we cut through its complexity to propose key properties of a successful public sphere: that it provides a place and a practice in which people as citizens (i.e., outside government and other institutional systems) can address together (maybe with those in government etc.) issues of social and political concern, in a way that gives access to all those with an interest, constitutes real dialogue between those involved, and leads to action (see Habermas 1989; Calhoun 1995; Fairclough forthcoming b). The notion of 'real dialogue' is complex and contentious, but we might say that it involves first, a symmetry between participants in their capacity to contribute to discussion, second, a freedom for all to represent their particular perspectives, and third, a simultaneous orientation to alliance and to developing a new shared voice on the issue in question. A question that arises about the conjuncture is whether practices are so ordered together that dialogue can indeed lead to action: in most cases they are not, i.e., this sort of public exchange 'leads nowhere', there are no channels to turn it into policy changes. So in that sense the nature of the conjuncture can be an obstacle. So too can the relationship between discourse and other moments of the social practice – for instance, it is questionable in such exchanges how sincere the discourse is, what its relationship is to beliefs and values, and whether the letters are strategically (and even cynically) designed to achieve certain outcomes rather than being properly communicative (Habermas 1984). A successful public sphere depends upon sincere engagement. Furthermore, the selection and articulation of genres and discourses can also be an obstacle – manifestly, for example the monological translation of the Professor's letter into official discourse by the Mayor, a strategy which excludes the emergence of any new, shared voice.

Function of the problem in the practice

The issue here is to look at whether and how the problematic aspect of the discourse which is in focus has a particular function within the practice. This may seem to be just focusing one aspect of the analysis above of obstacles to tackling the problem, but in fact in Bhaskar's account of explanatory critique this stage marks the shift from 'is' to 'ought' – the shift from explanation of what it is about a practice that leads to a problem, to evaluation of the practice in terms of its problematic results. Of course in actual analysis it may be difficult to keep the two rigidly apart, but the distinction is clear nevertheless. In the case of the Mayor's letter for instance, it is one thing to explain its construction of everything the police do as in accordance with procedure as a (typical) consequence of the network of practices and reflexive self-constructions which constitute official life in local government, but it is another thing to develop a critique of local government on the lines that it is the flawed character of local government that causes such problematic constructions – that such constructions have for instance an ideological function in local government which makes them indispensable, that therefore the only way to overcome the problem is to change the practices.

Possible ways past the obstacles

This is also part of the shift from 'is' to 'ought' – if the practices are flawed, then we ought to change them. The objective here is to discern possible resources for changing things in the way they currently are. In the terms of Chapter 2, whereas the previous two stages entail a focus on the relational logic of social scientific analysis, this stage involves a shift to the dialectical logic. The focus in the previous two stages was on how structural relations explain ('obstacles') and are responsible for ('functions') the problem at issue. It involves seeing the example as typical, and focusing upon its reproductive effects. For this stage by contrast, it is important that the data should fully represent the full range of variation within the practice in focus – in this case, the full range of variation in public debates and contestations between citizens and/or social movements and officialdom. The focus here is not so much reproduced structures but diversity of conjunctures, the range of what people can do in given structural conditions. This focus does still lead back to structures, but to an aspect of structures which does not get foregrounded in a relational analysis – their incompleteness, their contradictoriness, their gaps, i.e., the properties which keep systems open and make them amenable to transformative action. These properties manifest themselves in the variability of a practice, but also in tensions and contradictions within particular cases. Let us take an example from the Mayor's letter.

> The third incident to which you referred involved another woman. To the best of my knowledge, you are referring to a young woman who was attempting to interfere with the arrest of a man who had attacked a police officer, punching him and ripping the officer's holster in a strenuous effort to seize his gun. Throughout the struggle involving this man and the police officer, this woman kept screaming

and attempting to grab the man away from the officers. She was on the ground next to him when he was subdued but she was, to the best of my investigation, never struck with a baton or hit with a fist ….

There is a tension in the Mayor's letter around modality, i.e., around the Mayor's commitment to the claims he is making. Many are made as simple matters of fact without modal qualification, whereas others are modally qualified. In this extract, there is a mixture of the two: two claims are modally qualified (with *to the best of my knowledge* and *to the best of my investigation* – the latter seems to be a blend of the former and something like *on the evidence of my investigation*), the others are made as matters of fact. The issue is, whose voice is this? The Mayor has to speak for himself – he is putting his authority behind claims about what happened, and he has to 'own' those claims, otherwise he will be damagingly seen as insincere. Yet they are not his claims – he has no personal evidence of what happened. Presumably they are claims made to the Mayor by the police, but although the Mayor's letter refers throughout to his 'investigation', these claims are never attributed to anyone. Mostly they are made as the Mayor's own claims, but certain (perhaps the more contentious?) are modally qualified in a way which implies they belong elsewhere without saying where. The contradiction here is between the Mayor as a public individual who engages in public debate, and the Mayor as one link in an organisational chain. One might see the nature of such organisations as a reason why such exchanges fail as public spheres – the Mayor simulates being available for real dialogue, but the nature of the organisation means that he is not.

Reflexion on the analysis

Critical social research should be reflexive, so part of any analysis should be a reflexion on the position from which it is carried out. One issue here, as we saw in Chapter 2, is the relationship between the theoretical practice of the analyst and the practical practices which are analysed. Our reanalysis of the Smith texts has been purely an exercise in theoretical practice, i.e., we have obviously not had contact with the people concerned, used their perspectives to help determine what was problematic, nor produced an analysis designed in terms of its possible uptake within the practice. We recognise these as limitations. Moreover, we are coming from a particular position within the theoretical field, a particular knowledge interest, entailing a perspective on this example or others which for instance is oriented to problems, to power, to ideology, and so forth. There are of course other things to say about any discourse which are likely to arise from various other perspectives. We do not see the specificity of our perspective as a negative one-sidedness (as Toolan 1997 for instance suggests) – providing that specificity is made clear, and providing that other perspectives are recognised, focusing on problems, power, and so forth is not a problem.

THE INTERPRETATIVE PROCESS:
UNDERSTANDING AND EXPLANATION

Part of reflexivity is taking in the critical commentary of others on one's theoretical practice. To conclude this chapter, we discuss the question of how texts are interpreted in CDA in the light of criticisms made by Stubbs (1997) and Widdowson (1995). Stubbs (1997) notes that according to some critical discourse analysts, 'ideology cannot be read off texts in a mechanical way, since there is no one-to-one correspondence between forms and functions', and goes on to claim that 'if it is not possible to read the ideology off the texts, then the analysts themselves are reading meaning into the texts on the basis of their own unexplicated knowledge' and that 'the question of two possible sources of interpretative authority, text and audience, is not tackled by CDA itself.' There is the same misunderstanding here of what CDA's 'interpretation' of texts consists in, as we have criticised elsewhere in Widdowson (Fairclough 1996b). Interpretation is a complex, layered process, and it is necessary to make certain distinctions within it – first, between understanding and explanation as both parts of interpretation (Ricoeur 1977).

CDA takes the view that any text can be understood in different ways – a text does not uniquely determine a meaning, though there is a limit to what a text can mean: different understandings of the text result from different combinations of the properties of the text and the properties (social positioning, knowledges, values, etc.) of the interpreter. Part of CDA's analysis is analysis of understandings – we have located it above in the analysis of the conjuncture. We are aware that many analyses carried out within CDA have been partial in terms of the framework above and have not included analysis of understandings. However, CDA does not itself advocate a particular understanding of a text, though it may advocate a particular explanation.

An explanation re-describes properties of a text (including the range of understandings it gives rise to) by using a particular theoretical framework to locate the text in social practice. Useful here is Bernstein's distinction (1996: 135–7) between the internal and external 'languages of description' in the process of research: internal language refers to the properties of the theoretical framework itself, 'the syntax whereby a conceptual language is created', as the framework for CDA discussed in this chapter; external language relates the concepts of the framework to empirical material, thereby constructing the object of research (what are relevant relations for analysis), its workings (how these relations articulate together) and its potentialities (not only its actual effects but also its potential function). Explanation lies in the interplay between the two languages of description and it can be seen as a process of translation, whereby the (internal) conceptual language is used to re-describe specific empirical material, such as texts. It is an interpretation of the text in the terms of the theoretical framework, which crucially involves making invisible categories become visible. In CDA's case, this is possible by applying what in Chapter 2 we referred to as the logic of critical analysis: a relational/dialectical logic, oriented to assessing how the discourse moment works within social practice, from the point of view of its effects on power struggles and relations of domination. For instance, interpreting texts ideologically is not a part of understandings of texts but a part of explanations, in that it involves locating texts in social practice partly by reference to the theoretical category of ideology. This is the sort of thing that CDA does. And from this point of view, explanation is that aspect of critical social practice that makes critique possible, in so far as understandings, including the researcher's own, can be subjected to critical analysis, i.e., seen in terms of misrepresentations or unmet needs and their social effects analysed with a view to changing them. Of course there are always alternative explanations, and you have to argue for your explanation within both the domain of theoretical practice and relevant domains of practical practice; and within the latter, explanations may be practically tested for their epistemic value in action (see the discussion of relativism in the final section of Chapter 2). (The same is not true of your understanding.) One might argue that analysts, like everyone else, have to start from some understanding of the text, and that is so. But to gain the necessary distance from initial understandings, one has to be aware of the distinctiveness of one's own languages of description (the theoretical framework and the construction and analysis of the research object) and be reflexive in managing their interplay. As Bernstein says, in order to avoid circularity, it is necessary to keep the external language of description 'free' from the conceptual syntax as much as possible. This has both a pragmatic and an ethical dimension: pragmatic in order to avoid descriptions of the text that are self-confirming of the theory (Stubbs' circularity problem); ethical in the sense that text producers should themselves be able to engage (agree or disagree) with the description made of them. The ethical dimension not only makes room for people (e.g. as audience) as one possible source of interpretative authority, as in Stubbs' article, but is in fact a central concern in critical research in the sense of opening up channels and establishing a dialogue between theoretical and wider social practices (see Chapters 1 and 2).

NOTE

1. Stubbs (1997) claims that CDA 'aims to be a theory of the relation between cognition and the textual representation of reality', of how 'uses of language … influence a person's view of reality', yet tends to circularity in not providing independent evidence of cognition, and to vagueness when it comes to the actual 'mechanisms whereby such influences operate'. The emphasis in this version of CDA has been on sociological questions rather than psychological issues, though other work in CDA has given considerable attention to the mechanisms Stubbs refers to (van Dijk 1998). We do not see CDA as a theory specifically of the relation between cognition and text. The position we have set out above puts the focus on social practices and on dialectical relations between discourse and other moments, which include mental phenomena but also social relations and processes, and material activity. What would 'independent evidence' of cognition amount to? It would be 'non-linguistic' evidence, and since there is no direct way of examining mental phenomena, it would be evidence of them being internalised within other moments – the material or the social (though one should not exclude the (linguistic) evidence of what people reflexively say about what they believe and so forth). In a sense we have taken Stubbs' line of criticism on board in arguing that discourse should be analysed as a moment of social practices. This leads to explanations within a particular theoretical frame (see above) which constitute claims about the mediated causal effects of diverse mechanisms including, in SFL terms introduced in Chapter 3, the 'semologic' (the discourse mechanism) upon social life. Critical realism insists that the effects of each mechanism are mediated by others – so it makes little sense in its terms to isolate discourse and cognition and ask for evidence of the effects of the former on the latter. Within this theoretical frame, the aim is to produce explanatory accounts of some area of social life which show

the interplay of different moments of social practice, which can be tested argumentatively and practically against other accounts. For instance, one might point to texts like the Mayor's letter, ethnographies of police work which show what police do when dealing with an incident, and accounts of the procedures to follow in dealing with incidents in training materials, and postulate a belief about what the police do in dealing with incidents (maybe alongside other different beliefs) as both internalising a particular discourse of policing (realised in a particular language) and as internalised in the actions of police and letters such as the Mayor's.

APPENDIX

Part A: the Professor's letter
Bravo! Prof. Challenges Chief

Chief of Police
Berkeley Police Department
Berkeley, California

Sir:

001   Yesterday (Monday), September 9, between 6:15 and 6:30 pm, I was
002 personally witness to what must have been a classical exercise in the
003 performance of 'law and order' Wallace or Chicago style, only it was in
004 Berkeley. As a naturalized, non-native American citizen who has seen
005 first-hand experience with Nazi and 'SS' tactics, I find it most difficult to
006 believe what I saw,
007   I was walking toward my car parked off Telegraph Avenue. On Haste
008 and Telegraph I saw several (three, I believe) police cars with four men
009 each. In front of Cody's two men, for whatever reason, were being dragged
010 to one of the patrol cars. Many people were standing round, watching
011 quietly.
012   I was standing just below the corner of Haste and Telegraph opposite
013 Cody's and I saw a boy, 16 or 17 years old, walking up Haste and past two
014 policemen.
015   Suddenly a young policeman in his early twenties, with a cigar he had
016 just lit in his mouth, grabbed this young man, rudely spun him around,
017 pinned him against his patrol car, tore at his clothes and pockets as though
018 searching for something, without so much as saying one word of explanation.
019 Then he pushed him roughly up the street yelling at him to get
020 moving.

'Never forget'

021   I shall never forget the face of that policemen, his eyes bulging out, his face
022 distorted by a vile sneer, his whole countenance exuding hatred, his cigar
023 arrogantly sticking out of that obscene mouth. It was a frightening sight,
024 especially to someone uninitiated to police tactics such as I was.
025   Then several things happened: in a doorway a few yards away a young
026 woman of 18–19 years was standing holding a baby in her arms.
027 Suddenly two policemen, no, two uniformed thugs, were upon her,
028 seemingly trying to pull her into a car but at the same time trying to tear
029 the baby from her, tearing, pulling, pushing, quite oblivious to the tragedy
030 which might have ensued had the baby been dropped and likely trampled
031 upon in the melee.
032   Nearby another equally young girl was on the pavement and I saw a

033 cop's club repeatedly descending on her with all might!
034 What a sickening sight! A huge, strong man having the audacity to beat
035 up a young girl in open view of a hundred people!
036   I had moved out of the way in the meantime, across the street. Several
037 people were yelling at the uniformed hoods to lay off the girls and the baby.
038 Some people yelled 'pigs'. I would have joined them but I was unable
039 to say anything. Besides, such an epithet, I am now convinced, was much
040 too mild for the perpetrators of such bestiality.
041 Of course, I am only speaking of the 4–5 individuals actually involved
042 in those acts of violence, not the many policemen who were standing around
043 with their clubs ready, though these, because they failed to restrain their
044 comrades were no less guilty.

Hate

045   Then an empty beer can flew across the street hitting the pavement harm-
046 lessly. Immediately, the young, cigar-smoking cop sprinted across the
047 street charging like a vicious bull, the most vicious and horrifying look of
048 hatred and contempt on his contorted face, his club raised, shouting. If hate
049 could kill, that savage's look would have killed everyone in sight.
050 How can a man be entrusted with safeguarding the law and protecting
051 the citizens, all citizens, if he becomes so easily the victim of such neurotic
052 behavior that blinds him to all reason?
053   In a split second this savage and another cop were upon a young man,
054 clubbing him to the ground, twisting his arm on his back, then literally
055 sitting on the man's head.
056 Why? I presume that they thought that he had thrown than harmless
057 empty beer can, but I am ready to state under oath – and I will – that
058 that young man did in fact not throw the can. As all others around him he
059 was merely an aroused, ired, angered bystander.
060   But what's the difference? All the uniformed thugs wanted was some-
061 one to vent their spleen on.

Charges

062   I herewith state and charge that from all evident appearances the entire
063 fracas had been staged and organized by the police in an obvious attempt to
064 provoke the people there into a confrontation with the heavily armed cops.
065 Witness the presence of several squad cars with four men in each at the
066 scene already, or within minutes of the beginning.
067   I further charge that the policemen used force which was totally out of
068 keeping with the reality of the situation, and blatantly directed at a few,
069 selected victims.
070   I accuse the involved savage cops with actions and behavior totally
071 unbecoming civilized human beings, actions which degraded the concept of
072 justice and of true law and order.
073   The fact that only relatively few of the police were involved in the
074 actual perpetration of the crimes against the people, as described above, is
075 in no way a mitigating circumstance.

Not hippie

076   I am neither a hippie nor a beatnik. For the past four years I have been a
077 member of the faculty of the University of Santa Clara. I am what is
078 commonly referred to as a law-abiding, tax-paying, property-owning
079 citizen. As such, but not only as such, as a human being, I have the right to
080 demand an explanation for the events as outlined above.
081 I further demand a full investigation without delay in the events of
082 yesterday, with particular attention directed at the savage actions of the
083 cigar-smoking policeman, those who so violently and viciously struggled
084 with the woman and the baby, and those who clubbed a defenseless girl on
085 the pavement.
086   I am prepared, willing and able to identify the thugs involved and to testify
087 under oath before a court or grand jury on the events in the late afternoon
088 of Monday, September 9, 1968 at Telegraph and Haste.
089   I am determined to see the matter through and I will not allow myself
090 to be put off by a few meaningless words of reply from you.

> Ernesto G. Auerbach
> Santa Clara, California

cc. Mayor Wallace Johnson

Afterthought

Sept. 11, 1968

Editor:
091   As an afterthought I am sending you the enclosed copy of a letter to the
092 Berkeley Chief of Police. It is self-explanatory. Please read it. The incident
093 described in it is only a 'minor' one, perhaps, but to me it exemplifies what
094 is becoming more and more the standard operating procedure of the police
095 in this country.

> Sincerely yours,
> Ernesto G. Auerbach
> (*Berkeley Barb*, 12–19 September 1968, no. 161, p. 3)

Part B: The Mayor's response

September 26, 1968

Wallace Johnson
Mayor of Berkeley

The difficulties of law enforcement on Telegraph Avenue

096   The difficulty of law enforcement on Telegraph Avenue (the 2400 block) is
097 illustrated by a recent letter to the Mayor and the Police Chief. Pertinent
098 excerpts from this letter:

September 10, 1968

Sir:
099   Yesterday, September 9, between 6:15 and 6:30 pm ... I was walking
100 toward my car parked off Telegraph Avenue. On Haste and Telegraph I
101 saw several (three, I believe) police cars with four men each. In front of
102 Cody's two men, for whatever reason, were being dragged to one of the

103 patrol cars ... and I saw a boy, 16 or 17 years old, walking up Haste and
104 past two policemen.
105   Suddenly a young policeman ... grabbed this young man, rudely spun
106 him around, pinned him against his patrol car, tore at his clothes and
107 pockets as though searching for something, without so much as saying one
108 word of explanation. ...
109   Then several things happened: in a doorway a few yards away a young
110 woman of 18–19 years was standing holding a baby in her arms. Suddenly
111 two policemen ... were upon her, seemingly trying to pull her into a car but
112 at the same time trying to tear the baby from her, tearing, pulling, pushing.
113 ... Nearby another equally young girl was on the pavement and I saw a
114 cop's club repeatedly descending on her with all might. ... I had moved out
115 of the way in the meantime, across the street. ... Then an empty beer can
116 flew across the street hitting the pavement harmlessly. Immediately, the
117 young cop sprinted across the street ... his club raised, shouting. ... In a
118 split second this savage and another cop were upon a young man, clubbing
119 him into the ground, twisting his arm on his back, then literally sitting on
120 the man's head. Why? ... I am ready to state under oath – and I will –
121 that that young man did in fact not throw the can. ...
122   I herewith state and charge that from all evident appearances the
123 entice fracas had been staged and organized by the police in an obvious
124 attempt to provoke the people there into a confrontation with the heavily
125 armed cops. Witness the presence of several squad cars with four men in
126 each at the scene already, or within minutes of the beginning. ...

127   Before the Police Chief or I received the letter quoted, it had been
128 published in toto as a feature article in the local underground press.
129   Promptly upon the receipt of this letter I telephoned the man and suggested
130 he come to see me. He did. I listened to the full story of the incidents he
131 observed and assured him that I would investigate the incidents and advise
132 him of what I could determine. I did:

September 19, 1968

Dear

133   In accordance with our conversations on the subject of the incidents at
134 Telegraph and Haste on September 9, I have checked into the matter and
135 advise you as follows:
136   You referred to four incidents which you were able to at least partially
137 observe. The first concerned a young man who was frisked and who
138 appeared to be then released. In fact this man was a juvenile who
139 was arrested and charged with being a minor in possession of alcoholic
140 beverages. He pleaded guilty and the court suspended judgement. This
141 young man was one of three involved in the event which precipitated the
142 subsequent events to which you refer.
143   The second incident you referred to involved a young woman with a
144 child. Investigation revealed that this young woman was screaming vile
145 profanity at the police and was agitating the crowd. Two officers
146 approached her in front of 2441 Haste Street, informing her that she was
147 under arrest. The woman and an unidentified man standing next to her
148 were holding a baby. The man stated that the police officers were not going
149 to take her away and the couple locked arms. The officers attempted
150 to talk to the woman, but she continued screaming and swearing. At one

151 point another of the officers reached for the baby, intending to give it to the
152 man, who appeared to be her husband. One of the officers talked to the
153 woman and endeavored to start her toward the patrol car. It became
154 apparent to the officers that arresting her would be an extremely difficult
155 task, because of her attitude and because of the baby, and the officers
156 retired without arresting her. To the best of my ability to investigate this
157 matter, I do not find that there was any pulling, tearing, or shoving of the
158 woman in this incident.
159   The third incident to which you referred involved another woman. To
160 the best of my knowledge, you are referring to a young woman who was
161 attempting to interfere with the arrest of a man who had attacked a police
162 officer, punching him and ripping the officer's holster in a strenuous effort
163 to seize his gun. Throughout the struggle involving this man and the police
164 officer, this woman kept screaming and attempting to grab the man away
165 from the officers. She was on the ground next to him when he was subdued
166 but she was, to the best of my investigation, never struck with a baton or hit
167 with a fist. ...
168   The fourth incident you related involved the beer can and the man who
169 was arrested at the time the beer can was thrown. You are quite correct,
170 the man arrested was not the man who threw the beer can. The man who
171 threw the can was initially pursued by the officer but as he started this
172 pursuit he was body-blocked by the man who was arrested. This man was
173 caught and arrested after a brief struggle. He was charged with resisting
174 arrest. He pleaded guilty and was given a suspended judgement on penalty
175 of five days in the County Jail.
176   Regarding the last paragraph on the second page of your letter, there
177 is no evidence that the 'entire fracas had been staged and organized'. You
178 must keep in mind ... that these incidents you observed, however exciting
179 and unusual to you, represent a typical problem at the present time on
180 Telegraph Avenue. A simple arrest is likely to escalate to a major happen-
181 ing because so frequently a crowd of people gathers and tries to interfere
182 with the making of an arrest. In this case the arrest of three people
183 for drinking in public resulted in the several incidents you mentioned.
184 Because of the difficulty of making arrests in this area without interference
185 from the people in the vicinity, the Berkeley Police have found it necessary
186 to use more than one man at a time. ... Therefore it is not at all surprising
187 that when the crowd gathered because of the original arrest, additional
188 police officers were promptly summoned to handle the situation. ...
189   Thank you for relating to me your civic concern. I am sure we both
190 share a common desire to cultivate respect for law and law enforcement
191 officers, and at the same time to insure that professional conduct is
192 observed at all times.

Chapter 5

Narratives of late modernity and a research agenda for CDA

In Chapter 3 we argued that communicative interaction is a potentially creative social practice which is however shaped by social structures that it reproduces and transforms. And we suggested that analysis of communicative interaction correspondingly needs to combine interactional (hermeneutic, interpretative) analysis and structural analysis. That is, we should be sensitive to the particularity and specificity of communicative interactions, to what in particular is going on within them, without losing sight of the ways in which they work within social structures, social relations and social processes which transcend their local character. Or, to put it differently, in analysis we should adopt both an 'insider's' and an 'outsider's' perspective – both the perspective of someone practically engaged in a social practice for whom the issue is how social resources can be appropriated, and the perspective of the theorist aiming to describe those social resources. In the discussion of the intersection of face-to-face interaction with mediated quasi-interaction in Chapter 3, some of the distinctive ways in which communicative interactions work within the structures, relations and processes of specifically modern societies began to emerge. But we now need a more systematic consideration of the shifting place of communication and language within modern societies, and this is the objective of Chapter 5.

A striking feature of recent critical theories of modern social life is the degree to which they focus upon language. Language is seen as an important part of modern social life, and social analysis is correspondingly oriented towards language to a substantial degree. Earlier social theories were less language-centred – classical forms of Marxism for instance had relatively little to say about language. This change could be because theorists have come to realise that language is a more significant part of modern social life than they had thought, or because language has actually become a more significant part of social life in the course of modernity. We shall argue that it is both.

Classical Marxist theory has been a common point of reference for critical social theorists who have come to centre language in their theories – Habermas, Giddens and Baudrillard all positioned themselves in relation to Marxism relatively early in their careers through critiques and revisions of historical materialism, in which the poverty of the latter in its classical form with respect to language was a more or less central issue (Habermas 1976; Giddens 1995; Baudrillard 1972). Of course the issue is not simply language: rather, classical historical materialism has been subjected to more general critique and revisions which have included the question of language. A target for many theorists has been its tendency towards economic reductionism – to see other parts of society as effects of the economy and therefore epiphenomena. Theorists have moved towards the more dialectical views of society which are also part of the Marxist tradition, partly in response to changes in capitalism which have enhanced the effects of other parts of society on the economy – thus Habermas identifies the increasing intervention of the state to counteract the destructive effects of the capitalist market left to itself; and the growing incorporation of science into economic production as a productive force. These approaches have produced accounts of the state, of culture and of social interaction which are richer than those to be found in classical historical materialism, and have attributed greater autonomy to them in the constitution and evolution of social formations. The centring of language within reconstructions of historical materialism is tied in with this critique of economism: in particular, versions of historical materialism which centre culture and social interaction thereby also centre language. There is in this respect a broad tendency within and around Marxism ('Western Marxism') which includes also Gramsci, Althusser, Giddens and (earlier) Baudrillard amongst many others.

We begin this chapter with a review of critical theories of late modernity – different narratives of late modernity – focusing upon Harvey, Giddens and Habermas, but also referring more briefly to postmodernist and feminist narratives. Our method here is to read these theoretical texts from a linguistic perspective – to build up a picture of the language condition of late modernity on the basis of both what is said about language and what can be inferred about language. This emergent picture of the language condition of late modernity will then be used to define a research agenda for CDA within the interdisciplinary study of late modernity. Our aim is to attach CDA, not to a particular social theory but rather to a field of critical research which is also a field of contention between theories. In Chapter 6 we shift from the 'grand theory' of Chapter 5 towards more middle-range and local theories which focus upon late modernity in particular domains of social life, such as education. Our main theoretical resources here are Bourdieu and Bernstein, and we discuss how these theories might figure alongside CDA in transdisciplinary research projects, where the logic of one discipline is 'put to work' in the other without the one being reduced to the other. In Chapter 7 we focus upon poststructuralist theorisations which stress difference and the openness and contingency of late modern social life, arguing that CDA can both specify different relationships to the openness and creativity of discourse depending on social position, and contribute to critical research on dialogue across difference in late modern social life. In this part of the book, we are both using critical social research on late modernity to develop CDA, and arguing that CDA can make a major contribution to this research, both through developing its theorisation of the late modern language condition and by providing categories and frameworks which will allow detailed analysis of discourse to be productively incorporated within this research. We see ourselves as engaging in a conversation with our various theoretical sources here which is partly argumentative (we are critical of their views of language and discourse in some cases) and partly oriented to building cooperation.

The nature of late modernity is controversial, even within critical theory. For instance, Harvey's 'geographical–historical materialist' account (which we summarise shortly) is perhaps too strongly centred in capitalism and its transformations, and too slick in its reading of postmodernity as the 'cultural logic' (Jameson 1991) of the new economic formation, for others who see themselves as critical theorists. Different critical theorists are to some extent complementary to one another in focusing upon different aspects of late modernity. We have conjoined elements of different accounts on the basis of our judgement of what is particularly insightful about late modernity, especially from a language perspective. Of course, there are also major theoretical differences at issue – for instance, the centrality of capitalism in accounts of late modernity within the Marxist tradition contrasts with Giddens' insistence that there are four institutional dimensions of modernity (capitalism, industrialism, surveillance and state violence), none of which is privileged over the others. In conjoining elements of these theories, we are also therefore introducing tensions between different concepts and analyses. We believe that this is both appropriate and productive: appropriate because we are aiming to show how CDA can contribute to a tendentious field of research, not to show how CDA might strengthen the language dimension of a particular theory of late modernity, so it is right that we should keep tensions within the field in play; productive because we believe that doing so yields greater insights into the contemporary social use of language by foregrounding its contradictory properties, i.e., we assume that theoretical differences broadly reflect the contradictions of the domain theorised. Although it would be wrong to see the different accounts of late modernity we shall draw upon as simply divergent accounts of the 'same' reality, there is considerable common ground in the identification of key aspects of late modernity – for instance, in one formulation or another the perception of a threat to social life from the unrestrained expansion of technological systems and the instrumental rationality they are based in. A cautionary note is in order: while we shall endeavour to frame what each of the theories contributes to the account of late modernity in this chapter in terms of the broader theoretical project this material is taken from, it will inevitably be a highly selective view of these complex and sophisticated theories.

HARVEY

We shall begin this chapter with a very condensed summary of Harvey's 'historical-geographical' materialist analysis of late modernity (1990) which provides a useful frame for other theories. Harvey anchors his analysis of late modernity in economic changes within capitalism: in the transition from a 'Fordist' form of economic production to a system of 'flexible accumulation' which was described in Chapter 1. This transformation involves a qualitatively significant acceleration of processes of time–space compression which have been going on throughout modern society – a speed-up of the pace of life to the point where the present seems to be all there is, combined with a transcendence of spatial boundaries. The compression of time and place has provided a way out of the crisis of overaccumulation within Fordism which set off the shift towards the new economic regime of 'flexible accumulation'. The 'temporal fix' to the problems of Fordism has involved amongst other things an acceleration of the 'turnover time' of capital – the time it takes for capital invested to pass through the economic cycle and produce a profit; the 'spatial fix' has been an absorption of excess capital and labour through an expansionist implantation of capitalism in ever-wider areas of the globe.

Accelerating the turnover time of capital means a speed-up of production, which is achieved through increasing the pace of technological innovation and organisation change. (Lash 1993: 206–27) describes contemporary market conditions as increasingly 'innovation-intensive, design-intensive, and research and development-intensive'), which means an intensification of the labour process (so that those who are in work find themselves under increasing pressure) and a need for workers to constantly reskill themselves as existing skills become outdated. Speed-up also takes place in distribution and consumption. Speed-up in consumption is aided by a relative shift from material goods to services: the latter have a generally shorter 'lifetime' than the former. This shift involves capitalist penetration of many cultural domains which were previously outside or on the edge of the commodity market.

Harvey argues that these economic changes have profound cultural consequences. Contemporary societies are dominated by the volatile, the ephemeral and the disposable, not only in the domain of material goods but also in 'values, lifestyles, stable relationships, and attachments to things, buildings, places, people, and received ways of doing and being' (Harvey 1990). The sense of time and history is diminished. As Lyotard puts it (1984), the temporary contract becomes the hallmark of modern living. Long-term planning in such a context of volatility poses major problems for capitalism, and it deals with these both through being highly flexible in its response to market shifts, and through control of public communication, which allows it to 'mastermind the volatility' to a degree. Advertising becomes a pervasive cultural form, and most clearly manifests a shift in the dominant commodity form – from material goods to signs and images. Images of reality displace reality to the point where the line between the two becomes difficult to draw or – according to Baudrillard (1983, 1988) – disappears entirely: postmodern culture is the culture of the 'simulacrum', the perfect copy which cannot be distinguished from the real thing. Simultaneously there is a process of 'annihilation of space through time' – as the speed and cost of travel, transportation, and the communication of information and images have been dramatically reduced, spatial barriers have collapsed. This manifests itself in a changed experience of space (as well as time) in everyday life. Heterogeneous commodities (for example, foods), cultural practices (for example, musical styles) and built environments (architectural styles) are assembled in particular places, and there is a 'nightly assemblage of all the divergent spaces of the world as a collage of images upon the television screen' (Harvey 1989: 302). Or in Lyotard's words: 'one wakens to reggae, watches a western, eats Macdonald's foods for lunch and local cuisine for dinner, wears Paris perfume in Tokyo and retro clothes in Hong Kong' (1984: 76). Shifting experiences of time and space, but also an un-settling of senses of value which is rooted in the destabilisation of money in late modernity, underlie a general crisis of representation.

Harvey identifies two sorts of reaction to these changes: on the one hand an exploitation (and one might add celebration) of the possibilities they open up, for instance in the crossing of boundaries and hybridisation of practices; on the other hand a major defensive reaction which seeks to re-establish collective and individual identities and which has involved the thematisation of nation, religion, community and family. Both can be seen as exploring the new field of possibilities that has opened up, whether for purposes of innovation or conservation. Struggles to estab-lish collective identities often entail an aestheticisation of place and of politics, and a prioritising of being over becoming, which is a focus of contemporary philosophical debates. The resources for struggles to establish identities in the face of the ephem-erality of late modern culture are ironically those provided by that culture itself (for example, 'traditions' that are constructed for market purposes), and the outcomes of these struggles are immediately open to market appropriation. Moreover, the impetus to establish identities comes ironically in part from market pressures on organisations, places and persons to project distinctive images.

We have chosen to use Harvey's narrative of late modernity for two reasons. First, because it is a clear formulation of a dialectical and historical-geographical materialist account which anchors culture in economic change. This is in contrast to the post-modern position taken by fellow geographer Thrift (1996) which avoids claims about overall systemic change and thereby marginalises issues of power, focusing on (and perhaps tending to celebrate) the local experience of mobility. Our second reason for using Harvey's work is his orientation to discourse: he has developed elsewhere (Harvey 1996) an account of the dialectics of discourse which is close to our own position – which we have referred to in earlier chapters – and he sees the shift towards late modernity as constituted partly but substantially in language, and an orientation to language as crucial in its theorisation and analysis.

GIDDENS

Giddens has been concerned with the emergence and development of modernity throughout his career, and he has more recently focused upon late (or 'high') modernity, not only in terms of its institutional features but also in terms of its cultural characteristics and ways in which it reshapes daily and personal life. Some of the earlier work was located within a critique of historical materialism in its classical Marxist forms. Whereas for Marx modern society was fundamentally shaped by capitalism and the struggle between classes that it defined, and social change was fundamentally driven by the development of the forces and relations of production, Giddens sees modernity as a complex of four institutional dimensions including but not reducible to capitalism: industrialism, capitalism, surveillance and state violence ('industrialisation of war'). The third and fourth dimensions are connected to his claim that the development of the modern 'nation-state' – with its sophisticated capacity to exercise surveillance over its citizens as well as its monopolisation of technologically sophisticated means of violence – is just as constitutive for modernity as the development of the modern economy. Indeed it is the formation of the nation-state and, with it, the establishment of a particular relationship between economy and polity – their 'insulation' from each other – that defines modernity. The resources for power in modern societies are not only the 'allocative' (economic) resources that Marx focused upon, but also 'authoritative' resources including the technologies of surveillance which Foucault has so effectively analysed (1977). Giddens regards his project as a form of critical theory, though a critical theory 'without guarantees'. He rejects the 'providential' claims of Marxism that history provides people with the resources for resolving the problems it faces them with, the identification of the oppressed as privileged agents of change, and 'evolutionist' social theories (which for instance present socialism as 'the next stage' after capitalism) – but see Callinicos (1985) for elements of evolutionism in Giddens' own account of late modernity as time–space distantiation. The agenda of a critical theory can be specified in terms of the four dimensions of modernity: they define shifting configurations of problems which people are faced with in contemporary social life. Thus Giddens identifies as four key issues for contemporary critical theory the gap between rich and poor accentuated by contemporary capitalism, the destructive impact of industry on ecosystems, the repression of human rights in the context of intensified surveillance, and the threat of a major war.

The other side of Giddens' insistence upon the nation-state as a constitutive element of modernity is his claim that the emergence of the nation-state as a form goes in tandem with the emergence of a world system of nation-states – from the beginning, international relations between nation-states have been a defining feature of this form of state. This throws into question the dominant tradition within sociology of taking the individual 'society' in isolation as its object of analysis. The shape and development of any one 'society' involves for Giddens a combination of endogenous and exogenous factors – it is a product of a combination of internal and external forces. Late (or 'high') modernity is characterised by a shift in the nature of the world system involving a dramatic acceleration of time–space distantiation, which Giddens and others refer to as 'globalisation' – a widely used and controversial term.

We should understand globalisation in relation to Giddens' view of power. According to him, globalisation is related to a new modality of power characteristic of late modernity. As indicated above, Giddens draws upon theoretical geographers like Harvey in developing a social theory of modernity which centres time and space as a means for articulating power. An example of this centring comes up in Giddens' engagement with Marx: he agrees that the emergence of capitalist production depends upon the commodification of labour, but argues that this in turn presupposes the commodification of time and the emergence of 'clock time', which separates time from place and converts it into an 'empty' category (so that for instance labour can be measured in terms of time irrespective of its particular circumstances and contents). Social systems are defined by particular forms of 'time–space distanciation' which 'stretch' social relations across time and space to particular degrees and particular ways, but in all cases the specific time–space modality of a social system is its modality of power. Power is understood by Giddens as the 'transformative capacity' of social action;[1] and where an agent acts to transform the world in some way via the agency of others, we have 'domination', a particular form of power. Power is inherent in all social interactions, but the way it works depends upon the particular form of time–space distanciation (the particular social system) which the interaction is located within. For example, tribal or traditional societies work basically through face-to-face interactions where people are co-present, and depends for time–space distantiation on language itself, 'language as a time machine' as Levi-Strauss put it, which through its conventions permits the re-enactment of social practices across generations. But more complex societies depend upon modes of interaction in which people are separated in time and space. Giddens claims that 'all social interaction intermingles presence and absence' (1995: 38), and social systems differ in their specific ways of intermingling them. These differences can be specified in terms of the forms of mediation of social action, and the types of media they depend upon. The emergence of the media of written language and print constituted an important condition for increasing time–space distantiation in pre-modern and early modern societies, and the emergence of electronic media (telegraph, telephone, broadcasting, information technology), and especially their combination with print media, has been the basis for the dramatic further increases within the modern period. Different media intermingle presence and absence in different ways. Giddens has characterised the globalising tendency of late modernity (see shortly below) as 'action at a distance' – an extension in the spatio-temporal reach of power.

This intensification of time–space distantiation involves the 'disembedding' of social relations from particular places and contexts, and their generalisation across temporal and spatial boundaries. Disembedding can be seen as a particular regulative practice within social systems by which social relations are lifted out of their locales and reorganised to travel, so to speak. This is evident in the social use of language: generic forms such as the interview or advertisement increasingly transcend particularities of place and come to be techniques which are useable irrespective of time and place. Increasingly the balance between endogenous and exogenous forces shaping the development of discourse practices in a particular language is shifting towards the latter, so that commonalities of discourse practices increasingly transcend linguistic differences.[2] And social use of language in common with other resources for social interaction increasingly becomes a skill which has to be learnt and which requires recourse to experts and expert systems (see below). Disembedding is also evident in the practices of media (print, but particularly electronic) where 'news' items are lifted out of their contexts of production and circulate around the globe in the form of disconnected elements (the 'collage effect' of news), forming a new sense of familiarity with events far distant and thus creating a new 'global' consciousness. However, globalisation should not be understood as a unidirectional process of homogenisation and global integration – disembedding inevitably involves re-embedding in multiple new locales, where innumerable diverse interpretative resources are used to appropriate globalising effects in diverse ways (Featherstone 1995: 102–25). Globalisation is best seen as a dialectic of the global and the local: it entails an unprecedented degree of interpenetration between the global and the local, and between the systemic and the personal – the process of constructing self-identity in the contemporary world is profoundly penetrated by global processes and tendencies which individuals have to position themselves in relation to, and this work of self-construction itself profoundly affects global tendencies. In this respect globalisation is in fact a contradictory process which for instance sets off the revival of local nationalisms (Featherstone 1995: 111).

Globalisation is a major force in the 'detraditionalisation' of modern society, and the emergence of a post-traditional society in which, as Giddens puts it, 'traditions have to explain themselves' (1994a: 5) – i.e., traditions no longer shape social life in self-evident and unquestionable ways. One aspect of globalisation that has shaken the grounds of 'tradition' is the realisation that modernity produces risks that it cannot control – the realisation that science, technology and institutional forms of government are not inherently about human-centred progress. While modern life has reduced or eliminated many of the risks of earlier social forms (for example, death in child birth), it has manufactured new risks which are perceived as out of control, such as the risk of environmental degradation. The nature and perception of these risks undermines the Marxist 'providential' view of social change referred to above, and contributes to a sense that late modernity is a 'juggernaut' which we can ride and even steer but with no guarantees of a 'benign outcome' (Giddens 1991). Unlike Lyotard however, Giddens claims that the withdrawal from traditional belief systems does not mark a shift to postmodernity but a radicalisation of modernity itself (Giddens 1990).

In such a post-traditional context social life is reflexive in an enhanced way, in that people have to make choices and decisions about aspects of how to live their lives which might hitherto have been self-evidently given – how to conduct personal relationships, how to be a parent, and so forth. For the resources for these reflexive processes, people are dependent upon expert systems (for instance, in the concrete form of books or magazine features written by experts). Trust in the efficacy of expert systems becomes a vital condition for contemporary social life – for people's ontological security, their sense of being all right in the world – yet because of the radical doubt inherent in this social condition, in practice expert systems are am- bivalently oriented to with a mixture of trust and scepticism which constantly threatens to undermine them. So people do not uncritically draw upon the social materials available through expert systems; they are rather knowledgeable social agents who work reflexively on these materials in their own particular ways. The range of resources and the lifestyles available are considerably enhanced, in that one effect of globalisation is to give access to many cultural traditions, which can be drawn together in hybrid practices not chaotically but in ways which are informed by new principles of relevance. Globalisation has the contradictory effect of on the one hand opening up for the first time the basis for a truly universal subject, in that people throughout the world increasingly share common experience, yet on the other hand offering new resources for differentiation and fragmentation of subjectivity. Postmodernist accounts which focus solely on the latter are misleading.

The themes of self-identity and reflexivity in intimate relationships have become a major focus in Giddens' recent work on late modernity (1991, 1992). He presents the construction of self-identity in contemporary society as a reflexive 'project' which can be thought of as 'the sustaining of coherent, yet continuously revised, biographical narratives ... in the context of multiple choices as filtered through abstract systems' (1991: 5). Relationships with lovers, friends, children, etc. are shaped less and less by traditional norms, and increasingly take on the character of 'pure relationships' which are to do with the rewards that those involved can gain from them. Such relationships depend upon reflexive control, and democratic principles which have hitherto had force in different social domains come to be seen as having force within these relationships. In particular they come to be regulated through democratic dialogue, and the problematic of 'dialogical democracy' comes to be a central political concern which transcends the traditional division between the public and the private spheres (Giddens 1994a). Indeed the nature of the political is transformed: in conjunction and in tension with the emancipatory politics which has dominated modern society hitherto, there emerges a 'life politics' which focuses upon questions of how one should live in the late modern age, i.e., lifestyle.

As the routines of contemporary social life become detached from traditions which give them meaning, life is increasingly threatened by meaninglessness. Giddens refers also to the 'sequestration of experience', the exclusion from ordinary experience of decisive, problematic and morally challenging parts of life (death, old age, ill health). As daily life becomes more dominated by expert systems and questions of skill and performance, moral issues are backgrounded. In this context people are open to the demagogic appeals of nationalism and fundamentalism. At the same time contemporary social and religious movements are working towards a moral renewal in social life. Life politics has a central role to play here as a force which reinjects moral and existential issues into the public agenda. Centring individually or collectively posed questions of 'how to live' in the context of pressing issues of ecology (environmental exhaustion and the nuclear danger), the body (reproduction technologies, health) and globalisation (consciousness of global risks) re-politicises questions which have been treated as 'technical', and reinstates them as issues of debate in the public space. Giddens' view of public space is closer to Calhoun's (1995) and Fraser's (1992) 'spheres of public' than to Habermas's unitary 'public sphere' – it is a multicentred space in which different interest groups deliberate together to reach consensus on political action. The question of how networks and dialogical relationships are developed between different 'spheres of public' becomes a crucial one.

Giddens' work has attracted much debate and criticism. One widely shared line of critique is that he puts too much focus on the acts of individuals, seeing power more as a resource for action than a constraint on action, and that this furthermore leads him to underplay the different possibilities for action that are consequent upon different positions within social structures, and the different experiences of modernity of people in different parts of the world. (See for instance Callinicos (1985); Featherstone (1995).)

At this point we shall suggest a number of themes for CDA that arise out of the theories of Harvey and Giddens, and so move towards the specification of an agenda for CDA within late modernity. What we offer here is one linguistic reading of these theoretical texts which focuses (as we indicated earlier) on what is implied in them with respect to language, more than on what they actually say about language. Our reading is very selective, aiming to identify a small number of key themes. It seems reasonable to put Harvey and Giddens together in this way for this immediate purpose, because although their accounts of late modernity differ significantly, there are emphases in common (notably on time–space distantiation and globalisation).

We focus on five key themes: hybridity, globalisation, identity, reflexivity and commodification. Late modernity entails a radical unsettling of the boundaries of social life – between economy and culture, between global and local, and so forth – one aspect of which is an unsettling of the boundaries between different domains of social use of language. The result is a pervasive *discoursal hybridity* in interactions and text – the mixing together of different genres and discourses – which is a significant facet of the flux of late modern social life, for instance in the incorporation of cultural domains into the market (involving a 'marketisation of language'). The *globalisation of discursive practices* is one dimension of this hybridity, though it is a global–local dialectic wherein disembedded language practices increasingly flow across linguistic and cultural boundaries, but are assembled in distinctive hybridisations which contribute to the reconstitution of separate identities of place. Late modernity pervasively undermines individual and collective identity, and struggles over the construction of identities are a salient feature of late modern social life. These are substantively matters of *identification in discourse* – struggles to find a voice as part of struggles to find an identity. Late modernity is characterised by an enhanced reflexivity (for example, in the construction of identities) which is in part *linguistic reflexivity* – awareness about language which is self-consciously applied in interventions to change social life (including one's own identity). As commodities become increasingly cultural in nature they correspondingly become increasingly semiotic and linguistic, and *language becomes commodified*, subject to economically motivated processes of intervention and design (which entail linguistic reflexivity).

HABERMAS

Habermas's project is a political as well as a philosophical and social theoretical one: renewing critical theory so as to escape from the dead end which his predecessors in the Frankfurt School arrived at, and open up again a link between it and an emancipatory politics. According to the Frankfurt School, the emancipatory potential of reason had been eaten away in modern society by the progressive colonisation of reason by the economy and the state. Habermas argues that this diagnosis is based upon a reductive view of reason – equating the 'instrumental' rationality of modern technology and bureaucracy with reason as a whole. There is a different form of rationality inherent within modern society: communicative rationality. Instrumental rationality is about getting results: communicative rationality is about achieving understanding. The two forms of rationality are not in an either/or relation, because modern societies cannot do without a measure of instrumental rationalisation; but on the other hand instrumental rationality depends upon communicative rationality in crucial ways. The political project is not replacing instrumental by communicative rationality, it is (negatively) preventing instrumental rationality from spreading too far at the expense of communicative rationality with socially pathological consequences, and (positively) creating the social conditions in which the full emancipatory potential of communicative rationality can be realised.

Like Marx, Habermas sees an unrealised emancipatory potential within social life as it is. Unlike Marx, he locates this potential in forms of communication – in language. But whereas in his earlier work he located the potential in the specific historical forms of communication within the bourgeois 'public sphere' (the social spaces in which citizens deliberate on matters of social and political concern), in his later work he locates it in properties of communication per se – the 'universal pragmatic' properties of that form of communication that is oriented to reaching understanding ('communicative action'). These are 'validity claims' carried by utterances – claims to be comprehensible, true, sincerely said, and in accordance with social norms and values. These claims are of course often counter-factual in that people often do not speak the truth or with sincerity, but nevertheless they are implicitly there. It is these 'gentle but obstinate' presuppositions of communication which ground critical social science.

Unlike Giddens, Habermas maintains the evolutionary view of human society of historical materialism, but he gives a quite different account in which social evolution depends upon cultural innovation and learning as well as technology – on 'moral insight, practical knowledge, communicative action, and the consensual regulation of action conflicts' (Habermas 1979). The emancipatory potential of communicative action is progressively unleashed in the course of cultural innovation. Habermas envisages a dialectic between technological and cultural innovation: cultural innovations (including new forms of communication) occur in response to crises in economic systems, and create the conditions for technological innovations and the emergence of new systems (Habermas 1987a). Cultural innovation links forms of communication with forms of identity – so contemporary society sees the co-emergence of a more reflexive relationship to forms of communication (their validity claims are more readily questioned and argued) and 'post-conventional' identities, people who are not positioned within traditions but able to creatively remake themselves through creative reworking of inherited social resources (note the similarity with Giddens' views on reflexivity discussed above).

Habermas's account of modernity hinges upon the division between 'systems' and 'lifeworld', and processes of rationalisation. The phenomenological understanding of 'lifeworld' which Habermas is drawing upon is the unreflective background consensus which constitutes a necessary frame for social interaction (developed by Schutz and Gadamer). What Habermas refers to as the 'rationalisation of the lifeworld' is a process which points to the ambivalent status of the concept of 'lifeworld' in his theory, for rationalisation entails paradoxically an erosion of background consensus; i.e., more and more aspects of tradition are drawn into the sphere of communicative action and rational argumentation, as the potential of communicative action is progressively released into the lifeworld in the course of its rationalisation. For instance, the moral right of parents to control the actions of children in certain ways have in recent decades increasingly come to be thematised (therefore made open to challenge, justification and redesign) in argumentative discourse. (Legislation in Denmark in 1996 makes it illegal for parents to exercise any physical violence on children in public or in the home, for example.) The rationalisation of the lifeworld entails a process of abstraction and generalisation of communicative practices away from particular domains of life, and a separation of the forms of communicative action from their contents, so that general procedures emerge for argumentation over the truth, rightness or sincerity of communicative utterances which are applicable irrespective of the particular situations or contents of communicative interaction. Furthermore the increasing reflexivity of communicative action – the increasing capacity of people to use communicative action to reflect back on and redeem itself – is the basis for the increasing salience of critique of language (including academic forms of language critique such as critical discourse analysis). Increasing reflexivity moreover entails increasing transparency, which Habermas argues makes it increasingly difficult for communicative action to 'hide' ideologies (1987a: 187ff, 196). He suggests that ideology becomes displaced as a resource for domination by a fragmentation which obscures the interrelationships between parts of social life (1987a: 353–4).

Rationalisation of the lifeworld enables and brings about the 'uncoupling' – separation – of systems from the lifeworld which defines modern societies. With respect to systems, Habermas alludes to Weber's identification of modernity with a differentiation of cultural spheres of value – science and technology, law and morality, art. The differentiation of these systems within the 'sacred' domain of action (Habermas 1987a: 192) involves an unravelling of the validity claims which are woven together in communicative action, and a specialisation of each of these emergent expert systems around a particular validity claim – truth in the case of science and technology, rightness in the case of law and morality, truthfulness in the case of art. At the same time, within the 'profane' domain of action, the systems of the economy and the state (and their respective 'steering media', money and power) are uncoupled from the lifeworld, as systems which are built upon a specialised instrumental rationality (the rationality of 'getting results'). This is the rationalisation of systems. Habermas (unlike Marx) sees this as irreversible and not inherently negative – in fact, the viability of modern societies depends upon it. The argument is that the rationalisation of communicative action vastly expands its scope and scale at a potentially crippling social cost – if societies had to constantly reach consensus over everything through argumentation, they could not function. The steering media and the rationalisation of systems reduce this burden upon communicative action by converting interactions between people into routine and mechanical exchanges – a process of 'delinguistification'. The separation of systems and lifeworld is itself is a major evolutionary gain, according to Habermas. Pathologies arise not from the separation per se but from particular modes of connection between systems and lifeworld.

Systems that are uncoupled from the lifeworld at the same time remain dependent upon being institutionalised within the lifeworld – for example, the political system is institutionalised in the public sphere of the lifeworld (where people deliberate together on matters of social and political concern). There are thus channels between lifeworld and systems which in principle allow flows in either direction – systems can be shaped by lifeworlds, lifeworlds by systems. Habermas's argument is that under the conditions of contemporary capitalist society, the predominant flows are from systems to lifeworld – to the point where systemic practices 'colonise' the lifeworld and squeeze out communicative action. But excessive expansion of systems becomes counterproductive, and results in pathologies weakening the social anchorage of systems and impeding the growth of new cultural potentials which are a precondition for further systemic development. Corresponding to the two systems of money and power (the economy and the state), there are two divisions of the lifeworld (the private sphere of the family and the public sphere). Colonisation flows from the economy as the monetarisation (commodification) of the family and of the public sphere, and from the state as the bureaucratisation of the family and the public sphere. One pathology resulting from the systemic colonisation of the lifeworld in modern versus welfare capitalism is a change in social roles. In classical capitalism the grounding of the economy in the family and of the state in the public sphere are carried in the roles of worker and citizen respectively – they channel the influence of the lifeworld upon the systems. In the welfare state these two roles are weakened in favour of two others, the consumer and the client, which now channel the increasing influence of systems in the lifeworld, the colonisation of the lifeworld by systems.

The recent evolution of shopping might be used as an example of the colonisation (monetarisation, commodification) of the lifeworld. Shopping in the corner shop or in small, specialised town-centre shops (the greengrocers, the bread shop, the dairy, etc.) involves extensive communicative interaction. When shopping predominantly took this form a generation ago, it constituted a significant part of the lifeworld and a significant domain of communicative action. This has been progressively subjected to systemic colonisation, the incursion of instrumental rationality, and a delinguistification which has replaced communicative interaction by an exchange of money, as supermarkets have taken over from small shops. The vista that is now opening up of 'shopping' as a solitary activity carried out on the internet points to an intensification of this process, though at the same time older forms of shopping are being reinvigorated in particular domains (for example, 'craft').

Another pathological effect on the lifeworld which Habermas has given attention to is the undermining of the public sphere – of those spaces and practices where people as citizens deliberate together on matters of social and political concern, providing a channel from the lifeworld into the political system. In his early work (1989) Habermas charted the effect of mass communication in transforming politics into a spectacle in which people are increasingly spectators (clients) rather than involved citizens. More recently he has talked about the 'ambivalent potential' of mass communication – 'these media publics hierarchize and at the same time remove restrictions on the horizon of possible communication. The one aspect cannot be separated from the other – and therein lies their ambivalent potential' (1987a: 390).

As we have seen, Habermas sees the unrealised potentials of social life as a resource for change which can be released in periods of social transformation, when the systemic configurations which have blocked their realisation come into crisis. The 'carriers' for these potentials which effect their release are social movements, what in contemporary society are commonly referred to as the 'new' social movements – feminism, ecology, gay and lesbian movement, animal rights movement, fundamentalist groups, and so forth. What is politically distinctive about the new social movements in comparison with the trade unions and the labour movement is that their struggles are mainly over symbolic rather than material issues. They are resistant to the effects of colonisation of the lifeworld – for example, to the spread of the construction of people as consumers and clients rather than workers and citizens. They are largely defensive in nature – trying to defend the lifeworld against colonisation. But they may become offensive and so emancipatory – continuing in new forms the enlightenment tradition of struggles for universal emancipation. According to Habermas, this happens in the case of the feminist movement. Their struggles centre upon the revitalisation of public space through the generation of many diverse public spheres which draw upon modern communications media (print, broadcasting, the internet) and which are 'porous' to each other, which open up a struggle over the boundaries between systems and lifeworld (Habermas 1987b: 364–7).

We shall mention a couple of criticisms of Habermas which are particularly relevant here. First, Habermas has mainly been oriented towards the individual nation-state, in contrast with the global orientation in Harvey and Giddens which is called for by shifts in late modernity. Second, Calhoun (1995: 135) comments that Habermas understands power as 'simply and impersonally systemic', in contrast with Bourdieu, for whom power 'is always used, if sometimes unconsciously'. Habermas uses the term 'discourse' in a distinctive way to refer to the sort of communication which constitutes 'a step back from action' (Outhwaite 1994: 33) in order to evaluate and justify the validity claims which underpin action. Discourse is aimed at producing consensus; power is relevant in establishing the procedures which allow this to happen by guaranteeing open access and equal chances to contribute, but problematic differences of identity which would give rise to a power dynamic within discourse are assumed to be bracketed. Habermas's concept of the public sphere is along similar lines, and is essentially liberal (Calhoun 1995: 244). He is committed to the idea of a domain of communicative action characterised by the unfettered working towards consensus through argumentation – what he earlier called the 'ideal speech situation'. Critics such as Lyotard see this as covertly the tyranny of the universal – such a domain could only be achieved through a repression of difference. While we see the mobilising force of Habermas's idealisation, we believe that it is a problematic ideal as it stands because it does not acknowledge that the recognition of difference is a necessary complement to the search for consensus. We do not wish to go as far as Lyotard's (1984) agonistic alternative (also taken up by Billig 1991) of a space for unlimited verbal battle, but we believe that dialogue requires both expression and recognition of difference and localised construction of consensus – indeed that a discourse oriented to finding consensus is a possible local and occasioned achievement of dialogue across difference, which depends upon expression and recognition of difference (Fairclough forthcoming b, Barát and Fairclough 1997).

We said above that Habermas's theory can provide a research agenda as well as a theoretical grounding for critical discourse analysis. By way of summing up, let us briefly identify elements of that agenda (which not surprisingly overlap with themes identified from the theories of Harvey and Giddens). Habermas's theory analyses out the moments of a lifeworld–systems dialectic as they impinge upon the social use of language in modern societies: the rationalisation of the lifeworld as a linguistification of the sacred; the uncoupling of system and lifeworld; the colonisation of the lifeworld by systems; the defensive and offensive reaction of social movements to this colonisation. Each of these moments generates substantive issues for the research agenda of critical discourse analysis. The rationalisation of the lifeworld thematises *linguistic reflexivity*: there is a new field of research for critical discourse analysis in the diverse degrees to which and ways in which communicative interaction in the various spaces of modern societies reflexively turns back on itself and is reshaped through reflexivity. Critical discourse analysis itself can be understood as part of the increasing linguistic (and more generally social) reflexivity of late modernity (Fairclough 1997). Habermas also draws attention to the implications for ideology: how can a communicative practice which is open to reflection provide hiding places for ideology (Habermas 1987a: 352ff)? The uncoupling of system and lifeworld thematises both the separation and specialisation out of the discourses and genres of work, the state, science, etc. from communicative interaction in the lifeworld, and the theme of *linguistification/delinguistification*. The latter is another new and potentially rich theme for critical discourse analysis which centres the boundaries between language and other forms of semiosis (touched on briefly in Chapter 3), and between semiosis and other forms of social interaction and exchange. The colonisation of the lifeworld by systems links with an existing body of research within critical discourse analysis around themes of the systemic *colonisation of discourse* – commodification of language, technocratic discourse (Lemke 1995), bureaucratic discourse (Sarangi and Slembrouck 1996), mediatisation of for instance political discourse, and so forth. This can be fruitfully developed by focusing upon the unravelling of the synthesis of validity claims in communicative interaction by incursions of systemic discourses which one-sidedly focus truth (for example, technocratic discourse), rightness (for example, legalistic discourse), or truthfulness (for example, aestheticised discourse within politics). Here and throughout, the Habermasian perspective focuses upon spatial relationships between different types of communicative interaction (the separation of systemic types of communication from the communicative action of the lifeworld, the colonisation of the latter by the former, etc.) which harmonises with the centring in critical discourse analysis of 'orders of discourse' (Fairclough 1992a), socially structured configurations of discursive practices associated with particular social spaces, in terms of the shifting boundaries and flows between them. Finally the interventions of social movements in response to colonisation bring into the agenda *struggles over discursive practices* as part of social struggles, including a research agenda around the communicative construction of public space which centres upon the search for effective forms of *dialogue* (Fairclough, forthcoming b).

NARRATIVES OF POSTMODERNISM

Our account of critical narratives of late modernity and our agenda for CDA would be misleading is we did not include narratives which engage with the logic of postmodernism, either to embrace and celebrate it as in the case of Baudrillard and Lyotard, or to critique and modify it as in the case of feminist writings and Jameson (what Best and Kellner 1991 distinguish as 'extreme' and 'reconstructive' versions of postmodernism).

Our position is that postmodernist theories thematise important issues in contemporary social theory and provide a powerful critique of Western epistemologies. In both these senses, they fertilise and advance traditional Marxist and critical problematics. Indeed we share with postmodernist theories an indebtedness to poststructuralism – both its deconstruction of dominant objectivist and humanist theoretical practices, and its radical contribution to theorising the social world and the subject from the point of view of discourse. We do not however accept postmodernist social theories that abandon the project of social struggle and change; further, we do not agree with postmodern ontologies that conflate the social with discourse nor with epistemologies that advocate a 'just gaming' position for theoretical practice.

We will here refer to different theorists of postmodernism, keeping in mind that there is no such thing as a unified postmodern social theory, nor a unified position on what 'postmodern' actually means (Kellner 1988). But despite substantial differences, there are pertinent themes: the omnipresence of power and consequently the power–knowledge link which includes the widely theorised technology–power link in contemporary societies, and an 'agonistic' view of social struggle as an end in itself which renders the project of social change essentially futile (Lyotard 1984).

We begin from Foucault's post-structuralist account of power in modern societies, though we need to stress that not only did Foucault not recognise himself as a 'postmodern' writer, but in his late work he acknowledged his project's affinity to the critical school (Best and Kellner 1991). Foucault uses the term 'biopower' to refer to the radically modern form of power, which 'brought life and its mechanisms into the realm of explicit calculations and made knowledge/power an agent of transformation of human life' (1981: 143). Foucault's account focuses on the emergence of certain 'microtechniques' of power (such as the 'examination' in education and medicine) in institutions such as hospitals, schools, prisons and the military in the earlier part of the modern period, which are both based upon social and psychological knowledge, and continuously produce knowledge about the people to whom they are applied. Modern power is thus not domination from outside but discipline: the continuous action of techniques which are built into the very capillaries of social life, and which have the effect of normalising modern life. The concept of 'discourse' brings together the two productive aspects of social practice (its 'double economy'), both as positive activities of production and as sources and effects of technologies of power. Although Foucault took the view that all forms of power entail resistance, the concept of biopower lent itself to a bleak vision of modern social life as an 'iron cage', rather similar to the pessimistic visions that members of the Frankfurt School arrived at (Held 1980). There is an absence of an orientation to practice and to struggle (compare Gramsci's 'hegemonic' view of power – Forgacs 1988) which make Foucault's analyses 'terribly one-sided' (Taylor 1986: 81; see also Hall 1996a).

Foucault's post-structuralist critique of modernity in terms of disciplinary power is taken to the extreme, 'over-dramatized' in Kellner's words, by Lyotard and Baudrillard. Both see postmodernity as a 'post-industrial' society, where the primacy of the mode of production in defining social relations in replaced by the primacy of the mode of information. Both see technology and knowledge as the principles of contemporary social organisation, though each focuses on a different aspect of modernity.

The bleak vision of Foucault and the Frankfurt School is echoed in the fear of the 'tyranny of the universal' which is evident in Lyotard (Lyotard 1984). The focus of Lyotard's well-known book *The Postmodern Condition* is epistemological – it is a critique of modern knowledge, and an exploration of the conditions for postmodern knowledge. The postmodern is defined as 'incredulity towards metanarratives'. Lyotard's own implicit metanarrative is that modern society has generated univer-salising forms of knowledge (theory, science) which tyrannically suppress difference. The postmodern politics that Lyotard advocates is a politics of discourse centred upon the disruption of universal discourses and metanarratives – grand narratives such as historical materialism, or the narrative of the development of science as the progress of humankind, and discourses which are set up as universal codes that other discourses can be translated into (Haraway 1990). Theoretically, Lyotard focuses on the incommensurability of different 'language games' or discourses – the absence of any measure for comparing them or evaluating them, which leaves space for no more than local 'gamings', playful experimentations that bring forth the 'discontinuous, catastrophic ... paradoxical' nature of the social.

If Lyotard's critique of modernity focuses on metanarratives and on the impos-sibility of knowledge, Baudrillard's addresses the question of representation and of the impossibility of the real. In his own detailed narrative, postmodern society is 'hyperreality', the displacement of reality by signs as a consequence of technological change, entailing the 'implosion' of the social – the implosion of boundaries, most of all the boundary between image and reality. Media-generated systems of signs offer models for the conduct of everyday life. These systems are sets of binary oppositions that cancel out differences and maintain an essentially self-same system, which position individuals into an order of 'simulacra'. Social experience is only possible as 'spectacle' – it is fleeting and obsolete – and any attempt to theorise or historicise it is futile. This is a code-oriented account of social order (what Baudrillard refers to as 'cybernetic control') which shares Lyotard's nihilistic attitude towards social struggles – though Baudrillard's 'surrender' is not playful but deeply melancholic (Baudrillard 1988).

There are however post-structuralist accounts of modernity which do not follow Lyotard's or Baudrillard's dramatic twists. Though their focus is on the primacy of culture over the material and economic in late modernity, and they critique Marxist social theory for neglecting cultural difference, such accounts are closer to critical ones in so far as they are interested in articulating the postmodern problematic with a political project of resistance and social change (Featherstone 1995; Lash and Urry 1988; Lash 1993; Thrift 1996).

This holds true also for feminism. Although there is a danger of homogenising the internally diverse field of feminist studies, there are overlapping themes here too. Feminist writings draw on both post-structuralist themes, the critique of meta-narratives and the challenging of representation, but avoid the extremes of the postmodern accounts we referred to. There is a tense relationship between post-modernism and feminism (for example, Fraser 1998). On the one hand the post-modern critique of the universal and assertion of difference harmonises with feminist critiques of the covert masculinity of supposedly universal categories, such as 'man-kind'. However, the critique of the universal has been extended within the debate around 'essentialism' to a critique of any identity category which can be seen as suppressing difference, including the category of 'women'. This has led some feminists into a political concern with recognition of difference (for example, Mouffe 1992; Flax 1990) which others have criticised as compromising the emancipatory objectives of feminism (for example, Di Stefano 1990; Harding 1990; Bordo 1990). We would agree with Fraser and Nicholson (1990) that a critical synthesis of the postmodernist decentring of essential identities and a feminist commitment to radical politics can provide the basis for a powerful social theory which overcomes the limitations of the two, leading to political projects based on alliances and on working and dialoguing across difference.

This is also a position held by Haraway (1988), whose commitment to 'situated knowledges' and partial truths does not give way to thorough-going relativism but works towards conceptualisations of the object of science that allow for 'webs of connections called "solidarity" in politics and "shared conversations" in epistem-ology' (1988: 584). Haraway's 'cyborg', a half-human, half-machine creation, embodies and materialises the breaking of traditional patriarchal distinctions between human and machine, physical and non-physical. It is a metaphor for the social as a process of boundary-drawing, of constructing subjects out of available material–semiotic resources, including 'fundamental' biological categories, such as the body and sex, which once provided the basis for essentialist definitions of identities. The epistemological value of the cyborg lies in reconceptualising con-temporary (postmodern) subjectivities as multiple semiotic projects – the cyborg's 'prosthesis', says Haraway, 'is semiosis, the making of meanings and bodies' (1988: 599) – which can be constructed, deconstructed and, in the process, connected and reconnected with itself and with other subjectivities. From this point of view it is a useful concept to work with in CDA, especially with respect to the latter's concerns with hybridity: the cyborg's linguistic–semiotic aspects can be 'deconstructed' in terms of CDA's analytical categories (i.e., in terms of the dialectic within the semiotic moment), whereas the 'prosthetic' relationships the cyborg sets up between human and non-physical, and human and technology can help CDA define the dialectic between moments of the social (see Chapters 2 and 3), particularly under conditions of late modernity. Haraway's cyborg is in fact situated within an account of post-modernity as a post-industrial information society, so that the metaphor also stands for the tight link between knowledge and technology – an apparatus that constructs the body as both a natural and a technological object (see Haraway 1990: 212–5 for the 'informatics of domination', an account of women's position in contemporary society).

Foucault's disciplinary technologies and Baudrillard's cybernetic control are both important themes in Haraway's account, but in Haraway's radical feminist politics the focus is on concrete engagements with the 'social relations of science and tech-nology' and on struggles that can effectively rearrange existing sex (and race and class) relations. Haraway mentions and partly draws upon Jameson's attempt to connect the postmodern problematic with the critical project, and the two converge on the need for 'cognitive mapping' (Jameson 1988), for constructing a space that allows for systematic connections and structural explanations as the basis for a politics of alliance. Jameson's basic argument is that postmodernism is the cultural facet of a new (purer) stage of capitalism rather than its radical overcoming – and that the primacy of the mode of information over production (the post-industrial stage) was predictable in Marxism (Mandel 1972). On the other hand a concern with culture and its radical transformations is drawn into the Marxist problematic to enhance and transform it: the blurring of the distinction between high and low cul-ture and the canonisation and popularisation of high culture; the commodification and spectacularisation of modern culture with the loss of depth and continuity; the fragmentation of subjectivities and the radical change in the experience of space and time (for example, Jameson 1988). This is obviously not the place to unfold the richness and complexity of Jameson's accounts of the postmodern shifts in a range of cultural fields. Relevant for CDA is Jameson's theorisation of the 'cultural logic' of late modernity in terms of heterogeneity, fragmentation, pastiche and schizophrenia, which are at the same time positioned by Jameson within the field of social and economic relations, insisting on the structural determination of culture (but see Best and Kellner 1991: 191–2 for a critical account of his position). Jameson though is suspicious of discourse theory and analysis, which he understands as prioritising discourse as a dimension of reality which 'can be left to float on its own' (1991: 264), disconnected from other dimensions or 'moments' of a social practice in our termin-ology. We certainly recognise the danger of extreme forms of textualism in discourse theory and analysis (see Chapter 3), but we believe however that CDA puts forward a dialectical view of social practice that postulates a relationship of overdetermination between discourse and other (material, institutional, mental) aspects of the social without privileging the former. In Chapters 2 and 7 we choose to engage in a big way with the second influential 'reconstructive' postmodern narrative, that of Laclau and Mouffe (see Best and Kellner 1991: 303 for the grouping), which, despite its problematic aspects, is based on a theory of discourse operationable in CDA. To conclude, we believe that one important task in CDA is to pursue both Haraway's and Jameson's projects, seeking ways to articulate them with a CDA agenda – the apparatus of CDA can explicate their theoretical claims, whereas both Haraway's cyborg and Jameson's studies on postmodern culture can be redefined by and grounded in the particularities of discursive and semiotic practice.

CONCLUSION: A RESEARCH AGENDA FOR CDA

Our purpose in this section is to pull together themes from the narratives of late modernity we have been discussing to propose a research agenda for CDA. The main items on the agenda are major categories of problem for CDA as a form of explanatory critique (the framework which was described in Chapter 4). We have formulated the items as pairs of contrary terms, and as a dialectic, to try to capture some of the contradictory character of discourse in late modernity, as well as the different emphases of different theories. We also argue that to capture this complexity and often ambivalence of discourse on late modernity, CDA should be open in its analysis to different theoretical discourses which construct the problem in focus in different ways. Examples are given below. The items are as follows: colonisation/ appropriation; globalisation/localisation; reflexivity/ideology; identity/difference. There are two pervasive concerns within this agenda which cut across items and are therefore best not included themselves as items: power and hybridity. Given the orientation to problems, power and struggle over power are constant concerns for CDA. And given the instability and rapid shifts of late modernity, the horizon for the problems is a horizon of change which manifests itself discoursally as a pervasive hybridisation of types of discourse – the hybrid text (in the general, SFL sense) is the norm in late modernity. Needless to say, we are not claiming that this is 'the' agenda for CDA: we are offering it as a contribution to the important process of reflecting on what we are and should be doing.

Colonisation/appropriation

The dialectic of colonisation/appropriation is directed towards the movements of discourses and genres from one social practice to another within the network of social practices (in the terms of Chapter 2). Such movements can be construed as one practice colonising (and so dominating) another, or as the latter appropriating (and so dominating) the former. So the question of power is always at issue, as also is the question of hybridity – the movement of a discourse or genre from one practice into another entails its recontextualisation within the latter, i.e., a new articulation of elements into which it is incorporated, a new hybridity. We refer to a dialectic here because we see any colonisation as also an appropriation, and vice versa. This is not to deny that colonisation is more salient than appropriation in particular cases or vice versa but rather to accept that neither can fully eliminate the other – so the potential for subverting colonisation or appropriation is always there.

While the colonisation/appropriation dialectic works between any practices, what is most often at issue here is, in Habermas's terms, the relationship between the practices of social systems and the practices of the 'lifeworld' – in the context of the general problem of what he sees as the colonisation of the lifeworld by systems. 'Colonisation' is of course Habermas's concept, and it imposes a particular theoretical slant on this part of the agenda (for instance, colonisation leaves space for possible 'decolonisation'). CDA should also be open here to different theoretical discourses such as Foucault's discourse of 'normalisation' (as well as 'resistance' to normalisation); or Lyotard's discourse of the 'tyrannical' imposition of the 'universal' – which he would extend to Habermas's own consensual concept of 'discourse' (Lyotard 1984); or again, a Gramscian discourse of hegemony and hegemonic struggle, which we have used in an earlier formulation of CDA (Fairclough 1992a). The point is not to proliferate concepts for its own sake, it is to keep CDA oriented to a field of critical theorisation and research rather than a single theory.

Quite a lot of research previously carried out within CDA belongs here, including work on the marketisation of discourse (Fairclough 1995c), the spread of bureaucratic (Sarangi and Slembrouck 1996) and technocratic (Lemke 1995) discourse into new domains, conversationalisation of public discourse (Fairclough 1994), or within a different theoretical frame the spread of pedagogical discourse beyond pedagogical institutions (Bernstein 1996). One contemporary example is the colonisation of many different types of organisation by the discourse of 'total quality management' which incorporates a normative specification of organisational practices including discourse (for example, procedures for setting and auditing 'quality' targets).

Globalisation/localisation

The globalisation/localisation dialectic is really a particular form of the colonisation/appropriation dialectic. However, it merits being treated as a separate item because it is a form that is distinctive for late modernity and an important new feature of the social life of discourse, which moreover makes it increasingly difficult to justify taking a particular society as the object of analysis in CDA research. We refer to a dialectic here because not only do disembedded discursive practices (such as particular forms of interview, in work or politics) increasingly flow across linguistic and cultural boundaries, they are drawn into new articulations with each other and with local forms which vary from place to place and are shaped by and figure within local logics of practice. For instance, Hungarian television news has drawn upon dominant US and European models over a period of years, but it has integrated them into a distinctive practice of its own which accords with its own logic of practice (Barát and Fairclough 1997).

But the globalisation/localisation dialectic is played out as part of relations of struggle between globally dominant states and organisations, and not only national or local communities but particular groups within them – social struggles within these communities are mapped onto struggles on an international and global level. The concept of 'globalisation' tends to underplay this power struggle, and might indeed be seen as within an ideologically potent discourse which misconstrues a bid for global hegemony as a benign coming-together. For this reason we should be open to other discourses and narratives – such as the hegemonic project of 'neo-liberalism' as a 'Utopia' for groups such as the banks that they are struggling to impose globally, using the resources of discourse (including the discourse of globalisation) as well as other resources (Bourdieu 1998b).

Reflexivity/ideology

We have seen that late modernity has been characterised in terms of an enhanced reflexivity which can be said to include an enhanced reflexivity about discourse – people are generally more aware of their practices, and their practices are pervasively and deeply open to knowledge-based transformation. An example would be a relatively general and high level of awareness of practices including discourse which can be judged as sexist or racist. However, it is far from obvious that everyone shares a high level of critical awareness, or that people are aware of all their practices to the same degree. In the terms we adopt in Chapter 7, people in different positions in social life seem to be in different relationships to discourse and language, which furthermore vary from one social practice to another. At the same time, knowledge about discourse is a contested resource in social struggles – in what Fairclough has called the 'technologisation of discourse' (Fairclough 1996a), the knowledge-based engineering by managements of the discourse moment of organisational social practices figures as part of the engineering of organisational culture for instrumental purposes. Moreover CDA can itself be regarded as a manifestation within theoretical practice of a generally enhanced language reflexivity, and should reflect on its own position and role in knowledge-based struggles over discourse.

Enhanced discourse reflexivity would seem to go against discourse working ideologically, which requires a high level of naturalisation of discourse (Fairclough 1989) – ways of using language being taken as simply self-evident. Habermas has suggested this connection – that increasing reflexivity displaces ideology as a resource for domination, and that ideology is replaced in this role by fragmentation:

> in place of the positive task of meeting a certain need for interpretation by ideological means, we have the negative requirement of preventing holistic interpretations from coming into existence ... everyday consciousness is robbed of its power to synthesize; it becomes fragmented.
>
> (Habermas 1987a: 255)

Fragmentation certainly is a feature of late modern social life, yet we are not convinced that there is a simple displacement of ideology through heightened reflexivity.

Rather, while there may be an overall enhancement of discourse reflexivity, we see contrary pressures towards the naturalisation of discourse (for example, the 'quality' discourse which we referred to above as colonising a wide range of organisations) and towards greater reflexivity. These contrary pressures are comprehensible for instance in terms of the contradictions of contemporary organisations, which on the one hand need people who have thoroughly internalised the logic and values of the organisation, yet on the other hand need to be open to constant critical evaluation and possible transformation of their logic and values. Again, CDA needs to be open to different theoretical discourses, including both 'ideology' and 'reflexivity'.

Identity/difference

Different theoretical vocabularies again point to differences of emphasis. The concept of 'subject' is often associated with a structural focus on subjection, positioning, including positioning in discourse. This covers both a concern with the representation of particular social groups (for example, of women, or national or ethnic groups such as Arabs, in the press), and with how for instance particular genres set up particular discourse positions for people (for example, as doctor and patient in a medical examination). On the other hand, the concepts of 'identity' and 'self' tend to be associated with an interactional focus on people constructing their own individual or collective identities in discourse. The background to this perspective is the unsettling of identities in the flux of late modernity – the struggle to find identities is one of the most pervasive themes of late modernity and one of the sharpest focuses of late modern reflexivity. Collective forms include discursive aspects of nationalism and fundamentalism, in the frame of a global/local dialectic. But these struggles also include the calculated collective and individual constructions of image which are pervasive in contemporary consumer societies – finding an identity might be crucial for ontological security but it is also needed for business purposes.

Struggles over identity are also struggles over difference – for instance, discourse which uses *we*, the first person plural, to construct a universal subject, 'humankind', is for Lyotard part of the tyranny of the universal – it constitutes an identity which represses difference. But the question of how to dialogue and act with others who are different is quite as urgent in late modern societies as the question of who I am or who we are. Finding ways to dialogue across difference – recognising difference while also transcending it – is now widely seen as crucial to the survival of democracy (Touraine 1997; Giddens 1994a). Recall that for Giddens questions of 'dialogical democracy' are not simply public questions, they are also germane to the intimate sphere of personal relationships. CDA's task here is partly descriptive and partly normative, in the sense that it can contribute to social struggles around identity and difference by identifying unrealised potentials.

NOTES

1. This view of power links in with Giddens' statement that historical materialism remains viable as a theory only if it is based in the concept of praxis. Praxis is understood as a fundamental trait of human ontology: 'all human action is carried on by knowledgable agents who both construct the social world through their action, but yet whose action is also conditioned or constrained by the very world of their creation.' Or in Marx's words: 'Men make history, but not in circumstances of their own chosing'.
2. Giddens' critique of the focus within sociology on the individual society as the object of research carries over to linguistics. Given that discursive processes increasingly transcend language boundaries in the way we have suggested, the object of research for a linguistics with any interest in human social life (formalist linguistics has no such interest) should be refocused first, upon the discursive rather than the narrowly linguistic, and second, upon discursive relations across languages and societies.

Chapter 6

Language, space and time

In moving from Chapter 4 to Chapter 5, we are shifting from 'grand theory' – general theoretical accounts of late modernity – to middle-range and local theory which leads to a focus on the dynamics of late modernity within particular social fields. Bourdieu is mainly a middle-range theorist of the structuring of complex contemporary societies in terms of social 'fields'. Bernstein's interest is in one particular field, education, though he conceptualises the field of education in terms of a broad concept of 'pedagogy' which includes other fields – so he is similarly a middle-range theorist with respect to the theory's application potential. Language has a central position in both theories, and we shall argue that, taken together, they provide a mediating link between the theories of late modernity discussed in Chapter 4 and the critical analysis of particular types of discourse. They can provide this link because, while neither offers a 'grand' critical theory of late modernity, they are both oriented to trajectories of change in late modern societies. For instance, Bourdieu sees modernisation in terms of shifts in modes of social integration from inter-personal networks in traditional societies to fields (Fowler 1997; Calhoun 1995), and Bernstein contextualises shifts in configurations of 'pedagogical modalities' within the transition from pre-capitalist to late modern societies (see below).

Moreover, they are both critical theorists in the broad sense (see Chapter 2), although both distance themselves from the totalising theories of Marxism and the Frankfurt School and favour empirical research in specific fields. Both are concerned to trace the embeddedness of social practice within social relations of power and within class relations in particular, and both are concerned to discern the potential for transformation within actual social arrangements. And both are seeking to avoid the pitfalls of pure phenomenalism or pure structuralism through a constructivist structuralism which sees a dialectic relation between structure and agency, theorising language as a social practice within that dialectic (but see Atkinson 1995 on the particularities of Bernstein's structuralism) – though both tend to stress the continuity of structures and relations of power through changes in their forms of appearance, distancing themselves from postmodern claims about social fragmentation. Both have combined a Marxist view of the class basis of social relations of power with a Durkheimian emphasis on symbolic forms and modes of classification in sustaining social order, so that both foreground symbolic structures and meaning – and therefore language – in social reproduction and change.

Bourdieu and Bernstein differ in particular over the social significance of the 'content' of fields. For Bourdieu, the structure of the field in terms of the positions it sets up is everything; the particular content of the field is of secondary importance, because contents are arbitrary in the sense that the same field structure (and the same fundamental relations of power) can be sustained through radical changes in content (LiPuma 1993; Collins 1993; Hasan in press b). By contrast, Bernstein argues that the social analysis of education for instance calls for both analysis of the structure of the field of education and analysis of the pedagogical discourse of education (see particularly Bernstein 1996: 182–201). The latter entails detailed analysis of how particular pedagogical modalities operate within contexts of schooling, including analyses of classroom discourse (though Bourdieu has also discussed classroom discourse, in Bourdieu et al. 1994). Bernstein develops a theory of discourse which is lacking in Bourdieu, and therefore takes us closer to a coherent way of connecting language analysis with sociological analysis. This potential in Bernstein's theory is the basis of a long-standing relationship with systemic functional linguistics and particularly the work of Halliday and Hasan (Halliday and Hasan 1989; Halliday 1978, 1994a; Hasan 1986, 1992a, 1992b, 1996). However, we shall argue that there remains a gap in the theorisation of the connection between the linguistic and the sociological, and in available languages of description for sociologically relevant analysis of language, and that CDA can contribute to filling that gap.

BOURDIEU

To demonstrate the value and limitations of Bourdieu's sociology for CDA, we shall refer to his analysis of a post-election television debate (Bourdieu and Wacquant 1992: 257–8), which we reproduce at length below:

> The space of interaction functions as a situation of linguistic market and we can uncover the principles that underlie its conjunctural properties. First, it consists of a preconstructed space: the social composition of the group of participants is determined in advance. To understand what can be said and especially what cannot be said on the set, one must know the laws of formation of the group of speakers – who is excluded and who exclude themselves ... A second characteristic is the following: the journalist wields a form of domination (conjunctural, not structural) over a space of play that he has constructed and in which he finds himself in the role of referee imposing norms of 'objectivity' and 'neutrality'.
>
> We cannot, however, stop here. The space of interaction is the locus where the intersection between several different fields is realized. In their struggle to impose the 'impartial' interpretation, that is, to make the viewers recognize their vision as objective, agents have at their command resources which depend on their membership in objectively hierarchized fields and on their position within their respective fields. First we have the political field ... politicians ... occupy different positions in the political field: they are situated in this space by their membership

in a party but also by their status in the party, their notoriety, local or national, their public appeal, etc. Then we have the journalistic field: journalists can and must adopt a rhetoric of objectivity and neutrality, with the assistance of 'politologists' when needed. Then we have the field of 'political science' within which 'media politologists' occupy a rather unglamorous position ... Next is the field of political marketing, represented by advertisers and media advisors who dress up their evaluations of politicians with 'scientific' justifications. Last is the university field proper, represented by specialists in electoral history who have developed a speciality in the commentary of electoral results. We thus have a progression from the most 'engaged' to the most detached, structurally or statutorily: the academic is the one who has the most 'hindsight', 'detachment' ...

The discursive strategies of the various agents, and in particular effects aimed at producing a front of objectivity, will depend on the balance of symbolic forces between the fields and on the specific resources that membership in these fields grants to the various participants. In other words, they will hinge upon the specific interests and the differential assets that the participants possess, in this particular symbolic struggle over the 'neutral' verdict, by virtue of their position in the system of invisible relations that obtain between the different fields in which they operate. For instance, the politologist will have an edge, as such, over the politician and the journalist, due to the fact that he is more readily credited with objectivity, and because he has the option of calling upon his specific competence, i.e., his command of electoral history to make comparisons ... The resultant of all these objective relations are relations of symbolic power which express themselves in the interaction in the form of rhetorical strategies. It is these objective relations that determine for the most part who can cut somebody off, ask questions, speak at length without being interrupted, or disregard interruptions, etc., who is condemned to strategies of denegation (of interests and interested strategies) or to ritual refusals to answer, or to stereotypical formulas, etc. We would need to push further by showing how bringing objective structures into the analysis allows us to account for the particulars of discourse and of rhetorical strategies, complicities, and antagonisms, and for the moves attempted and effected – in short, for everything that discourse analysis believes it can understand on the basis of discourse alone.

The example is a particularly useful one for our purposes because it applies Bourdieu's theoretical framework in the analysis of a communicative interaction which brings together agents from various different fields. Before commenting on it further, we shall briefly sketch out central aspects of Bourdieu's theory.

Bourdieu views modernity as the increasing differentiation and autonomisation of fields, and his theory of fields gives substance and specificity to the insight which is captured in different ways in Habermas's theory of the uncoupling of systems from the lifeworld, and Foucault's theory of power in modernity – that modernity entails a radical change in the mode of social integration and regulation. The strength of Bourdieu in comparison with these other theorists is that the differentiation of fields and associated habituses more readily allows empirical investigation of shifts in the social practices of late modernity than the more general and abstract categories of the latter (Calhoun 1995: 207). And from the specific perspective of CDA, field theory is complementary to analysis in terms of orders of discourse (Fairclough 1992a – see further below).

A *field* for Bourdieu is a network of positions defined by a particular distribution of capital (for example, in educational institutions or the political system) which endows that field with its own specific practical logic: the way people who occupy these positions act within the space (the strategies they adopt) depends upon the quantity and composition of the capital they are endowed with – composition in the sense of in what proportion different types of capital are combined. Capital may be economic, social or cultural. All forms of capital are convertible into 'symbolic capital', once they are (mis)recognised as and have the effects of forms of power. 'Linguistic capital' is the power conferred upon a particular linguistic form, style or dialect associated with the legitimacy and prestige of particular social positions – it is crucial in the conversion of other forms of capital into symbolic capital. Differences of capital between different positions are differences of power. But Bourdieu is not simply saying that the positions people occupy in structures shape how they act in a deterministic way – their strategies (including whether they act to preserve or subvert the structure of the field) also depend upon their social trajectories, and how the volume and composition of their capital are shifting over time. And as this implies, Bourdieu does not construe fields as static structures but as spaces of struggle in the course of which they can be restructured, and the boundaries which separate them from other fields redefined, strengthened or weakened (in interactions such as this one). Also at issue, as the example shows, are relations of dominance–subordination between fields. The 'field of power' is a 'meta-field' in which agents with power in the various specific fields contest the relative exchange values of the different capitals accumulated in different fields. Bourdieu also refers to the 'social space' or 'field of class struggle' also penetrated by other social divisions (gender, race, etc. – cf. Bourdieu 1990) in terms of 'homologies' between it and specific fields such as the political field.

An agent operating within a field is endowed with a particular *habitus*, a practical sense of 'the game', a set of dispositions to act, which is determined by structure of positions in the field and the particular social trajectory (and history) of that agent (the example does not use the word 'habitus', but it alludes to the concept for instance in referring to 'resources'); an inculcated and incorporated effect of structures with a transformative capacity which entails that it cannot be reduced to rules or norms (Calhoun et al. 1993, 'Introduction'). Field and habitus constitute two spaces of inscription of the social – in places or institutions, or in bodies. The habitus is the social in an embodied form. The habitus shapes how agents act on particular sorts of occasion – how successfully in terms of generating 'profit' from the 'investment' of capital, how creatively or normatively, how subversively or conservatively. The concept of habitus displaces two opposed but equally unacceptable conceptions of action – a structuralist conception of action as merely an epiphenomenal effect of position in structure, and a rationalist conception of it as rational choice – while maintaining both a sense of structural determination of action and a sense of agency. Social analysis on this account centres upon the relationship between habitus and field. That relationship may be a close match – so the habitus of those highly endowed with capital and power in a particular field often seems to be perfectly adjusted to the structure of the field. Conversely, there may be tension between habitus and field. In Bourdieu's early research on Algeria for instance he claimed that sub-proletarians in Algeria could not, because of their conditions of life, attain the 'rational habitus' demanded for action within the capitalist economic field. Rapid social change may transform field structures and produce overlaps between fields – of the sort illustrated in the example – faster than people's habitus can change. While habituses could thus be the source of resistance within fields, commentators have argued that Bourdieu's emphasis on the 'profits of distinction' arising from a habitus well adjusted to a field pushes habitus in a more adaptive direction (Pujolar 1997; LiPuma 1993). Whereas Bourdieu's emphasis is on unrationalised practical sense, he recognises that agents can in varying degrees become conscious of their dispositions and consciously change them – they can become reflexive – and in so doing become to that extent the rational subjects postulated in an illegitimately universal way by rational choice theorists, and in an intellectual rather than just a practical relation to their action. This is where Bourdieu sees the possibility for instability in the system (Calhoun 1995).

The potential of all forms of power to be transformed into symbolic capital makes the latter the basis of symbolic power, 'a power of constituting the given through utterances, of making people see and believe, of confirming or transforming the vision of the world and, thereby, action on the world and thus the world itself' (Bourdieu 1991: 170). Notice that Bourdieu describes the post-election debate as a struggle for symbolic power whose nature depends upon the symbolic capital which the different categories of agent bring to the debate (though without recognising the capacity to mediate as a form of symbolic capital). A central element in this is linguistic capital. Bourdieu argues that there has been a unification of the linguistic field (or 'market') in the modern period which has led to all local and class dialects being structured together within a single field in relations of subordination to the 'legitimate' (standard) language. An agent's linguistic capital depends upon access to positions within the linguistic field and especially access to the legitimate language. In specific fields such as the field of politics, this linguistic capital manifests itself as access to more or less powerful 'styles', where a style is 'an element of the mechanism … through which language aims to produce and impose the representation of its own importance and thereby help to ensure its own credibility' (1991: 76). This implies – without explicitly formulating – a close relationship between two linguistic aspects of symbolic capital: the capacity to 'constitute the given', and the capacity to do so in a legimated style which gives 'credibility' to that 'vision of the world'. As we shall show below, these two aspects of language are not theoretically reconciled in Bourdieu's work.

Let us return to the example to explore the value and limitations of Bourdieu's theory for CDA. Bourdieu insists that interactions are constrained by prestructured fields and criticises (as 'discourse analysis') purely interactional analysis which makes no reference to fields. Sociological analysis of fields provides a frame for specifying what we have argued in Chapters 2 and 3 to be the necessary structure-oriented side of CDA. We might say that a field is a social order which can be characterised from the particular perspective of language as an order of discourse. Bourdieu's account suggests that the relevant structural frame for CDA is not the individual order of discourse, but the the structured configuration of orders of discourse within a field and across fields (see the section on field and order of discourse below).

Bourdieu describes the debate as 'a situation of linguistic market' and locates it in a 'preconstructed space', but he does not fully recognise a specific 'journalistic field' of which the debate is one particular function. This has two implications. First, the preconstructed space is simply a matter of the predetermined composition of the group of participants; second, although Bourdieu acknowledges that their 'space of interaction is the locus of intersection between several different fields', the dynamics of this intersection is explained exclusively on the basis of the journalist's 'form of domination ... over a space of play that he has constructed and in which he finds himself in the role of referee'. What is lacking here is a theory of contemporary forms of mediation, such as television, as an institutional complex or field with its own structural logic and forms of capital. In the journalistic field, interactional practices are regulated not only 'conjuncturally' but also structurally, and so the intersection of fields in Bourdieu's example gives rise to a complex interaction that goes beyond the 'struggle to impose the "impartial" interpretation'. This brings out a layering dimension of field structure which is not apparent in Bourdieu's text. The journalistic field, itself constituted by an articulation of agents and habituses specific to journalism with the other fields Bourdieu refers to, is a site of mediation between (in Habermas's terms) systems and lifeworld (or: the public and the private) which transforms the boundaries and nature of publicness. One feature of this transformation is manifest in the tension between the language of the political, academic, etc. systems and the language of ordinary life (more informal and personal), which emerges as a pervasive 'conversationalisation' of media discourse (see Fairclough 1994).

In being articulated together within the journalistic field, the various systemic fields as well as the lifeworld are transformed, in that the boundaries and relations between them are redrawn. One aspect of this process is that the political field becomes mediatised, but also conversationalised through the relationship with the lifeworld in which it is placed within the journalistic field. The mediatisation of politics means not only that the language of politics changes (for example, becomes more journalistic as well as conversational), but also that media events such as this programme come to be significant political events in their own right. Given the power of the journalistic field within the social configuration of fields, mediatised politics arguably comes to radically reshape the political field overall (Fairclough 1995a; Thompson 1995). We would argue that this calls for the journalistic field to be theorised in terms of a specific form of 'media capital' (see Calhoun 1995: 155 for a general critique of Bourdieu for his neglect of mediation, including information technology, as a crucial aspect of modernity and late modernity). Media capital generates profits of distinction for particular habituses (media-friendly politicians, for example) and combines with other forms of capital (cultural, economic, etc.) to maximise their overall symbolic capital.

The increasing significance of media capital is asserted as it becomes convertible into power within the field of politics itself (or, as Bourdieu himself recognises in a recent study of television (Bourdieu 1998a), within the academic field). Conceptualising the interaction in Bourdieu's example as a practice in the journalistic field with its own specific logic and forms of capital – and moreover as field of tension which cuts across the systems–lifeworld divide – allows us to rethink the 'symbolic struggles' that are played out in the course of interaction in ways which are complementary to and enrich Bourdieu's own account. We would agree with Bourdieu that the interaction is (partly) a struggle over the imposition of an 'impartial' interpretation, based on the resources agents bring from their positions within fields which are in a prestructured relation to each other. Field struggles in this sense are both struggles over 'classifications', the boundaries between fields (including the systems–lifeworld divide) and their hierarchisation, as well as struggles over 'profits of distinction' accruing from access to and recourse to legitimated languages and styles. But increasingly in television the legitimated styles include everyday conversational style. And moreover, symbolic struggle should be understood as something more than people acting with the single motive of accumulating capital (Dreyfus and Rabinow 1993: 41–2). This is important in order to disentangle the two views of struggle that remain unresolved in Bourdieu's work: classificatory struggles, and struggles for profit (capacity to constitute the given, and capacity to do so in a legitimate style which gives credibility to a vision of the world). In focusing on symbolic struggle as struggle for *access to* legitimated capital ('objective' rhetorical styles in the example), Bourdieu essentially plays down the crucial issue that *linguistic capital per se*, in the form of discourses as representations of social processes and relations, is part of the struggle for the constitution and classification of social (field) relations. This is a neglect on Bourdieu's part of what we referred to earlier on in this chapter as the 'content' of fields.

What we wish to stress though is the point that struggles are enacted in the course of communicative interaction, and that communicative interaction is the discursive facet of the constitution (and reproduction) and reconstitution of the social, including the structuring of positions within and relations between social fields. This entails an analytical focus upon communicative interaction which Bourdieu consistently resists. In rightly arguing that a purely interactional analysis (which is how he sees 'discourse analysis') which ignores field and habitus is indefensible, he effectively backgrounds interactional analysis altogether. Yet the 'balance of forces between fields' must surely be a cumulative outcome of interaction as well as a structural precondition for interaction. It is only through analysing interaction that the subtle yet fundamental changes in the discursive practices of journalism which discursively contribute to changes in the balance of forces between fields can be traced – mixing of genres and discourses, ambivalence of meanings, hybrid identities, shifts in political representations. Acknowledging the social significance of linguistic capital as discourse, constitutive social representations, relationships and identities, can broaden the concept of practice in Bourdieu's theory. The specifically discursive dimension of practice allows for conceptualising local interactions as sites of struggle of competing and contradictory representations with a potential to change dominant classifications (see further below). The discursive dimension of practice can address two problematic issues of Bourdieu's theory: first, that field positions and relations are treated only as a given preconstructed structural frame for interaction – they are not treated as worked (and potentially changed) in the course of interaction (Cicourel 1993; Collins 1993; Hasan in press b); second, as a result, that field relations are contradictory only in systemic (as opposed to interactional) terms (Collins 1993: 127–8), which tends to reify structures and leave their social genesis and change unexplained (Fowler 1997: 25–6). The unified linguistic field is charac-terised in the same static, non-contradictory way (Pujolar 1997; Woolard 1985).

We want to draw upon the concept of 'articulation' (Laclau and Mouffe 1985; Hall 1996a), introduced in Chapter 2, as a resource for theorising and analysing the connection between discursive and non-discursive facets of the social, which we believe can usefully complement Bourdieu's theory of symbolic struggle. An articulation is 'any practice establishing a relation between elements such that their identity is modified as result of the articulatory practice', and an element within an articulated whole is a 'moment' of it (Laclau and Mouffe 1985: 105). Articulation implies that all elements of the social (non-discursive and discursive) continuously enter into shifting relationships with each other, with discourse playing the key role of constituting these relationships in meaning. The way we use the concept of articu-lation implies that discourse has its own generative force which cannot be reduced to the struggle over 'profits of distinction'.

We agree with Hasan (in press b) that Bourdieu's view of language denies the specificity of semologic, reducing the semiological to the sociological by treating language as an epiphenomenon, differences of style which constitute merely one of various ways of realising sociological categories. While this account has the strength of locating language firmly within social relations of and struggles over power, in refusing to recognise the specificity of language and semiosis it also cuts itself off from accounting for the crucial discursive aspect of the constitution of the social which we referred to above. This might be seen as part of a more general tendency in Bourdieu's analyses to give the symbolic order less autonomy from the social order in analyses than he does in his theoretical formulations (LiPuma 1993). The concept of articulation operationalises in concrete terms Bourdieu's view on the constitutive force of language (on which his 'symbolic power' already depends) as a force that works with but also independently of the logic of legitimate styles in the service of upwards social–field mobility (Chouliaraki and Fairclough 1999).

In the light of the above, the debate is an articulation of agents, and therefore an articulation of habituses, which is framed, as Bourdieu points out, at a more abstract structural level by an articulation of fields (itself a cumulative outcome of occasioned articulations like this one). One facet of the articulation of fields is an articulation of orders of discourse, and one facet of the particular articulation of agents and habituses in the debate is an articulation of voices, where an agent's voice can be conceived (like an order of discourse) as a particular configuration of discourses and genres (see further below). But the debate is not only an articulation of voices, it is also an articulation of bodies and their accoutrements (perhaps including, if people are filmed in their own locations, articulations of place) – habitus is an embodiment of the social, with specific bodily dispositions. Part, but only part, of the articulatory analysis of this event needs to be an analysis of articulation in discourse, another part being an analysis of other semiotic modalities (Kress and van Leeuwen 1996) that encompasses practices related to the body and physical space.

The concept of articulation applies to different facets of the social and helps us to see their interconnection, but the actual nature of articulatory processes – how diverse elements are worked together – differs from one facet to another. For instance, the logic of bodily articulation of people within the same social space is a quite specific logic which cannot be reduced to the logic of articulation of voices, or vice versa. In particular, the logic of semiotic systems ('semologic' – Hasan in press b) is quite distinctive. Hasan points out that semiotic systems are characterised by having a formal potential ('lexicogrammar', grammar plus lexicon, in the terms of systemic-functional linguistics) which determines their meaning (or 'semantic') potential. An articulatory change in discourse changes the formal potential within a particular social space (for example, within the political field) and hence its semantic potential by opening up new combinations of forms (for example, it might combine the forms of political discourse with the forms of conversation and of journalism).

However, while we recognise that systemic–functional linguistics is the one major linguistic theory within the English-speaking world capable of productively connecting with sociology, we believe that CDA has a crucial mediating role between them. Hasan refers to a dialectic between language and society and 'the co-genetic logic' that governs their 'co-evolution', but she does not give an account of that co-genetic logic. We argue that this co-genetic logic centres upon the concept of articulation, and that CDA is oriented to articulation in its specifically discursive forms.

BERNSTEIN – SYMBOLIC CONTROL AND DISCURSIVE PRACTICE

Bernstein's concerns to some extent overlap with Bourdieu's, but to some extent extend them in ways we have already pointed to in our critique of Bourdieu's analysis of the post-election television debate. Both are concerned with questions of social space, the division of social territory into fields (in Bourdieu's terminology) and the subject positions and forms of consciousness set up through that division. Both are therefore concerned with questions of classification, with degrees of insulation between social practices (fields) and social subjects (and so habituses), with 'what can go with what', seen as effects of power which impose arbitrary divisions through symbolic violence. As Bernstein has put it, both are concerned with what he calls 'relations between' (Bernstein 1990: 167, 1996: 19). But Bernstein differentiates his own project from Bourdieu's in terms of a concern also with 'relations within' – an orientation to specifying not only 'locational principles' but also 'interactional principles'; a concern not only with space but also with time; a concern, that is, with what goes on in the course of social interaction, including 'the selection, organisation, sequencing, criteria and pacing of communication' (Bernstein 1990: 34) – and a consequent opening to discourse and discourse analysis in contrast with Bourdieu; a concern therefore with the process of symbolic control, with the transformations that take place in the course of interaction, with the transmission and acquisition of (in Bernstein's terms) codes and code modalities, and thus forms of consciousness ('habituses' for Bourdieu). Thus Bernstein can identify in Bourdieu's work, in contrast with his own, a neglect of the specific 'grammar' of symbolic control, of specific 'devices' which link particular relations of power to particular forms of consciousness – which socially distribute particular subjectivities, potentially including embodied subjectivities, i.e., habituses, in unequal ways. His particular focus of research has been upon pedagogic discourse and the 'pedagogic device' – though he works with a broad conception of the pedagogic which centres upon but transcends education in the narrower sense to include any 'fundamental social context through which social reproduction and production takes place', for instance social interaction between doctors and patients (Bernstein 1996).

The power relations whose symbolic effects Bernstein is primarily concerned to specify are social class relations: 'class relations generate, distribute, reproduce and legitimate distinctive forms of communication, which transmit dominant and dominated codes, and … subjects are differentially positioned by these codes in the process of acquiring them' (Bernstein 1990: 13). Bernstein's earlier work on 'restricted' and 'elaborated' codes sparked off an extended academic and political controversy which has distorted subsequent reception and evaluation of his theory and the major transformations it has undergone (Labov 1972; Stubbs 1983; Stubbs and Delamont 1976; King 1981; Gibson 1984; Harker and May 1993). A code is a 'regulative principle, tacitly acquired, which selects and integrates relevant meanings, forms of realisation and evoking contexts' (Bernstein 1981: 328; see also 1990: 101) – that is, it links meanings, texts and contexts. 'Restricted' and 'elaborated' identify different 'orientations to meaning' in terms of which codes vary. A restricted orientation to meaning is 'particularistic, local and context-dependent', whereas an elaborated orientation to meaning is 'universalistic, less local, and more context-independent' (Bernstein 1990: 96). Educational systems privilege elaborated orientations to meaning, and also unequally distribute access to socially powerful elaborated code modalities in ways which reproduce and increase class differences in access to education, which are manifested in the different resources children bring to education. This is not a simple equation between orientation to meaning and social class – the claim is not for instance that restricted orientations are working class and elaborated orientations middle class. Both orientations figure in social practice irrespective of class, in ways which vary from context to context, but there are

nevertheless class inequalities in the distribution of restricted and elaborated orientations. Bernstein's more recent elaboration of the concept of code has shifted the
focus of attention from the restricted–elaborated distinction itself to the workings
of 'pedagogic discourse' and to the specification of the diverse 'code modalities'
generated from codes which effect specific distributions of power and forms of
control within particular practices, thus differentially shaping interaction in its
orientation to meaning and forms of text (Bernstein 1996: 92; see though Bernstein
1981 and 1971 for initial formulations of code modalities). In particular, different
code modalities realise different pedagogies; shifts in pedagogic modalities are linked
to shifts in the division of labour within the fields of production and of symbolic
control, i.e., shifts in the form of capitalism (1990: 133–64, 1996: 54–81, but also
1997). The concepts of 'classification' and 'framing', which are used to differentiate
code modalities, have been developed in this more recent work and assumed
considerable importance in the theory of pedagogic discourse (see below).

The pedogogic device

Bernstein characterises the 'pedagogic device', the specific mechanism of symbolic
control within pedagogy, in terms of three types of rules: distributive, recontextualising and evaluative. Distributive rules control the social distribution of two forms
of knowledge, the mundane and the esoteric, the thinkable and the 'unthinkable'
(the 'yet to be thought'), knowledge of what is and knowledge of what might be.
Pedagogical regimes ensure restricted access to the 'unthinkable'. 'Through its distributive rules the pedagogic device is both the control of the "unthinkable" and the
control on those who may think it' (Bernstein 1990: 183). This control is effected
through the distribution of codes: elaborated meaning orientations and codes

> are the media for thinking the 'unthinkable', the 'impossible', because the mean-
> ings they give rise to go beyond local space, time, context and embed and relate
> the latter to a transcendental space, time, context. A potential of such meanings
> is disorder, incoherence; a new order, a new coherence.
>
> (Bernstein 1990: 182)

In a different terminology which we met in Chapter 4, elaborated meaning orientations subject meanings to time–space disembedding (Giddens 1991).

From the point of view of recontextualising rules, pedagogic discourse is a
combination of two strands, both of which Bernstein calls 'discourses': a regulative
discourse and an instructional discourse, a discourse which is to do with the role of
pedagogies in constituting social relations and order (the 'hidden curriculum'), and
a discourse which is to do with pedagogy in the transmission and acquisition of
knowledges. According to Bernstein, the regulative discourse is dominant in all
pedagogies, so any pedagogic discourse can be seen as a particular way of embedding
the instructional into the regulative. It can be characterised moreover as 'a principle
for appropriating other discourses and bringing them into a special relation with
each other for the purposes of their selection, transmission and acquisition' (1990:

183–4). Indeed Bernstein suggests that pedagogic discourse is not really a discourse in its own right, but rather such a recontextualising principle which removes discourses from the practices they primarily belong in and relocates them within its own practice. We understand recontextualisation as a condition for the constitution of any practice in discourse; as van Leeuwen puts it (1993: 204–5), 'the practical knowledge of a social practice, the knowledge of how to perform as a participant of this practice, is knowledge in an "unrepresented" state. As soon as the practice is represented (taught, described, discussed) it is recontextualized'.

In this process discourses are abstracted from their social bases and power relations, and relocated as imaginary practices involving imaginary subjects. It is in the relocation of discourses through recontextualisation that ideology is at work – 'every time a discourse moves, there is a place for ideology to play' (Bernstein 1996: 24). The 'imaginary' is not in contrast with the 'real', rather it precisely draws attention to how practices or subjects are ideologically constructed as unproblematically real through recontextualisation in ways which mystify the arbitrariness of the divisions between them by disguising the principle of classification, the specific logic of the recontextualising practice, which effects those divisions. Notice that ideology is defined in a relational way which we drew upon in our account of ideology in Chapter 2: 'ideology ... is not a content but a way in which relationships are made and realized' (Bernstein 1996: 30–1).

Here is an account of pedagogic discourse in Bernstein's own words:

> We shall define pedagogic discourse as the rule which embeds a discourse of competence (skills of various kinds) into a discourse of social order in such a way that the latter always dominates the former. The rules constituting pedagogic discourse are not derived from the rules regulating the internal characteristics of the competences to be transmitted. In an important sense, pedagogic discourse, from this point of view, is a discourse without a specific discourse. It has no discourse of its own. Pedagogic discourse is a principle for appropriating other discourses and bringing them into a special relation with each other for the purposes of their selective transmission and acquisition. Pedagogic discourse, then, is a principle which removes (delocates) a discourse from its substantive practice and context, and relocates that discourse according to its own principle of selecting, reordering and focusing. In this process of the delocation and the relocation of the original discourse the social basis of its practice, including its power relations, is removed. In the process of the de- and relocation the original discourse is subject to a transformation which transforms it from an actual practice to a virtual or imaginary practice. Pedagogic discourse creates imaginary subjects.

> (Bernstein 1990: 183–4)

We see considerable potential in this conception of a discourse as a device for recontextualising other discourses in ways which accord with its own distinctive logic. It is particularly useful in explicating discursive aspects of what we have called, after Harvey, 'internalisation' (see Chapters 1–3) – i.e., the specific regulative capacity of discursive practice in appropriating and 'setting in motion' other practices under its own order (see also below on recontextualisation, genre and intertextuality). It can for instance be productively extended to the discourse of television news (Chouliaraki 1998b, in press), or we suggest the discourse of advertising. Furthermore, in defining pedagogical discourse as 'specializing meanings to time and space' (Bernstein 1996: 49), Bernstein points to how recontextualisation links to the processes of time–space compression in modernity we discussed in Chapter 5: the concept of recontextualisation equips discourse analysis to be used as a resource in the detailed specification of time–space disembedding and re-embedding.

Evaluative rules regulate (i.e., provide criteria for judging) the production of texts in pedagogic interactions. 'Text' is defined here as any semiotic act that attracts evaluation, including linguistic but also bodily acts (Bernstein 1996: 32). Evaluative rules distribute discourses unequally between groups of acquirers according to time (the age of the acquirer) and space (the context of transmission) (Bernstein 1990: 186), selectively determining what is to be learnt and how (the contents and forms of transmission). For example, Chouliaraki's (1995) study of a secondary school 'learner-centred' classroom analysed the ways in which the evaluative rules regulated the distribution of discourses and genres between categories of pupils in such a way that while 'competent' pupils produced highly sophisticated texts (mixing lifeworld with instructional discourses), 'dependent' pupils produced texts drawing only on a regulative discourse of classroom procedures. So within an overall ('progressivist') weakening of relations of power between transmitter and acquirer, the evaluative rules selectively weakened controls to a greater or lesser extent according to the category of pupil. This is a case where evaluative rules distribute 'specialised consciousnesses' (Bernstein) on the basis of different meaning orientations, which are actually based on differences of social class.

Pedagogic modalities, classification and framing

Bernstein distinguishes two 'generic types' of pedagogic practice, each of which generates a number of different code (specifically, pedagogic) modalities: 'visible' and 'invisible' pedagogies. Visible pedagogies are characterised by rules which are explicit for acquirers as well as transmitters – rules relating to appropriate conduct in educational interaction, to the sequencing and pacing of learning (embodied for instance in syllabuses and curricula), and to criteria for evaluating practices (in terms of what counts as legitimate or illegitimate). The focus in visible pedagogies is on transmission and what the acquirer can do, on performance, and they stratify children according to performance on the assumed basis of inherent ability. Class-related differences in outcomes are built into visible pedagogies in that they set their starting positions in ways that are differentially accessible to acquirers according to their class-linked family background, and presuppose an involvement of the family in the learning process which is actual or non-actual in class-relative ways.

Invisible pedagogies are characterised by rules which are visible for the transmitter but invisible for the acquirer. The focus in invisible pedagogies is on acquisition and the internal development of the learner rather than on the learner's (external) per-formances. Acquirers are differentiated in terms of the particular and unique ways in which competences that they have in common are realised. Class-related differences in learning outcomes for invisible pedagogies are linked to an uneven distribution within the family of the competence to understand the implicit rules of invisible pedagogies (recognition and realisation rules). Invisible pedagogy is based on a code which is 'intrinsically more difficult, initially at least, for disadvantaged social groups … to read and to control' (Bernstein 1990: 79) than a visible code, because it is itself modelled on what goes on in families within a fraction of the middle class.

The emergence and relative salience of different pedagogic modalities is linked to shifts in the relationship between the field of pedagogy and the field of production (the economic field). In the case of visible pedagogies for instance, there is a tra-ditional modality based upon claims for the autonomous value of knowledge, which mystifies its effects, unevenly distributing forms of social and cultural capital which are convertible into economic capital. But with the shift towards a post-Fordist form of production and a neo-liberal political economy, there has arisen a different, 'market', modality of visible pedagogy. Its features include the packaging of instruction, periodic mass testing of acquirers, and 'performance indicators' which are used to evaluate effectiveness. In his more recent work Bernstein has elaborated on the connection between particular pedagogic modalities and particular social identities, particular forms of consciousness, and has developed an account of how these shifting identities are framed within changes in capitalism (Bernstein 1996; see also Bernstein 1997 on invisible pedagogy in relation to changes within the middle class).

The generic types of pedagogy and their different code modalities are differ-entiated in terms of the categories of 'classification' and 'framing'. Classification measures degrees of insulation between categories (between practices, between discourses, between subjects). Where categories are strongly insulated from each other we have 'strong classification'; where they are weakly insulated we have 'weak classification'. The boundaries which are constituted through classification are seen as effects of power – for instance, power relations position subjects in particular ways through the insulations they secure between categories of subject. Classification is a manifestation of what Bourdieu calls symbolic violence: it inherently involves the suppression of contradictions and dilemmas.

Framing is a matter of the regulation and control of interaction – it 'refers to the principle regulating the communicative practices of the social relations … between transmitters and acquirers' (Bernstein 1990: 36). When the regulation of com-municative practices is controlled by the transmitter we have 'strong framing'; when the acquirer has a greater degree of control over their regulation we have 'weak framing'. Visible codes are characterised by both strong classification and strong framing, invisible codes by both weak classification and weak framing. It is the category of framing which brings to the theory the concern with interaction and process-in-time which we earlier described as distinguishing Bernstein's project from Bourdieu's. Framing relates to 'the selection, organization, pacing and criteria of communication and the position, posture and dress of the communicants, together with the arrangement of the physical location' (Bernstein 1990: 37). While classification constitutes 'voice', framing constitutes 'message'. Message is constrained by voice, yet message also has the potential to transform voice:

> there is a dynamic relation between voice and message. Whereas in the first instance the latter limits the former, the former is also the source of change in the latter and so in itself. In other words, social relations within the social division of labour have the potential of changing that social division of labour. Message is the means of changing voice.
>
> (Bernstein 1990: 35 – note that the original contains an error
> which we have corrected; but see also Bernstein 1981.)

In the voice–message dialectic, Bernstein locates a possibility for social change that is absent from Bourdieu's work. Although for both theorists classification is symbolic violence which, in insulating categories or positions from each other, construes the contingent as necessary and suppresses contradictions and dilemmas, in Bourdieu, classification (the positioning of voices) is the primary site of contradiction and struggle, and message is just an arbitrary realisation of voice (recall the discussion above; see also LiPuma 1993; Bernstein 1996: 196). For Bernstein, on the contrary, if contradictions and dilemmas are suppressed in voice, they re-emerge in the process of interaction, in message, as 'sources for a "yet-to-be-voiced", for alternative discourse, other subject relations of power' (Bernstein 1990: 39). This difference has major consequences for the two theorists' views of the possibilities for change, for instance within education. Whereas Bourdieu argues that it is only through structural changes in class relations that change can come about (for example, Bourdieu 1977: 127), Bernstein views change also as a possibility arising out of local, interactional practice both within pedagogic discourse and in the contexts of primary socialisation (family, peer group relations, etc.). In this sense his theory provides, in our opinion, a more sensitive resource for exploring social dialectics, contradiction and change.

BOURDIEU, BERNSTEIN AND CDA

Working across disciplines can be understood in a superficial way as an 'inter-disciplinarity' which consists in applying the theoretical categories and methods of different disciplines to the same issue or problem in a way which leaves them untouched. It can be understood on the other hand as 'transdisciplinary research' (Halliday 1993; see also Dubiel 1985; Kellner 1989) in which the boundaries between disciplines and their categories are put at risk. In Chapter 2 we put forward a view of critical social research as maintaining a weak boundary both between theoretical practice and the social practices it theorises, and between theoretical practices (disciplines) themselves. This is how we see the relationship between the sociological theories discussed in this chapter and CDA. Putting the categories of one theory to work within another involves a process of translation – to claim otherwise is to reduce crucial differences between theories in the objects of research and logics. We find it helpful to think in terms of an 'internalisation' (Harvey 1996) of sociological categories within the categories of CDA, and vice versa, a relationship we spell out in some detail below in our discussion of 'field' and 'order of discourse'. Where categories are connected in this way within transdisciplinary research, we can say that the categories of one theory are 'grounded' in another, in the sense that the categories of one theory are partially motivated and formed within the logic of the other theory, as well as within the logic of their own theory. The internalisation of a theoretical category within another theory is also the internalisation of its theoretically specified relationship to other categories – for instance, of order of discourse to genre and intertextuality, or of field to habitus. Internalisation is therefore a catalyctic process, whose outcome is not a simple duplication of the categories and relational logic of one theory within another but a more open effect of the reworking of the former within the latter.

Transdisciplinarity depends upon theories being 'exotropic', i.e., being open to dialogue with other theories (Hasan in press a). This depends on how a theory defines its 'problematic' (Hasan) and, within it, its 'object of research' (Bourdieu). For instance, CDA is exotropic in that it defines its object of research (discursive aspects of contemporary social change) within a problematic shared with other theories, namely the dialectic between social systems and social action in contemporary societies. In particular, CDA of a communicative interaction sets out to show that the semiotic and linguistic features of the interaction are systematically connected with what is going on socially, and what is going on socially is indeed going on partly or wholly semiotically or linguistically. Put differently, CDA systematically charts relations of transformation between the symbolic and the non-symbolic, between discourse and the non-discursive. Different theories can be brought together to make complementary contributions to this problematic, and each theory can be specified in terms of its relations of 'relevance' (Hasan) to others and to the overall analytical focuses of CDA. Three such analytical focuses can be identified within CDA, each with their respective theoretical practice: (a) analysis of communicative interaction, incorporating (i) interactional analysis, and (ii) linguistic and semiotic analysis (both (i) and (ii) being textually oriented analyses); (b) interdiscursive analysis which identifies the discursive resources (genres, discourses) that are drawn upon in the interaction and maps them onto social orders of discourse; (c) sociologically informed analysis of the social structures and sociocultural practices which the interaction is a facet of.

The theoretical practice informing (a) is discussed in Chapter 8 (systemic functional linguistics), the theoretical practice informing (c) – social-theoretical accounts of late modernity – was discussed in Chapter 5. This chapter discusses (b) in terms of ways in which the 'conceptual syntax' (Bernstein 1996) of sociological theories such as Bourdieu's and Bernstein's can be usefully internalised in the project of CDA, by establishing compatabilities and 'relevances' between them and (different aspects of) interdiscursivity. So CDA can be thought of not as a single theoretical practice but rather as a recontextualising principle that draws together other theoretical practices under a dialectical logic.

We now comment upon particular relations of 'relevance' between the sociological categories of Bourdieu and Bernstein and the categories of CDA.

Field and order of discourse

CDA has been working for some time now with the concept of 'order of discourse' (adapted from Foucault) as the discursive aspect of hegemonies open to articulatory struggle and change (Fairclough 1989, 1992a, 1995b). But this conception of the structuring of discursive space has not hitherto been systematically linked to an overall integrated theory of the structuring of social space and its regulations. A transdisciplinary connection between CDA and field theory can begin to make that link, thus providing a chart or topology of social relations where the more general social theories of time–space, such as those of Harvey and Giddens (see Chapter 5), can be explored in concrete terms and on the basis of empirical data – as for example with the relationships between the field of politics and media discussed above. (See Calhoun 1995: 207 and Fowler 1997 on Bourdieu's capacity to mediate between the abstract and the empirical.)

We have already indicated a relationship between Bourdieu's category of 'field' and the CDA category of 'order of discourse'. An order of discourse is a socially structured articulation of discursive practices (including both genres and discourses) which constitutes the discursive facet of the social order of a social field, such as politics, media or education. We can say that an order of discourse is the specifically discoursal organisational logic of a field – a field seen specifically in terms of its discursive practices. In this sense the analysis of an order of discourse can be seen as part of the social analysis of a field. However, the concept of field is a difficult one (see Bernstein 1998, for example) and its relationship of relevance to order of discourse needs to be spelt out. We prefer to look upon both field and order of discourse are heuristic as well as descriptive concepts. In terms of description both conceptualise more or less bounded institutional complexes (for example, the political field, the scientific field, onto which the political or scientific order of discourse can be mapped). One gain for CDA in internalising the concept of field would be in elaborating the category of order of discourse in the light of Bourdieu's theoretical articulation of relationships between different levels of field – between individual fields (see below on shifting boundaries between fields and between orders of discourse), but also between fields and the 'field of power' (a meta-field in which agents with power in the various fields contest the relative value of their different capitals), and the 'field of class struggle'. For example, Bourdieu has shown that the degree of relative autonomy between particular fields and the field of power is an important stake in social struggles and can have major implications for the forms of socio-cultural practice enacted there (see for example Bourdieu and Collier 1988 on struggles for autonomy from the field of power within the academic field and the types of academic practices these struggles entail).

The logic of Bourdieu's theory also demands that any analysis in terms of orders of discourse should be framed within an analysis of field, habitus and forms of capital, i.e., of the particular agencies and their social base which partly enable a discursive practice and are partly constituted by it, as well as of the discursive potential that agents bring to the practice, much along the lines of Bourdieu's analysis of the post-election television programme discussed earlier. In terms of research design, incorporating Bourdieu's concepts in CDA implies more detailed (large-scale, including ethnographic) empirical projects than CDA has engaged in so far, so that a 'charcoal sketch' of field relations and structures and habitus can work as a backdrop for more detailed analysis of discursive practices. Since the discursive practices of an order of discourse include semiotic modalities other than language, one question about an order of discourse is what relationships are set up between semiotic and material activity in a field. A crucial issue here is what systematic distributions can be traced between the semiotic modalities available in a field, including language, and material practices associated with specific field positions. These are important questions that need to be addressed in empirical studies which are yet to be done.

As we said above, field and order of discourse are heuristic as well as descriptive concepts, in the sense that they are also dynamically oriented to struggles which shift their boundaries. In Bourdieu's words,

> the boundary of the field is a stake of struggles, and the social scientist's task is not to draw a dividing line between the agents involved in it by imposing a so-called operational definition … but to describe a state (long-lasting or temporary) of these struggles and therefore of the frontier delimiting the territory held by the competing agents.
>
> (Bourdieu 1990: 42–3)

It is in this respect that field has most to gain from internalising order of discourse. We have already pointed to this in the commentary on Bourdieu's analysis of the post-election programme: in focusing on processes in interaction, CDA can trace the emergence of a journalistic order of discourse (and field) from the articulation of orders of discourse (fields), which Bourdieu's analysis misses. Fairclough (1995d) is an analysis of a late-night political television programme which has precisely this focus. The paper argues that the programme shows the emergence of a new political discourse in television through the articulation of three different orders of discourse – those of the political system, the media and the private sphere of the 'lifeworld' – which constitutes the articulation of (in Bourdieu's terms) three different fields. The paper also points to problems which the negotiation of this emergent discourse causes for the politicians involved in the programme, manifested in ambivalence and disfluencies, which can be seen in Bernstein's terms as the manifestation of a voice–message dialectic (see further below) – the emergence in the course of interaction of contradictions which are suppressed in the constitution of this new composite political voice.

The analysis of orders of discourse is oriented to variable strengths of boundaries and flows between discursive practices, both within and between orders of discourse (corresponding to Bourdieu's focus on relationships between individual fields referred to above). The particular contribution of CDA here is interdiscursive analysis – the claim is that the link between communicative interaction and text on the one hand and social structures and processes on the other is mediated by the way in which social orders of discourse are drawn upon, which is the focus of interdiscursive analysis. Given the interest in social change, there is an emphasis on how boundaries and flows of orders of discourse are shifting in late modern societies. Drawing on the terminology of systemic functional linguistics, the analysis has both a 'choice' (paradigmatic) and a 'chain' (syntagmatic) dimension. Choice analysis asks to what extent a particular type of communicative interaction draws upon a mixed resource of discursive practices (genres and discourses) with low maintenance of boundaries within and across orders of discourse, or conversely sustains these boundaries. Social change is discursively realised in shifts in these boundaries. The key concept here is articulation (see Chapter 2): genres and discourses can become disembedded from particular orders of discourse and circulate as free-floating elements capable of being articulated together in new ways, as the manifestation of processes of social change in discourse. As with choice relations, so with chain relations the emphasis is upon shifting articulations. Chain analysis charts channels between discursive practices within and across orders of discourse which systematically connect one discursive practice with another (for example, in Chapter 3 we suggested how everyday conversation is systematically linked with mediated quasi-interaction). An important point is that a particular communicative interaction may be simultaneously located within a number of chaining practices.

CDA's choice and chain analyses suggest elaborating Bourdieu's analysis of relations between fields (centring upon the concept of 'homology' and capital convertibility) to include changing discursive relations: relations produced in the 'recontextualisation' (Bernstein) of one discursive practice within another or the 'colonisation' (Habermas) of one discursive practice by another. Setting this issue against the broad canvas of the critical analysis of neo-liberalism which Bourdieu engages in within his more recent work (Bourdieu 1998b), the production of such relations across fields is a move towards the production of a translatability of all discourses into certain dominant 'codes' (Melucci 1996), thus ensuring a convertability of capital across fields, which neo-liberalism as a rational Utopia from the perspective of international finance (Bourdieu) is committed to achieving. We suggest that interdiscursive analysis is a key dimension of analysis of field relations which can foreground the potential for social change in the complexity and hybridity of late modern forms of practice, something that Bourdieu has been accused of neglecting (for example, in Lash 1993).

Habitus and voice

The internalisation within CDA of the relationship between field and habitus is potentially particularly productive. Bourdieu sees the social as doubly inscribed, in places (fields) and bodies (habituses), so that there may be tensions when habituses are not well synchronised with fields, notably in circumstances of rapid social change. However, habitus is basically a descriptive concept – it describes how a specifically socially positioned agent 'looks' in terms of bodily dispositions (for example, posture, dress) as well as linguistic dispositions (for example, dialect, style). It cannot account for how such a habitus has come about – as LiPuma puts it (1993: 24), 'although the habitus appears at first glance to be a bridge between the social and the psychological, the system and the agents, it cannot make the connection because the relationship of individual agent to social classification is not developed.'

We propose to use Bernstein's concept of 'voice' in a way which allows the theoretical relations of Bourdieu's theory to work within CDA. In Bernstein, 'voice' is related to the subject's ability to distinguish between contexts of discursive practice: where and when it is appropriate to say what (an effect of the subject's 'recognition rules'); it is on the basis of 'voice', of what is understood as appropriate, that the subject can then manage a particular interaction and produce a specific 'message' (an effect of the subject's 'realisation rules' – see Bernstein 1990: 15). 'Voice' manifested in 'habitual ways of being, doing, saying over the total range of semiotic exchange' (Hasan in press a) can be seen as 'linguistic habitus', dispositions to use language in particular ways which agents are differentially endowed with depending on the fields they are operative in, their positions within those fields, and their different social trajectories. In CDA terms, 'voice' can be specified, like an order of discourse, in terms of particular configurations of discourses and genres available for each subject, in particular relations to each other. Furthermore, for any socially positioned subject these discursive configurations of 'voice' (and the 'messages' produced) obey the principles of power and control specific to the practice in which the subject participates (Bernstein's coding modality – see above). In the analysis of a specific discursive practice, such as the television programme discussed by Bourdieu (see above), we should separate the question of what orders of discourse are brought together from the question of what voices are brought together. Such a procedure allows CDA to explore relations and tensions between the discursive practices in place within a particular conjuncture, and the specific discursive endowments of agents operative within them – a potentially powerful and explosive mix as the television example indicates, though Bourdieu's analysis does not bring that out. This is a new perspective for CDA.

But Bernstein's theory enhances Bourdieu's conception of habitus by incorporating a voice–message dialectic: classification constitutes voice, framing constitutes message, and while voice constrains message, message also has the potential to transform voice. The contradictions which are suppressed in constituting and demarcating voices re-emerge in the course of interaction, and can undermine the division between voices. It is perhaps helpful to think about the classificatory division of voices on two timescales: structurally, in terms of relatively permanent divisions; and conjuncturally, in terms of the specifically occasioned conjunctures of fields, habituses, voices, etc., such as the television programme we have been referring to, where the effect of the regulative principle of the practice of television debate on the classification of voices is open to analysis. The dialectic of voice and message is also accessible at this level of analysis. For instance, Fairclough (1995d) investigates on the one hand the conjunctural constitution of composite voices for politicians in a television political panel debate (voices emerge for professional politicians which mix voices of politics, entertainment and ordinary life), and on the other hand the emergence in the course of the programme of contradictions which are suppressed through the imposition of these hybrid voices as an act of symbolic violence. Specifically, the politicians find it hard to sustain a balance between the hybridised voices, and there are communicative breakdowns as a result.

Recontextualisation, genre and intertextuality

In contrast with Bourdieu, Bernstein explicitly recognises the role of textual and linguistic analysis in sociological analysis (analysis of pedagogical practices): 'the text is the form of the social relationship made visible, palpable, material. It should be possible to recover the original specialised interactional practice from the analysis of its texts in context' (Bernstein 1990: 17). His theoretical categories are oriented to text and interaction, and are in that sense closer to the categories and logic of discourse analysis. Bernstein's account of the recontextualising rules of the pedagogic device points to the complex articulation of various discourses within pedagogic discourse in configurations which are determined by the recontextualising principle. Chouliaraki (1998a) has discussed 'translation' relations between Bernstein's categories and the discourse analytical categories of genre and intertextuality. She suggests that the category of genre maps onto Bernstein's coding modality and can be specified in terms of classification and framing properties; the categories of classification and framing can accordingly be internalised within the category of genre. This perspective can be put to work within discourse analysis by regarding a genre as an ordering device for articulating discourses together in particular ways – the recontextualising principle is materialised discoursally in the genres characteristic for a particular pedagogy. The theoretical gain for CDA is a conception of a genre as a device for simultaneously constituting particular degrees of insulation between subjects (classification), and controlling interaction through time (framing), which can be worked and developed in discourse analytical and linguistic terms. The application to pedagogic discourse of the intertextual and interdiscursive analysis which constitutes a central element of CDA (see the outline framework in Chapter 4) constitutes a resource for analysing in fine detail the concrete effectivity of the recontextualising principle in particular pedagogical interactions. This is what is gained from Chouliaraki's suggested translation relations for Bernstein's theory.

We wish to suggest that CDA also constitutes a resource which is sensitive enough to the detail of social interaction to identify the emergence within it of the 'contradictions and dilemmas' which Bernstein argues are suppressed in the process of categorisation (and so in 'voice') but re-emerge in 'message'. Volosinov argued that the dialogical interactions of everyday life constitute a sensitive barometer which register subtle processes of social change before they solidify into fully fledged social forms (Volosinov 1973; see also Chapter 3). Discourse analysis and the linguistic analysis it draws upon allow such subtleties to be picked up and analysed.

There is a specifically intertextual aspect to the suppression and emergence of contradictions. Recontextualisation involves a selective appropriation and ordering of other discourses. If we think of discourses as meaning potentials, recontextualisation entails suppression of some of the meaning potential of a discourse in the process of classifying discourses, establishing particular insulations between them. Recontextualization suppresses contradictions between (the meaning potentials of) different discourses. However, when different discourses are worked together in interactions these contradictions may re-emerge. In this case Bernstein's theory on the one hand enriches intertextual analysis by introducing the question of contradictoriness into it, but the CDA focus on intertextuality on the other hand enriches Bernstein's theory by elaborating the question of the suppression and re-emergence of contradictions in the direction of intertextuality.

CDA has used the Bakhtinian concept of intertextuality formulated by Kristeva (1986) to conceptualise 'the property texts have of being full of snatches of other texts, which may be explicitly demarcated or merged in and which the text may assimilate, contradict, ironically echo and so forth' (Fairclough 1992a). Intertextuality has been central to the recent focus of CDA on discursive aspects of contemporary social change. However, the concept of intertextuality must be combined with a theory of power (Fairclough 1992a suggests Gramsci's theory of hegemony) if we are to avoid the problem identified by Hasan (1992b: 519–20): 'the ever-enlarging circle of intertextuality implies almost unlimited access to any voice; it is not clear at what point, why, and how the material basis and the forms of communication constrain this pervasive intertextuality'. Coding orientation, the modalities of power and control operating in specific social contexts (as classification and framing) embed intertextual relations in a theory of social regulation and explain why certain intertextualities but not others are possible in a particular discursive practice (Hasan 1992b; Chouliaraki 1998a: 11).

Overall, Chapter 6 offers a principled framework for explaining systematicity and order in the social, i.e., the structural end of (particularly) discursive practice, whilst at the same time taking into account the structure–agency dialectics of discourse (in Bernstein's voice–message). However, as the yet-to-be-voiced already implies, the closure of the social is always an unfinished project. It is to theories that foreground the unfinalisability and openness of practice that we now turn.

Chapter 7

Discourse, difference and the openness of the social

In this chapter we focus upon 'postmodern' theorisations of late modernity which stress the openness and contingency of late modern social life. One way of seeing such theories is as theories of complexity – attempts to come to terms with the great complexity of late modern social life (Cilliers 1998). We see such theorisations as contributing to the field of critical social scientific engagement with late modernity which we are trying to locate CDA within, although they also in some respects undermine the critical project – critical theory needs to reassert itself against them through partly assimilating them, which is what we are aiming to do here. The emphasis on the openness of the social includes an emphasis on social difference, on the diversity and fluidity of social identities, linked to a critique of 'essentialism' (claims that for example 'women' have certain essential, stable, common properties). These properties of the social are associated in postmodern theories with discourse – with the discursively constituted nature of the social, and theories of social constructionism. These theories are widely taken to entail a rejection of realism in favour of relativism (Parker 1998). While we owe to postmodern theorists our understanding of the discursively constituted nature of the social, this is sometimes mistakenly (Mouzelis 1990: 27) taken to entail that the social is radically contingent, not constrained by structures – we argue on the contrary that the discursive constitution of the social is also in part the discursive reproduction of structures.

We shall proceed in this chapter by first sketching out Laclau and Mouffe's influential 'post-Marxist', discourse-based political theory. We select this as our starting point because it is an attempt to bring together Marxism, and especially Gramsci's theory of hegemony, with the postmodern discourse theory of especially Derrida and Foucault. While we find Laclau and Mouffe's account of processes of discursive articulation valuable, we also associate ourselves with criticisms of their theory for developing a one-sided focus on the contingency of the social which eliminates social structures. Our particular contribution to this argument is that people stand in differing relationships to discourse depending precisely on their positions in social structures – in particular that the degree and nature of the openness (or closure) of the discursive practices they are involved in varies according to their social class (position in the labour process – categories of workers in the new capitalism – Gee etc.), gender (Haraway), race (Bhabha) and generation (Lury). We look at these differing relationships to discourse in relation to different metaphors which have been recently used in theorisations of social life and identity (for example, play, masquerade, mimicry), and also consider with particular respect to discourse the view that social life has been 'aestheticised'. We then frame the post-modern emphasis on difference, the openness of discourse and the incommensur-ability of discourses in relation to tendencies in late modernity towards totalitarian imposition of codes – in Marcuse's famous terms from the 1960s, the 'closure of the universe of discourse' (Marcuse 1964). We argue however that merely responding to this threat with assertions of difference runs into the opposite danger of fragmen-tation, and that the question of living with and dialoguing across difference is a major focus of research for CDA. A focus on difference and the incommensurability of discourses easily slides into relativism, and we sketch out in contrast a realist view of discourse.

LACLAU AND MOUFFE

Laclau and Mouffe (1985) aim to redirect socialist strategy towards a 'radical democratic' politics on the basis of a new theoretical formulation of Gramsci's concept of 'hegemony' which pushes it in a postmodern direction and links it to postmodern theories of discourse, those of Derrida and Foucault in particular. Hegemonic struggle is conceived as struggle to articulate different social antagonisms (for example, working class, feminist and anti-racist movements) together through articulating different discourses together – political struggle becomes struggle in and over discourse.

The theory is grounded in Derrida's view of discourse. Derrida's critique of certain concepts of 'structure' leads him to a view of discourse as 'a system of differences' whose elements are in constantly shifting relations ('an infinite number of sign-substitutions come into play' … 'the domain and the play of signification' is ex-tended 'infinitely') which preclude the fixing of meaning (Derrida 1978). Discourse is inherently open, and no hegemonic bids to achieve its closure can ultimately prevail – there is always a 'surplus of meaning' which subverts it. Laclau and Mouffe locate the openness of discourse in what they call the 'field of discursivity', which consists of 'free-floating [non-articulated – see below] elements'. These elements are not just linguistic: Laclau and Mouffe reject the distinction between the discursive and the non-discursive and refuse to identify the discursive simply with the linguistic (see below), so these elements are social (including linguistic) elements in a broader sense.

Social life by its very nature involves bids to limit the openness of discourse, to achieve closure, to fix differences and meanings. Laclau and Mouffe conceptualise these processes as processes of 'articulation' which lead to the constitution of sep-arate 'discursive formations' (confusingly called just 'discourse' in the following quotation):

> we will call articulation any practice establishing a relation among elements such that their identity is modified as a result of the articulatory practice. The struc-

tured totality resulting from the articulatory practice we call discourse. The differential positions, insofar as they appear articulated within a discourse, we will call
moments. By contrast, we will call elements any difference that is not discursively
articulated.

(1985: 105)

But the fixities produced through articulation are never more than partial:

the practice of articulation consists in the construction of nodal points which
partially fix meaning; and the partial character of this fixation proceeds from the
openness of the social, a result, in its turn, of the constant overflowing of every
discourse by the infinitude of the field of discursivity.

(1985: 113)

The elements articulated together in a discursive formation are not only linguistic –
they include 'institutions, rituals and practices'. Laclau and Mouffe are drawing
heavily on Foucault's theory of discourse (the conceptualisation of discursive
formations is his), but also pushing it in a direction which leads them to reject
Foucault's distinction between discourse and non-discourse – the social is nothing
but discourse. They reject the idea that this is a form of mentalism (and therefore
idealism) – a discursive formation is material not mental, it combines language with
other elements, some of which (such as forms of physical activity in work) are
manifestly material, but in fact all its elements (including language) have their own
particular forms of materiality.

Laclau and Mouffe associate themselves with the post-structuralist view of the
subject (in the theories of Derrida, Foucault and others) as discursively constituted,
in the articulation of discursive formations, and therefore an effect of social processes
rather than (as in the Enlightenment view) their point of origin. One consequence
of this view is that subjects appear as dispersed and fragmented. However, this itself
says nothing about the important question of the relationships between discursively
constituted subject positions. To address the question, Laclau and Mouffe draw upon
the concept of 'overdetermination' in Althusser's early work. The concept of overdetermination belongs to the field of the symbolic. For Althusser everything social is
'overdetermined', which means that the social constitutes itself as a symbolic order.
Take the category of 'woman', for example. The category is symbolically constituted
– discursively constituted in Laclau and Mouffe's terms. There is no prior essence of
'woman', only diverse discursive formations in which social divisions are constituted
in the dimension of gender. But the concept of overdetermination sees these not
as separate and fragmented but as each having others present within it and having
potentially contradictory effects within it – gender relations and the category of
woman in politics for instance internalise and are worked by gender relations and
the category of woman in the family and in the workplace. Relations of equivalence
are set up across discursive formations so that the category of woman emerges as a
general category. This is what Laclau and Mouffe write about the 'logic of overdetermination' in Althusser: Althusser

foreshadowed ... a break with orthodox essentialism ... through the critique of every type of fixity ... This was the logic of overdetermination ... far from there being an essentialist totalization, or no less essentialist separation among objects, the presence of some objects in others prevents any of their identities from being fixed. Objects appear articulated not like pieces in a clockwork mechanism, but because the presence of some in the others hinders the suturing of the identity of any of them.

(Laclau and Mouffe 1985: 104)

Laclau and Mouffe anchor the impossibility of sustaining social closure in the social relation of 'antagonism', which they define as the situation whether 'the presence of the "Other" prevents me from being totally myself' – for instance, the antagonism between peasants and landowners in contemporary Brazil is based upon landowners depriving peasants of land, i.e., the resources they need to be peasants. Antagonism manifests itself in a subversion of the social, which takes the discursive form of setting up relations of 'equivalence' which subvert differences. They give the example of the existence of the dominant power in a colonised country being manifested through a variety of contents: difference of dress, or language, or skin colour, or customs. A relation of antagonism between coloniser and colonised can subvert the differences between these contents and others by constructing them as equivalents – if the process goes far enough, the positive identity of the coloniser can be dissolved into the purely negative identity of the 'anti-colonised'. Every society and practice is characterised by tension between the creation of differences and the subverting of differences through 'equivalence'. But antagonisms have different effects in different sorts of society – in colonial contexts they can lead to a full polarisation of the society, whereas in developed capitalist societies they tend to be limited within particular social spaces.

The concept of hegemony helps conceptualise power struggles within developed capitalist societies in particular. Hegemonic struggles are antagonisms which take the form of struggles over the articulation of discursive practices – they presuppose free-floating elements and weak boundaries, i.e., the 'incomplete and open character of the social'. Ideology is understood within this theory as 'the non-recognition of the precarious character of any positivity, or the impossibility of any ultimate suture' (Laclau 1983) – although this conception is obviously tied to the particular categories of their theory, it accords with a view of ideology as suppression of the contradictory character of the social which is found in Marx. Laclau and Mouffe differentiate their view of hegemony from Gramsci's in that they do not see a society as a single field of hegemonic struggle but many such fields, and in that they do not see hegemonic struggle as necessarily class struggle – other social relations (for example, gender) are also at issue. Hegemonic struggle involves the setting up of equivalences between different struggles – for instance, between anti-sexist, anti-racist, and anti-homophobic struggles. Power is therefore not a matter of fixed relations between social classes which manifest themselves throughout social life, but rather the construction of 'nodal points' which achieve a certain (though always limited) permanence for articulations and relations of equivalence between different struggles, brought together around some positive hegemonic project. Laclau and Mouffe conceive of socialist strategy in late modern society as 'radical democracy', extending as far as possible the chain of equivalences between different democratic struggles. The 'logic of equivalence' is seen within this strategy as limited by a 'logic of autonomy' – the setting up of equivalences between struggles does not entail the erosion of the differences between them, though their objectives are changed through co-articulation in a shared hegemonic project.

If hegemonic struggle around the strategy of radical democracy is one trajectory made possible by the openness of the social in late modernity, there are also other inherent potentials of bourgeois democracy. They argue that it is important to recognise that the openness of the social is also the possible ground for totalitarian attempts to impose closure through the apparatus of the state, and for a fragmentation and dissolution of the social. Radical democracy is conceived as a trajectory which can avoid these opposite dangers.

Laclau and Mouffe provide valuable resources for theorising and analysing the openness and complexity of late modern social life – they capture the instability and flux of social practices and identities, and the pervasive dissolution and redrawing of boundaries, which characterise late modernity. Like the postmodernist theorists they draw upon, they provide the sort of critique of essentialism that has been theoretically and politically attractive for instance to feminists (Fraser and Nicholson 1990), both in their critique of concepts of a 'human essence' which turn out to covertly allow the male to stand in for the human, and in their critique of no less terroristic universal constructions of an essential 'woman' which cover over differences between women linked to social class, race, sexuality and so forth. Yet unlike much postmodernist theory, they retain a belief in modernity's potential for emancipation and, indeed, radical democratic politics is an extension of rather than a radical break from modern democratic societies. This commitment makes them sensitive to the problems that arise from going no further than asserting difference – through their use of the concepts of overdetermination and hegemony they open up questions about the conditions of emergence of alliances and of general identity categories such as 'women' which transcend without suppressing difference. The theory also points to the power of language and other forms of semiosis in these processes, working with other moments within discursive formations. We regard Laclau and Mouffe as providing valuable conceptual resources for the analysis of change in discourse – in particular their conceptualisation of 'articulation' and 'equivalence/difference'. We believe that these can be fruitfully internalised and 'put to work' within critical discourse analysis, and indeed we have already drawn upon the concept of articulation in earlier chapters (on 'equivalence' see also Fairclough forthcoming c). However, we also have certain problems with their theory, particularly their insistence on the unconditional openness of the social and the abandonment of the discourse–non-discourse distinction, both of which are related to the way they use the concept of 'discourse'.

Laclau and Mouffe provide two different levels of explanation for the impossibility of a full closure of the social: that the field of discursivity is inherently open, and that differences and boundaries are subverted by social antagonisms. The first of these is Derrida's view of semiosis as an infinite play of signification which precludes the fixing of meaning. What is Derrida's contribution, and what are its limits? Derrida has helped us to understand the specific logic of the semiotic, its specific power. Systemic linguistics gives a rather different formulation of the openness of the logic of the semiotic ('semo-logic', as Hasan calls it): the logic of the semiotic generates wordings ('lexicogrammar' in terms of systemic functional linguistics) which constitute meanings, which are meaning-making, so that any difference of wording entails a difference of meaning, though what that difference is is a matter for social negotiation (for example, what a speaker intends does not determine how a listener interprets). We might take this as a specification of the Derridean notion of the infinite play of signifiers. In the terms of critical realism, this is the specific 'mechanism' (or generative power) of the semiotic. According to this view, social practices involve the simultaneous operation of different mechanisms of which semiosis is one, no mechanism works on its own, all mechanisms are mediated by the operation of others. The infinite possibilities of semiosis are constrained and limited by the effects of other mechanisms within social practices – the semo-logic and the socio-logic intersect in specific contexts of meaning-meaking (Hasan in press b). What this means is that the open logic of semiosis may be more or less freely in play, or may be in play in different ways, for different groups of social agents within different social practices. This could be seen as already implicit in Laclau and Mouffe's second argument for the openness of the social: different forms of social life, different types of society, give rise to different forms of antagonism, which entail different degrees and forms of access to the possibilities of the semiotic.

However, this is an instance of the unacknowledged presence in Laclau and Mouffe's theory of social-structural elements (noticed by Mouzelis 1990: 29) which they claim to have eliminated on the grounds of the radical contingency of the social – or rather to have replaced with their concept of 'nodal points', structures viewed as always provisional and immediately open to new articulations. The basic problem with this is that it is unable to explain which social forces have greater capacity to effect articulatory changes and why. We need a concept of structure not as provisional but as relative permanence – open to change but with relative stability (see Chapter 2). Mouzelis (1990: 29; see also Geras 1987; Best and Kellner 1991; Coombe 1998) also argues that it is only by reference to social structures that one can differentiate between articulatory practices with respect to Laclau and Mouffe's ultimate concern – hegemony and socialist strategy: how otherwise can we know which articulatory practices may be important within hegemonic struggles and which articulatory practices may be quite unimportant? Laclau and Mouffe's one-sided focus on contingency projects the contingent in an undifferentiated way. We would claim that the degree and the form of the contingency of the social depends upon how persons and practices are positioned within social structures. We argue below that positioning in terms of class, gender, race, and age relations affect the contingency of the semiotic in particular.

We do not agree with Laclau and Mouffe's abandonment of the distinction between discourse and non-discourse. They give two arguments for doing so. On the one hand, discourse for them (as for Derrida) stands for the contingency of the social, and their rejection of non-discourse is really just another way of asserting this contingency. On the other hand, the argument that everything is discourse follows from claiming that language (more generally: semiosis) is always articulated with other elements of the social within discursive formations, so that anything that is constituted socially is constituted through such articulated discursive formations and therefore through semiosis, and semiosis and language belong no less than other elements in the 'field of objectivity' – they are material not 'mental', possessing their own specific forms of materiality. But the two arguments are separable – we broadly accept the second, but not the first. Against the first, we have argued that contingency is structurally constrained. We therefore need a distinction between structures and contingency – what Laclau and Mouffe call 'discourse'. However, using their terminology gives the misleading impression that the articulations of language and other social elements thematised in the second argument are relevant only to the contingency of the social and not to structures – on the contrary, one effect of the discursive constitution of the social is reproducing structures (Mouzelis 1990; Harvey 1996). Also, using 'discourse' to mean contingency creates confusion given that in most usage 'discourse' means language and the semiotic – the fact that Laclau and Mouffe feel it necessary to emphasise that discourse for them is not just language points to the likely confusion (Torfing 1998). We prefer the terminology of Chapter 2, according to which 'discourse' is the semiotic moment dialectically related to other moments in social practices. We therefore believe that there is a need for two distinctions which they reject: structures versus what we call 'conjunctures' (the domain of the contingent), and discourse (meaning semiosis) versus other elements of the social such as physical actions.

RELATIONSHIPS TO DISCOURSE

In this part of the chapter we want to develop the argument raised above that the openness of the social is relative to particular social practices and categories of social agents through the idea that different social agents are positioned in different relationships to discourse. In so doing we are generalising and giving a discursive focus to the argument of Lury (1996). Lury discusses the claim that late modern 'consumer culture' involves an aestheticisation and stylisation of everyday life. Not only is there an increasing aesthetic element in the production and design of goods, their use is also increasingly tied to aesthetic practices linked to the construction of self-identity through consumption. Lury argues however that people are positioned very differently and therefore have different possibilities for access in this process according to class, gender, race, and age or generation. These differences give rise to different metaphors for the active relationship of social agents to the resources of consumer culture, such as 'play', 'masquerade' and 'mimicry. By contrast, generalised accounts of the reflexive construction of the self in late modernity (as in Giddens 1991) overgeneralise a particular (white, male, middle class) social position.

We want to take up this perspective of Lury's by looking at various forms of openness in discourse, involving various relationships to discourse (and especially relationships of people to 'other' discourses coming to them from 'elsewhere' in social life). An example will make the issues clearer. The following is an extract from a meeting in a large textile manufacturing company. The researcher (Farrell) contextualises it as follows:

> the company depends for its survival on maintaining certain international automotive clients. These clients require that their suppliers adopt certain specified, 'quality' practices, practices that revolve around team based work organisation and documentation of process. They provide a manual to guide the development of these processes, and they inspect and assess the company at regular intervals.
>
> (Farrell 1997)

The extract[1] is from a meeting of mainly supervisors discussing meetings they have recently convened in accordance with the required 'quality' practices. Participants are: Sally – the facilitator, a workplace literacy teacher employed by the company under a government scheme; Ben – Warping Shed Supervisor; Grace – Weaving Shed Supervisor; Peter – Production Coordinator; James – a Warper; and Mary – Mending Room Supervisor.

Ben we thought you know maybe maybe I should be the facilitator for Grace's group or something where I'm away from the people a bit and um
Sally yeah
Ben just have a background in what's going on but just sort of keep them on the right track and let them they've got to really then rely on each other instead of relying on the supervisor to do the work
Grace well I think kind of in the groups that are gonna come along that's what's gonna have to happen. I mean I know the the first ones that start off I think we have to go down this path to try to direct people onto the path and therefore we kind of will be in charge of the meeting but then we have to get people to start their own teams and us sort of just being a facilitator rather than
James the team leader
[..] yeah
Grace I mean it's hard to get started I think that's where people are having trouble and that's why they're kind of looking to you Ben and you know things like that
Peter I'm not the only one I'm having trouble maintaining the thing
[..] yeah
Peter I just can't maintain it at the moment you know a couple of days you know a couple of days crook there and you know just the amount of work that builds up it just goes to the back of the queue sort of thing it's shocking
James so what you really want is the um you've got a a group you start a group and you want one of those people to sort of come out and [..] facilitate the group

Peter just to maintain the group you know like just to keep it just keep the work flowing

Ben what I'm trying to get across

Peter cause

Ben is I'm too close to those people because I already go outside of the group and then I'm their supervisor outside on the on the floor where maybe if I was facilitating another group where I'm not I'm not above them you know I'm not their supervisor or whatever

[..] yeah

Ben um I can go back to my job they can go back to theirs and they still um you know it's this their more their team than

Sally yours

This is a discussion of how to handle to team meetings that the supervisors have convened, which we see as manifesting a particular open relationship to discourse centred upon the negotiation of the meaning of 'facilitate/facilitator' through setting up relationships of equivalence and difference between this expression and others. These equivalence–difference relationships are roughly summarised below: there is a relationship of difference between the columns, and a relationship of equivalence between items within each column.

facilitate/facilitator	team leader
keep them on the right track	relying on the supervisor
let them … rely on each other	direct people onto the path
people to start their own teams	be in charge
maintain the group	supervisor
keep the work flowing	

This table slides over the various specific ways in which relations of equivalence and difference are interactionally and textually set up – for instance, the difference between 'facilitator' and 'team leader' is set up collaboratively by Grace and James (with James completing Grace's sentence) using a contrastive structure with the conjunction/preposition *rather than*. Another striking feature of the extract which underlines the negotiative work that is being interactively performed is the hedging – the many expressions like *just, sort, kind of,* most of which are associated with setting relations of equivalence.

But the main point about the extract for present purposes is that the term *facilitate/facilitator* belongs (along with *team*) to the new 'quality' discourse which is being imposed on this company. In this extract we see people working the new term into a set of relationships of equivalence and difference with familiar terms and expressions, and in that sense making a step towards assimilating it into the discourse of this workplace. Notice that this is an articulatory relationship between discourses, not simply between expressions. This is a form of openness in which innovative articulatory work is going on interactionally, but it is obviously a special and constrained form of openness in that these people are required for their survival to assimilate textually mediated practices and discourses. Perhaps the metaphor of 'mimicry' is the most appropriate one here – they have to learn to mimic a discourse which originates elsewhere and outside. Bhabha (1994) has analysed mimicry in the relationship between colonised people and colonisers – and indeed there is a neo-colonial feel to this relationship between an Australian company and its US-based multinational client. But Bhabha sees mimicry as ambivalent – it can end up throwing the practice or discourse mimicked into question. More concretely, acquiring a discourse imposed from outside is shown here to be a matter of hybridising it with existing discourses, assimilating it through setting up relations of equivalence and difference. The original discourse is recontextualised in Bernstein's terms, made part of something different, and caught up in trajectories of discursive change which those who imposed it could not predict or control. Even in a (neo-)colonial relationship, colonisation by a discourse is always simultaneously appropriation of that discourse which can loosen the coloniser's control. This is a basis for ideological struggle (see Chapter 2).

Mimicry is one relationship to discourse within workplaces in the new global economy, but it is not the only one. The new capitalism entails a new division of labour and a new stratification of workers – according to one recent analysis (Reich, discussed in Gee et al. 1996), into a small elite of 'symbolic–analytic' workers (scientists, systems analysts, management consultants, etc.), and two other large groups: 'routine production' workers (for example, factory workers) and workers in 'in-person services' (for example, shop assistants). Symbolic–analytic workers are highly educated and charged with innovation, while the other two categories (the vast majority) need only limited educational qualifications and are expected to work in mainly routine ways. The workers in the above example are routine production workers, though in lower managerial positions which are relatively less routine and more innovative. But the relationship of symbolic–analytic workers to discourse tends to be a very different one. We shall illustrate this with a rather extreme example of the discourse of management consultancy, a book by a well-known management 'guru', Tom Peters, called *The Tom Peters Seminar* (Peters 1994). The subtitle is *Crazy Times Call for Crazy Organizations*, and this immediately illustrates a striking feature of the book – its hybridisation of different discourses: the mixture of the discourse of showbusiness and academic discourse in the main title (modelled on television programme titles of the type 'The Tom Peters Show', but substituting *seminar* for *show*), and of business discourse (*organization*) with everyday conversational discourse (*crazy*) in the subtitle. A great deal of discoursal hybridity is packed into a short title, as into the book as a whole. Another example is from a diagram on the second page which sums up the contents of the chapters – for instance, *Crazy times/ More intellect/Imagination* (Chapter 1), *De-construction/Spunky units* (Chapter 2), *Every person a business person* (Chapter 3), *Leveraging knowledge* (Chapter 6), *From TGW to TGR and Wow!* (Chapter 8), *Perpetual revolution* (Chapter 9). The assembly of a diverse set of discourses is obvious.

Hybridisation of different discourses is a feature of both this example and the previous one. What then is the difference? In the second example the discourses are more diverse than in the first – they are drawn from a wide range of different fields. Some of the collocations are surprising and even shocking: for example, *leveraging* and *knowledge*, but even more so *de-construction* and *spunky*, *TGR* and *Wow!* The central claim of the book is that contemporary business organisations have to work in a 'crazy', 'paranoid', 'revolutionary' way, constantly 'disorganising' and 'destroying' and starting again; we might see that claim as enacted in the discursive practice of the book – its particular forms of hybridisation of discourses. But an important difference between the two examples is that the writer here is in a relatively powerful position, in contrast with the workers' need to appropriate the 'quality' discourse to survive. His discourse is not mimicry, it is what we might call a 'playful' relationship to discourse, a rhetorical tour de force performance (the book is dedicated to Evelyn Peters, 'a talker who raised a talker') which sets up shocking equivalences across discourses to bounce readers into this 'revolutionary' way of thinking about work. Jameson (1988) calls this type of hybridisation 'pastiche' – drawing upon, imitating and experimenting with cultural resources as if there were no norms – for instance, freely combining the 'sacred' (for example, scientific discourse) and the 'profane' (casual, even 'vulgar', conversational language). In contrast with satire, pastiche works 'without that still latent feeling that there exists something normal compared to which what is being imitated is rather comic' (Jameson 1988: 16). Pastiche is, according to Jameson, quintessentially postmodern. To sum up then, what we are suggesting is that the openness and hybridity of discourse within contemporary economic production takes different forms according to how people are socially positioned within processes of production, entailing different relationships to discourse.

Contemporary party politics shows a rather different open relationship to discourse. Two recent developments in politics have been widely commented upon: the marketisation of politics (the New Labour spin doctor and now minister Peter Mandelson summed up the 1997 election victory as 'product positioning, packaging, advertising and communication. Politics is no different.' *The Guardian*, 30 April 1998), and the increasing similarity of mainstream parties in terms of policies (implied in Mandelson's formulation – 'product positioning' means policies are determined by the shape of the political market as much as by long-standing political ideologies). As differences in policy decline, differences in style become more prominent – the 'packaging' element of Mandelson's formulation. What are the implications for discourse? Politicians put a great deal of effort into designing new styles, experimenting with new articulations and hybridisations of discursive practices. This may be playful in a sense, but its playful and experimental nature are not shared with political publics – on the contrary, the strategic ducking and weaving of politicians is hidden as much as possible between claims to steadfast commitment to positions and principles.[2] Unlike management consultancy, the openness to discourse in contemporary politics is primarily stylistically motivated – the issue is the development of a political style and image. Whereas the focus in management consultancy is primarily heuristic – generating new perspectives and possibilities by hybridising discourses in new ways – the focus in political discourse is aesthetic – generating a new style. The aestheticisation of political discourse distances it from a commitment to rational argumentation, with worrying implications for democracy. In Best and Kellner's terms (1991: 290) the aestheticisation of politics 'fails to provide a language to articulate what are arguably indispensable concerns with autonomy, rights and justice; it is individualistic in its emphasis on desire and pleasure; and it is irrationalist in its rejection of theory and rational critique.'

If late modernity is characterised by an 'aestheticization of everyday life' (Featherstone 1991), aesthetically focused relations to discourse can be seen as part of that. But again the question arises, what positions in social life entail aesthetic relations to discourse or particular forms of aesthetic relations to discourse? Featherstone has linked aestheticisation of everyday life to positions in 'consumer culture'. On the one hand, producers of commodities proliferate images which are aesthetically designed to constantly 'rework desire' as Featherstone puts it – the proliferation of images in late modern society leads, according to Baudrillard (1988), to the breakdown of the distinction between image and reality. On the other hand, there is a tendency (implicit in the concept of 'lifestyle') for consumers to live their life as 'a work of art', an object of aesthetic design. But do all consumers experience this aesthetic relation to life and to discourse, or experience it in the same ways, or is it relative to specific social positions?

The particular form of discursive openness which is most evident in advertising (and to some degree invests political advertising – see above) is central to the first aspect, involving a constant aesthetically driven search for novel articulations of discursive practices which generate apparently limitless imaginary constructions of reality that help sell commodities. The political advertising referred to above is really just a specific case. This particular form of discursive creativity has involved a relative displacement of language in favour of visual image (or, in Lyotard's terms, of '*discours*' in favour of '*figure*' – Lyotard 1971; Lash 1988) – novel visual articulations seem to have on the whole more commercial impact than novel linguistic articulations, though there is usually a configuration of the two in advertising (as in print and television media more generally). Indeed according to Kress and van Leeuwen (1996), there has been a more general restructuring of relationships between different semiotic forms in late modernity which has broadly enhanced the role of visual images, and advertising has been an important part and influence in this general development.

The second aspect of aestheticisation of everyday life (living one's life aesthetically) suggests that people's discursive practices are partly aesthetically motivated within lifestyle choices – that for instance people adopt language varieties according to how they want to constitute and project themselves. But there are two provisos here. First, that the idea of people living their lives as works of art and choosing their lifestyles is more plausible for some people than others – for young middle-class people more than old working-class people, for instance. Second, there may be differences in this process for different social groups which include different relations to discourse. Lury (1996) for instance discusses gender differences in aesthetic consumption, contrasting playfulness, mastery and self-possession in the self-presentation of men with women's 'masquerade' – a knowing, ironic and playful relationship to the consumer goods which provide the resources for constructing femininity that recognises how different femininities can be selected and constructed for different circumstances. Some of these resources are discursive, and masquerade is also one aesthetic relation to discourse.

Finally, cynicism (Billig 1992) is another form of the relationship to discourse, which Billig discusses in relation to British people's attitudes towards the monarchy. Similarly in Chouliaraki's (1998b) study of media reception, young audiences reworked and demystified the ideological effects of a news discourse which emotionalised and aestheticised a conflict between Greek and Turkish Cypriots in Cyprus that led to the killing of two Greek Cypriots. Whereas the news discourse constructed the victims within a mythological nationalist discourse as 'brave young men', 'heroes' and martyrs', one audience group consistently reworded their account in a distancing and even ironic way. Such discursive practices seem to manifest a subtle form of resistance to the highly emotional language of media – a form cynicism as 'existence in resistance, in laughter, in refusal'. This may not be a rebellious practice but, as Billig (1992) claims, it shows a 'knowingness' which is one aspect of late modern reflexivity.

The relations to 'other' discourses discussed above are all unequal relations, in the sense that the 'other' discourse is either externally imposed or used creatively as a resource to achieve particular effects (for example, particular images). These relations to other discourses are therefore non-dialogical, if by dialogue we understand an equal and open exchange between individuals or groups of people. Yet dialogue and dialogical relations to discourse are a matter of primary concern for the radical democratic politics which Laclau and Mouffe's theory is directed towards. We shall delay our discussion of them however until the end of the next section, for reasons which will emerge there.

'THE CLOSURE OF THE UNIVERSE OF DISCOURSE'

Laclau and Mouffe argue that hegemonic struggle around radical democracy is only one of the possible trajectories from the openness of the social in late modernity – another is totalitarian attempts to impose closure on the social, using the resources of the state. There is not a simple division into totalitarian and non-totalitarian societies; totalitarian tendencies are evident alongside others in for instance 'western democracies' like Britain, and these tendencies are partly constituted in discursive practices. The order of discourse of such a society is the site of contradictory movements – the proliferation of difference, the negotiation of difference, and totalitarian movements of closure.

It is unfashionable to metaphorise discourse in legal terms as a 'code' which people are subject to (like the penal code), but some relationships to discourse are more or less code-like. Some code-like relationships to discourse manifest the persistence of traditions – for example, ritual in conservative religious communities, or routine in certain sorts of families. But more significantly there are totalitarian tendencies which are more or less successfully imposing code-like relationships to discourse now.

One example is the normalising imposition of a configuration of neo-liberal economic and managerial discourses on a wide range of public and private organis-ations, schools, universities, hospitals, as well as commercial companies. A specific generic form within this complex is the 'mission statement', public statements of the purpose or 'mission' of an organisation which are 'rhetorically designed in order to ensure maximum employee "buy-in"' (Swales and Rogers 1998). In one British university with which we are familiar, not only the institution as a whole but also particular departments within it are required to produce mission statements, and their activities are then measured in terms of whether they accord with their mission statements – this attempted codification of discourse is part of a normalisation and policing of social practices. Organisations are free to arrive at quite different state-ments of mission – the codification is roughly speaking in the form of organisations and not their content.

The insistence by postmodern theorists on the irreducibility of difference and the 'incommensurability' of discourses is in part a political gesture in the face of such totalitarian tendencies – of what Lyotard and others have referred to as the 'tyranny of the universal' in modern societies: the sweeping away of difference in the name of a spurious 'universal' which in fact is the tyranny of the powerful – in the case of this example, the attempted universalisation of one organisational form which sweeps away others. This critique of the spuriously 'universal' harmonises with feminist critiques which have shown how the supposedly 'universal' is gendered – is in fact the tyranny of the male. This perspective is concretely illustrated by Readings (1992) in applying a Lyotardian theoretical framework to a legal dispute over a mining com-pany in Australia conducting blasting tests for minerals, which a group of Aborigines saw as disturbing the 'dreaming' of the green ants so that the 'universe world' might come to an end.

> It might seem that the Aboriginal evidence is funny. It's not obviously evidence. But common law is flexible … the judge's tolerance extends to admitting that the rough weight of speech acts, 'hearsay', may achieve a mysterious transformation into the supposedly 'universal' language of evidence – 'palpable truth', but only by becoming universally exchangeable, palpable; the tolerance that admits Aboriginal evidence, that lets it speak in court, silences the Aboriginal in its translation. In gaining value as evidence, the Aboriginal voice is abstracted from its locality just as the mining company gives land value in abstracting minerals from their location. In order to become evidence, Aboriginal language must be 'mined'.
>
> (Readings 1992: 34)

There is a fear that the liberality of contemporary social life in the law and elsewhere – its apparent openness to all discourses – is a covert tyranny which is reducing all discourses to powerful 'universal' codes through insisting upon their general translatability.

Melucci (1996) puts forward a similar perspective in his work on social movements: that the focus of struggle in contemporary societies is 'hidden codes that make individuals and groups predictable and dependable social actors', a struggle on the part of the dominant powers to impose such codes and on the part of social movements to resist them. Similarly Haraway in her influential 'Manifesto for cyborgs' (1990) states:

> communications sciences and modern biologies are constructed by a common move – the translation of the world into a problem of coding, a search for a common language in which all resistance to instrumental control disappears and all heterogeneity can be submitted to disassembly, reassembly, investment and exchange ... The world is subdivided by boundaries differentially permeable to information. Information is just that kind of quantifiable element that allows universal translation, and so unhindered instrumental power (called effective communication). The biggest threat to such power is interruption of communication.
>
> (Haraway 1990: 182)

Haraway goes on to argue that cyborg politics is essentially a politics of language – 'the struggle for language and the struggle against perfect communication, against the one code that translates all meaning perfectly, the central dogma of phallocentrism'.

The repression of difference through the imposition of discourses with universal pretensions should be a focal issue on the agenda of CDA. It should include the discourse of nationalism which is a mainly invisible precondition for political communities in for instance contemporary Western Europe. Its totalitarian character lies in its capacity to articulate, assimilate and rework other discourses on the principle of an essential unity based on common blood, land and history (Calhoun 1995; Harvey 1996), including democratic and egalitarian discourses (see Phillips 1999 on the case of Denmark; see Billig 1995 on 'banal nationalism'). Approaching the issue of nationalism from a CDA perspective means denaturalising its articulatory practices, and searching for new articulatory principles for the constitution of social and political communities. This can be an important contribution towards the struggle against totalitarian tendencies and the closure of the social.

THE FRAGMENTATION OF THE SOCIAL AND THE QUESTION OF DIFFERENCE

But Laclau and Mouffe identify two dangers consequent upon the late modern openness of the social – totalitarianism, but also social fragmentation. In terms of their own concern with radical democracy, without alliances between different social struggles the left will remain fragmented and no substantial change to relations of domination can be achieved. The need for such alliances entails that it is not enough to simply assert difference as postmodernists such as Lyotard have tended to do, it is also necessary to negotiate difference, to work across difference without suppressing it.

This brings us back to the question of a dialogical relation to discourse which we referred to at the end of the last section, for negotiating difference means bringing different discourses into dialogue. What does dialogue mean here? One influential account of dialogue across difference is that of Habermas, where the focus is on procedures for open and equal deliberation on issues of common concern which can lead to consensus. Critics – notably Lyotard (1984) – have argued that Habermas's account amounts to the suppression of difference through a spurious consensus which is a form of the universalism referred to above. Lyotard's alternative is an agonistic view of dialogue which Billig (1991, 1996) has also argued for. In Billig's account dialogue is argument, though in a recent formulation (Billig 1996) he seems undecided whether argument is fighting in words (which would bring him closer to Lyotard) or reasoning (which would bring him closer to Habermas). But the general drift of this view of dialogue is that the priority is ensuring that difference is not suppressed or reduced – that rhetorical processes of argumentation are available for different discourses to connect with (including oppose) each other.

But neither the Habermasian nor the Lyotardian version of dialogue is adequate – the former sidesteps the problem of a non-repressive negotiation of difference, the latter risks an unconditional assertion of difference which neglects the need to work across difference. In Chapter 5 we discussed relationships between different theories in transdisciplinary research and proposed that one theory be seen as internalising others, putting them to work within its own logic without reducing its logic to theirs. A dialogical relation to 'other' discourses can be thought of in similar terms. Laclau and Mouffe suggest that there is a 'democratic equivalence' between different struggles (within the strategy of radical democracy) in so far as there is 'the construction of a new "common sense" which changes the identity of the different groups, in such a way that the demands of the different groups are articulated equivalentially with those of the others' (1985: 183). In a similar vein Butler envisages alliance as 'a difficult labour of translation in which social movements offer up their points of convergence against a background of ongoing social contestation' (1998: 38). Again, Bhabha also talks about the creation of new political objects by opening up

> a space of translation: place of hybridity ... where the construction of a political object that is new, neither the one nor the other, properly alienates our political expectations and changes, as it must, the very forms of our recognition of the moment of politics.
>
> (Bhabha 1994: 25)

All are suggesting that alliance means convergence (though convergence seems to go further in Laclau and Mouffe's formulation) – a process in which different groups change, and the difference between them is reduced yet never quite overcome. Convergence requires a process of negotiation, not an elimination or suppression of difference but 'constant renegotiation of the forms of its presence' (Laclau 1996: 30; Bhabha 1994: 25–6). Negotiation covers a variety of relations to the discourse of the other, including the relations we have reviewed above (mimicry, pastiche, cynicism, etc.), but also the 'negotiation' from positions of strength between antagonists where identity 'remains uncontaminated by the process of negotiation' (Laclau 1996: 32). We are talking about a particular form of negotiation and dialogue where each discourse internalises others so that its development is inflected by others without it being reduced to others.

An example might be how feminist political discourses have internalised Marxist and postmodernist discourses, incorporating some of their concepts but appropriating them in ways which accord with their own logics. One way of conceptualising this is in terms of circumstances in the feminist movement where social practices become disarticulated and their parts cease to be moments and become merely elements available for new articulations. Fraser and Nicholson (1990) sketch out a process by which discourses such as that of 'biological difference' emerged within Marxist feminism as part of the struggle for the primacy of gender over class, later to be replaced by a discourse of 'public/private division' which asserted the primacy of gender without the essentialism and determinism of the earlier discourse. The two discourses were elements internalised within the discourse moment of feminist theoretical practice in its dialogue with Marxist discourse. But these different articulations of and dialogues between discourses emerged and changed as part of the emergence and change of social movements, political parties and campaigns. It is in this process that the 'fit' between discourse and other social moments comes into focus (Collier 1998), and that the actual (our existing discursive constructions of reality) comes up against the potential (what might be constituted as reality), which entails different (articulations of) discourses coming up against each other. This is the terrain on which the debate between realism and relativism belongs (Parker 1998; Potter 1996). We can actually distinguish two types of relativism (Bhaskar 1986; Collier 1994): epistemic relativism, according to which first, all discourses are positioned, i.e., generated out of and reflective of particular positions in social life, and second, reality is always discursively mediated – we have no access to reality except through discourses; and judgemental relativism, according to which all discourses are equally good or bad constructions of reality – there is no way of evaluating discourses in terms of their fit with reality. We have no problem with epistemic relativism, but we reject judgemental relativism. In our view the comparative strengths and limitations of different discourses are constantly being judged in the course of practice. We can think of this in terms of the articulation of the discourse moment within other moments of social practices – how good is this discourse for thinking (perceiving, feeling, evaluating)? how good is it for acting materially? how good is it for relating socially (for collaborating, for getting others to do things, etc.)? – i.e., how effectively and productively is the discourse internalised within the mental, material and social moments of the practice?

PUBLIC SPHERE

But that is very abstract. What is needed is research, including discourse analytical research on actual forms of dialogue in politics, and in other domains, with the objective of arriving at detailed accounts of the practices of dialogue in late modern societies which can discern the obstacles to, practices of and potentials for non-repressive dialogue across difference.[3] We see this as a matter of CDA taking the 'public sphere' as an object of research (Fairclough forthcoming b). The concept of the public sphere relates to the social spaces and social practices in which people as citizens dialogue on issues of social and political concern in ways which can affect policy and shape social change. The pioneering work of Arendt (1958) and Habermas (1989) established that there is a crisis of the public sphere in contemporary capitalist society, and that the reconstruction of the public sphere is a priority in the struggle to defend and extend democracy. One corollary of the emphasis on difference in recent social and political theory has been the recognition that there are many public spheres in contemporary societies (for example, the public spheres of the different social movements) and not the unitary public sphere which Habermas discerned in earlier capitalism. This has been an important issue in feminist theory and politics in the context of the feminist contestation of the public–private divide and the under-standing of the private as political (Fraser 1989; Calhoun 1995). The question of how dialogue occurs across different public spheres becomes part of the problem of working across difference (Benhabib 1996; Calhoun 1992; Meehan 1995). Public spheres are social practices (see Chapter 2), which means that while they have a discursive moment they are not simply discourse. Public spheres are practices of social and political action, conjunctures where people assemble resources for doing something about issues or problems, and where dialogue is a primary activity (but quite likely to be dismissed as 'just talk' if people cannot 'get things done').

CONCLUSION

This chapter has focused upon the complexity of late modern social life in terms of the openness and contingency of its discourse. We see it as part of an integrated set of perspectives developed in Chapters 5, 6 and 7 which we believe can be fruitfully 'operationalised' in the critical analysis of discourse in late modernity, in terms of the framework we set out for CDA in Chapter 4. That framework envisages CDA as focusing on the discourse aspect of conjunctures of social practices. In analysing any conjuncture the perspective of Chapter 5 is important in locating it within the wider dynamics of late modern social life so that the social and cultural processes which impinge upon it can be fully appreciated – for instance, in terms of totalising and fragmenting tendencies within late modernity. The perspective of Chapter 6 emphasises structure, closure and, in Bakhtin's terms, the 'centripetal' aspect of the discourse, its tendency to sustain and reproduce structures. This is a matter of specifying the field of social practices or the intersection of fields in or at which the discourse is located, and the diverse habituses brought to it by different social actors (Bourdieu); and of seeing what is included and what is excluded from the social potential of discourses as a manifestation of classification values, and seeing the genre and the way it sequences these discourses as a manifestation of framing values (Bernstein). The perspective of Chapter 7 by contrast emphasises action, openness and contingency, and, in Bakhtin's terms, the 'centrifugal' aspect of the discourse, its tendency to transform and diversify. The focus here is on creative articulation and hybridity. These three perspectives are not alternatives, they are part of the wider picture. And they are also needed when it comes to specifying possible ways of overcoming obstacles to change.

NOTES

1. We are grateful to Lesley Farrell for permission to use the extract.
2. We are grateful to Celia Ladeira Moto for the view of political discourse as centred in a tension between political ideologies and political strategies which she is developing in her doctoral research on political discourse at Lancaster University.
3. For example, the project 'Democracy in Language – the study of discursive practices in Danish institutions' (Danish Research Agency, University of Copenhagen). This uses CDA with other quantitive and qualitative methods to study dialogue in media, workplace, etc.

Chapter 8

Critical discourse analysis and linguistics

In this chapter we extend the 'conversation' we are engaging in with other theories and disciplines in the direction of linguistics, and specifically the linguistic theory which we believe has most in common with CDA and most to offer CDA, systemic functional linguistics (SFL). CDA has developed in a close relationship with SFL, especially in Britain and Australia. The 'critical linguistics' which developed in the 1970s at the University of East Anglia (Fowler et al. 1979; Hodge and Kress 1993) was specifically built upon SFL, and the version of CDA which we work with ourselves has used SFL as its main resource for textual analysis. Also more recently the 'social semiotics' which has pushed critical analysis of discourse towards analysis of images of various sorts has explicitly anchored itself in SFL (Hodge and Kress 1988; Kress and van Leeuwen 1996; Thibault 1991). Our main motivation in writing this chapter is a sense that the version of CDA which we work with would gain from extending its so far limited relationship with SFL (essentially just using a systemic grammar of English as a method in text analysis), not only in terms of using SFL as a resource for analysis but also towards a theoretical dialogue over such issues as the relationship of semiotic to social change, and the nature of what systemicists have called 'semologic' (Hasan in press b) – the generative power of the semiotic, or its generative 'mechanism' in the terms of critical realism (see Chapter 2).

It is no accident that critical linguistics and social semiotics arose out of SFL or that other work in CDA has drawn upon it – SFL theorises language in a way which harmonises far more with the perspective of critical social science than other theories of language. SFL views language as a semiotic system which is structured in terms of strata. Language connects meanings (the semantic stratum) with their spoken and written expressions (the stratum of phonology and graphology). Both meanings and expressions interface with the extra-linguistic – meanings with social life, expressions with for instance bodily processes such as those of the vocal mechanism. The stratal organisation of language means that the link between meaning and expression strata is mediated by a stratum which does not itself directly interface with the extra-linguistic – lexicogrammar, i.e., grammar plus lexis (vocabulary), where lexis is not radically different in nature from grammar but rather 'most delicate' grammar, grammar taken down ultimately to individual lexical items (Halliday 1961; Hasan 1987). But although lexicogrammar does not directly interface with the social, it is historically shaped through processes of semogenesis – the historical production and change of the semiotic – which open the language system to social shaping. More specifically, lexicogrammar is seen as functionally grounded, shaped by the social functions it serves, and in particular built around the intersection of the 'macro-functions' of language – the ideational function (language in the construction and representation of experience in the world), the interpersonal function (language in the enactment of social relations and the construction of social identities), and the textual function (language in the specifically semiotic – textual – form of productive practice). The grammar is structured as three major 'networks' of grammatical systems (transitivity, mood and modality, and information – including theme/rheme and given/new – see Halliday 1994a) corresponding to these three macrofunctions; and every clause in a text (as well as lower- and higher-level grammatical units) is seen as grammatically constituted simultaneously as semiotic production (textual function) which constructs the world (ideational function) while enacting social relations between its producers and others who inhabit that world (relational function). Thus the social is built into the grammatical tissue of language – an example of what we referred to in Chapter 2 as the 'internalisation' of other moments of social practice – so that the semiotic constitution by the social and of the social is constantly at issue in language analysis.

REALISATION AND INSTANTIATION

In SFL the specificity of the semiotic and the relationship between the semiotic and the social are discussed in terms of two principles of 'realisation' and 'instantiation'. The relationship between strata is one of 'realisation': each of the strata defines a potential, a set of possibilities – a meaning potential (semantics), a wording potential (lexicogrammar), an expression potential – and the two former potentials are realised in the terms of the strata below. But the relationship is rather complex, because language is organised as a 'meta-redundant' system – the meaning potential is realised not simply in the wording potential, but in the realisation of the wording potential in the expression potential (Halliday 1992, 1995; Lemke 1984, 1995; Martin 1997). This form of embedded realisation relationship can however be extended upwards in a way which links language to the social – we can say the options of the 'context of situation' (the immediate, extra-linguistic, situational context of text) are realised in language – i.e., in the realisation of the meaning potential in (the realisation of the wording potential in the expression potential) – the bracketing here perhaps helps to get across the embedding. The context of situation can also be conceived of in terms of a (situational) potential, which can be specified in terms of possible values for three variables – the 'field' (the activity which the language is a part of), the 'tenor' (the social actors involved and the relations between them), and the 'mode' (the part language plays in the activity) – which correspond respectively to the ideational, interpersonal and textual macrofunctions.

If realisation is about looking at the semiotic space in terms of its internal relations, instantiation is about language as an open dynamic system in relationship to its (social) environment. Language is conceived as both system and text (or system and instantiation), and these are seen as just different perspectives on the same thing – looking at language in the long term or in its immediacy. There is a focus on the dialectic of system and text in the process of semogenesis, the production and change of the semiotic, incorporating phylogenesis, logogenesis and ontogenesis – the history of the system, the history of the text in the sense of the process of the text in time–space, and the (linguistic) history of the person. Semogenesis is shaped by both the logic (or generative power, 'mechanism') of the social ('sociologic') and the logic of the semiotic ('semologic'). In terms of the latter, language is a resource for making meanings, and the formal basis for meaning-making is the syntagmatic and para-digmatic relations specified in the semantics and lexicogrammar – the possible combinations of meanings and forms, and the set of options available at any given position in syntagmatic structure. This meaning-making capacity is the semologic, the specific logic or generative power of the semiotic. In terms of the former, the sociologic, the text is a specifically semiotic form of social production (Matthiessen 1992), and we might add that like any form of social production it is 'joint action' – overtly so in dialogue, more covertly so in the case of mass mediated (for example, written) text – and so is always located in and participates in the social process (Halliday and Hasan 1989).

This conception of text locates the SFL theory of language within what we have called structuralist–constructivist social theory – it sees language dialectically as structured and structuring. Texts as instantiations on the one hand draw upon and instantiate the system, but on the other are located in specific and potentially new ways in social life, so that in principle every instantiation opens the system up to new impetuses from its social environment. Texts are thus channels for socially driven changes in the language system – logogenesis is phylogenesis in a local, instantiated form. More specifically, logogenesis draws attention to the processes of change which go on in the course of a text, which can be a matter of specific movements within the existing potential of the language (for example, 'nominalising' what begins as a verbal process, i.e., converting it through a process of 'grammatical metaphor' into a noun-like 'nominalisation' – for instance, 'she criticised them' being nominalised as '(her) criticism') or a matter of a text extending the existing potential, for example by a mixing of different types of discourse which manifests itself as new collocations (such as perhaps 'back-scratching skills'). The meaning potential of language can be elab-orated in this way through for instance increasing the range of language varieties or through an extension of 'grammatical metaphor' (this concept is explained below). Language is an open system, in the sense that it is open to socially driven shifts (shifts driven by the sociologic) which ensure that its meaning-making capacity is extend-able without limit.

DIVERSITY AND VARIATION IN SFL

We believe that CDA complements and extends this view of language, and we want to argue this through a discussion of how SFL and CDA treat variation and diversity in language. Both take the view that first, one aspect of difference *between* social practices is semiotic difference, and second, there is also (in the terms of Chapter 2) difference *within* the semiotic (discourse) moment of any social practice which is part of differences and struggles within its social relations. Let us take these in turn for SFL.

The semiotic difference *between* social practices is treated in terms of the categories of dialect, register and genre. Particular values for the three variables of context of situation – field, tenor and mode – are realised through particular choices within the meaning potential (in turn realised through particular choices in lexicogrammar) which together constitute a particular 'register'. Registers are thus language varieties associated with particular contexts of language use, as opposed to dialects which are language varieties associated with particular groups of language users. One way of formulating the difference between dialect and register is that the former does not affect or increase the potential of the semantic system, whereas the latter does (Halliday 1995). The term 'genre' is reserved for the structuring of particular types of discourse in terms of sequentially ordered 'stages' – for instance, in a buying and selling encounter in a local shop the sequence of: greetings + request for goods + compliance with request (there might be a number of sub-sequences of request + compliance) + payment + farewells. Halliday and Hasan (1989) see the field, tenor and mode values of a context of situation as specifying a 'generic structure potential' for that context of situation (specified as a particular ordering of elements, some obligatory and some optional) which particular texts select from – i.e., each has all the obligatory and some, all or none of the optional elements. The precise nature of the relationship of register and genre is a matter of debate (see Hasan 1995; Martin 1985, 1992; Thibault 1989).

Semiotic difference *within* a social practice is treated in terms of the category of 'coding orientation', taken from Bernstein (Hasan 1973). Differences in social membership – especially social class but also for instance gender and ethnic group membership – correlate with different coding orientations. These are realised as particular 'semantic styles', 'integrated fashions of speaking' (in the terms of Whorf 1956), which lead to particular selections for a wide range of otherwise unconnected features within the meaning potential associated with any particular register or genre – choices in meaning and therefore in lexicogrammar are systematically skewed in particular directions. This concept of 'semantic styles' is extended to include ideologies (Hasan 1986) – we return to this below.

It is evident from this brief account that the SFL approach to language variation, like the macrofunctional view of language system, gives concrete operationalisation to the theoretical claim of a dialectic between the semiotic and the social, and indeed to the concept we discussed in Chapter 2 that moments of the social internalise other moments. Not only does language on this account internalise differences in social membership and relations and in situational context, the context of situation itself is constructed as internalising language – as semioticised – in that the categories of field, tenor and mode project the macrofunctional organisation of the language system into the context of situation. Yet there is a consistent gap between the sort of theoretical formulations of the dialectics of the semiotic which we summed up above and the way the dialectic is operationalised in analyses – for instance, in the recent contributions by Halliday and Hasan to a multiple analysis project whose data was the defence of a doctoral thesis which we discuss below (Halliday 1994b; Hasan 1994). We believe that this operationalisation of the dialectics of the semiotic is only partially successful, because first, it consistently leans too heavily towards (a) the semiotic as opposed to other moments of the social, and (b) towards the system rather than the instance (or text); and second, it does not recognise the social structuring of semiotic hybridity as itself constituting a system – what CDA calls the 'order of discourse'.

A focus on language and the semiotic on the part of linguists is hardly surprising, but that normal disciplinary inclination can become problematic for a theory which aims to be dialectical – other moments of social practices (in our terms) tend to be bundled together within and reduced to the 'context' of language and the focus is on how language internalises them, in a one-sided way which gives no account of how they internalise language or how language constitutes part of the 'context' for them. It is not that the dialectic is suppressed in the analytical papers – Halliday for instance does point out in the example referred to above that 'we' ('you' and 'me') are not only the creators of the text, 'we' are also created by it – it is that the apparatus of SFL does not allow the analyst to do it justice, it pushes the analyst to the side of the semiotic and of language in particular. That is why we think it is important to frame analysis of discourse within analysis of social practices conceived as articulations of diverse moments, as we argued in Chapter 2. Focusing on social practices directs attention to links and relations of internalisation between all the various moments, so that it is possible to assess the work the semiotic moment does in each particular practice. In this way relations between 'doing, being and saying' (Hasan 1996) can be explored in specific cases without automatically privileging the semiotic.

The apparatus of SFL also pushes the analyst to the side of system, for despite claims that every text (instance) 'perturbs the system' (Halliday 1992), the analysis of texts is overwhelmingly an account of what choices the text makes from the potential of the system, of the text as an instantiation of the system.[1] All texts are seen as making particular choices from the meaning and wording potentials, being 'in' a particular register (Halliday 1992) and 'members' of a particular genre (Hasan 1994). This leads to difficulties with hybrid texts – texts which mix discourses, genres or registers. We discuss this in relation to Hasan's (1994) analysis of the dissertation defence text referred to above in terms of its generic structure potential, in which she argues that the text contains parts which might be taken to be extraneous to the genre of dissertation defence. Hasan argues that instances of discourse types which are different from the main discourse type of a text may be treated as parts of that text (as 'subtexts') in so far as they 'functionally support' the main text – for instance, one subtext in this case is constituted by joking, which is different from the main discourse type of dissertation defence yet functions to ease tensions which have built up in the social relations between participants and therefore does constitute a part of the main text. Hasan introduces the concept of 'permeability' for relations between discourse types in such cases. By contrast a confrontation between two of the participants over alleged sexist bias in academic life which comes at the end of the interaction is seen as a different text (a 'separate text running parallel to the dissertation defence discourse', Hasan 1994: 165) on the grounds that its field and tenor are different from those of the main text and it does not function to support the latter in any way. (Halliday's analysis of the same text in the same volume names this part of the text the 'post-mortem' (1994b: 184) and suggests it is either an optional element of the dissertation defence text type, or falls outside it and indicates a change of register.) Notice that the category of 'text' itself is here pushed to the side of the system – as well as being used for the semiotic event itself, the dialogue of the dissertation defence, it is being used more abstractly and systemically for the parts of the event which instantiate the genre plus other elements which 'functionally support' them.

Hasan's concept of 'permeability' seems to be put forward as a way of resolving the difficulty which hybrid texts cause SFL, yet we see it more as a cautious move from the side of system to contain the messiness of events: permeability accommodates hybridity but selectively and marginally. The difficulty in dealing more fully and dynamically with hybridity lies in the way the concept of instantiation is operationalised – the claim that a text is an instance of a contextually correlated selection from the potential specified in the system, that a text therefore is an instance of a register (is 'in' a particular register) or a 'member' of a genre. Although there is indeed a need to show how the instance is anchored in the system, this is making the instance fit the the system. In the difficult business of grasping the dialectic of structure and event, we believe it is necessary to be as fully as possible open to the specificity of events as events, at the same time as reiterating how they are constrained by and reproductive as well as productive of structures. Otherwise the analysis runs the risk of becoming a systemic reduction of interaction, a theoretical objectification of practice, which the ambiguity of 'text' referred to above is a symptom of.

This is another reason for the focus we are suggesting for CDA on social practices. We argued in Chapter 2 that the concept of practice helps mediate between social structure and social event, and that the ambivalence of the concept is actually a virtue from this point of view – the notion of 'practice' suggests both the relative permanence of the way things are normally done, and the actuality of what is happening now. We used the concept of 'articulation' for configurations of elements which range in permanence from relatively stable long-term articulations (structures) to less durable medium-term articulations (conjunctures) to momentary articulations which are likely to be transitory (events). Within the discourse (semiotic) moment of a practice, the elements that are articulated together are genres and discourses. We want to see a genre as a specifically discursive structuring or ordering of a social practice, a regulative device through which relations of power are realised as forms of control; and we want to see a discourse as a construction or representation of one social practice from a particular perspective within another social practice (see Chapter 6; see also van Leeuwen 1993 for a distinction between genre and discourse along these lines). A genre is itself an articulatory device which controls what goes with what and in what ordering, including what configuration and ordering of discourses, and like the concept of articulation the concept of genre applies within different timescales. Genre therefore needs to be understood in a more abstract way than in SFL as the ordering and regulative facet of discourse, and not simply used for the staged structuring of relatively permanent types of discourse such as the dissertation defence (see also Kress and Threadgold 1988; Threadgold 1989 on the SFL view of genre; Chouliaraki 1995). Structures, conjunctures and events all have generic properties. The staging of individual genres such as dissertation defence can be described at the level of structures, but at the level of conjunctures and at the level of events genre involves mixtures of such individual genres, relatively stabilised mixtures at the level of conjunctures and more or less transitory mixtures at the level of events (which can be seen as locally motivated reworkings of more stabilised mixtures). One facet of genre at the level of conjunctures is the sort of mixing of formal and informal (for example, dissertation defence and conversation) which we have in this example – formal genres are more or less and differently hybridisable with informal genres in socially different times and places.

From this perspective, we are not happy with Hasan's analysis of 'office space' as 'a separate text running parallel to the dissertation defence discourse', but we shall argue this with reference to our other reservation about SFL's treatment of the dialectics of the semiotic – that it does not recognise the social structuring of semiotic hybridity (what we call the 'order of discourse') as itself constituting a system. In the cases where Hasan's concept of permeability does accommodate hybridity, it gives only an interactional motivation for it, rather in the spirit of linguistic pragmatics. For instance, as we saw above, Hasan treats joking in the example as a strategy for easing tension (Hasan 1994: 162–3). We have no quarrel with this, but what the analysis misses is the generic conditions of possibility for the joking to have this function in this example. Such articulations between the formal and serious discourse of organisational procedures and informal and often non-serious conversational discourse (for example, joking) are not unusual – on the contrary, they are absolutely characteristic in interactions within organisations in this culture and an important facet of its complex public–private dialectic. The specific forms of combination between the two are part of the ordering and regulative constraints of genre at the level of the conjuncture. But we would argue that the same applies in the case of the 'office space' (Halliday's 'post-mortem'), which deals with a charge which the doctoral candidate made during the dissertation defence that the university department concerned at some point discriminated against single women in its employment policy. The 'post-mortem' is a relatively informal conversational exchange interpolated within the formal business of dissertation defence; the formal business is not over, it carries over through 'office space', which performs the crucial function of 'repairing' the threatened legitimacy of the institution at an earlier point of the defence activity. It is another typical form of combination between the formal and the informal. The combinatory possibility is available and used in this case to manage aspects of the formal business which are not easily dealt with within the formal procedure – it is 'functionally supportive' in that sense (as Corsaro 1994 argued in a commentary on Hasan's analysis) – just as the joking is used to ease tension.

The point we wish to make is that in both cases the local function of the hybridity in this specific text depends upon a social (conjunctural) structuring of semiotic diversity which includes certain combinations of the public/formal/serious and the private/informal/non-serious while excluding others, which constitutes a system which the specific text draws upon and works in a particular way. Specifically, the practice of discourse defence at a conjunctural level includes a discourse genre which allows for such movements between formal procedure and informal conversational discourse – in a different time and place that might not be so, or might be movements of a different type. The generic analysis of this text needs to refer to this hybridity – treating the example in this case as two separate texts running in parallel means subordinating the sociosemiotic logic of the text to the logic and categories of the system, and missing this hybridity. The system here we refer to as the 'order of discourse' – an open system characterised by shifting boundaries and flows between its constitutive elements. This social structuring of semiotic hybridity, of compatibilities and incompatabilities, of boundaries and flows, defines a potential (that of the order of discourse) which may be variously drawn upon as well as reworked in texts, and a necessary systemic frame for making sense of what is done in a specific instance such as this one (i.e., in the discourse moment of a specific practice). The focus is on 'interdiscursivity', the combination of different discourses and genres. We see this focus of CDA as contributing to the long-standing commitment of SFL to specifying, via analysis of the dialectic of system and instance, the openness to each other of social and semiotic systems.

The discourse of people differently positioned within a social practice will differ. Correspondingly, the discourse moment of any social practice needs to be conceived of as constituted not as a single articulation of elements, but rather as a spread of articulations of elements potentially in contestation. Social relations of class, gender and ethnicity are constituted in such discursive differences within particular practices and across networks of practices – coding orientations which transcend particular practices can be understood in terms of structural relations and trajectories within these networks. Recall that we understand ideologies within this framework, in terms of the network of social practices, as the colonisation of the reflexive moment of a social practice by discourses from other social practices – discourses which, in Bernstein's terms, are recontextualised, thereby rendered imaginary and thus open to working ideologically. Whether and how discourse works ideologically can be determined only by looking at how the discourse moment of a practice articulates with other moments of that practice within the network of practices. This seems to be implicit in some formulations in Hasan (1986).

Let us conclude this discussion by briefly referring to another attempt to deal with discursive hybridity within SFL. Martin (1997: 33) approaches the issue by using Halliday's concept of 'grammatical metaphor' (which we discuss below) as a model for a concept of 'contextual metaphor'. Just as grammatical metaphor, for instance where a finite clause appears as a nominalisation, sets up a tension between the actual (metaphorical) grammatical form (nominalisation) and the non-metaphorical grammatical form it metaphorically replaces (finite clause), so contextual metaphor sets up a tension at the contextual level between the actual (metaphorical) genre and the non-metaphorical genre it substitutes for. For example, in an educational context what is non-metaphorically a report might appear in the genre of narrative, but a tension (and thus ambivalence) between the two might be set up by certain features of the narrative which retain its identity as a report, such as an exceptional amount of technical information about the 'characters' in the narrative. This is an attempt to disentangle the articuatory practice in hybrid texts, which however runs into the difficulty of determining what is metaphorical and what is non-metaphorical in most cases of textual hybridity and therefore of determining what 'at a deeper level the text is intended to instantiate' (Martin 1997: 33). We are suggesting that the category of interdiscursivity locates genre in a particular (conjunctural) network of discursive practices (other genres and discourses) which the genre appropriates and recontextualises in normative or transformative ways.

INTERDISCURSIVITY AND SCIENTIFIC DISCOURSE

As an example of how CDA complements SFL and might be used as a resource by systemic linguists, we want to briefly discuss Halliday's work on the history of scientific discourse in English (Halliday 1993, 1995), which we believe fits well with this CDA framework. Halliday discusses the development of 'the new technical registers of science and learning' in the early modern period in Europe with particular reference to Galileo and Newton (the examples below are from Newton). He identifies 'syndromes of grammatical features' which constitute the 'semantic character' of scientific discourse. There are a number of these grammatical features, but let us just mention those involving grammatical metaphors (Halliday 1993: 19). Processes and properties are metaphorically worded as nouns in nominalisations (for example, the diverging and separation of the heterogeneous rays), and logical relations are metaphorically worded as verbs (such as cause, follow), both features being manifested in, 'perhaps, a newly emerging clause type "happening a caused happening b"' (for example, 'all Bodies by percussion excite vibrations in the Air ...'). Halliday traces aspects of the social trajectory of this new scientific discourse, noting how it came to be seen as alienating because of its remoteness from commonsense constructions of experience, and even eventually unsatisfactory for scientists as their views of reality changed – as they came to see it as fluid and probabilistic rather than fixed and deterministic. Halliday also discusses how scientific discourse was transformed into bureaucratic discourse, and 'technocratic discourse' which 'combines the bureaucratic with the scientific ... obscuring the issue at stake ... to persuade us that ... we should leave every decision to the experts'. Halliday concludes that this 'nominalising, metaphorical grammar' has become in some ways dysfunctional in contemporary societies.

What Halliday is tracing here can be read in CDA terms as shifting articulations (shifting boundaries and flows) between types of discourse and orders of discourse within various social practices that recontextualise scientific discourse in significant ways (see Chapter 6 for recontextualisation). Newtonian scientific discourse itself developed through recontextualising (not pace Halliday just 'carrying further' – 1993: 18) the theoretical discourse of classical antiquity within an enlightenment discourse of progress grounded in the radical socio-economic and technological developments of modernity (for an analysis of this latter discourse, see Halliday 1988). And it has in turn been recontextualised within other institutional discourses which have co-evolved with the increasing specialisation of institutional domains in modern Western societies and new techniques of power and regulation, thus giving rise to bureaucratic and technocratic discourses. Contemporary recontextualisations of specialised (including scientific, bureaucratic and technocratic) discourses with discourses of the lifeworld partly manifest a suspicion towards elitist discourses, as Halliday suggests (1993: 20) – as well as a disrespect towards the (Newtonian) scientific project overall. However, the relationship is more complex than this formulation suggests: this is not a 'move to plain English', but an articulation of 'plain English' with other institutional discourses (mediatised political discourses, for example) which brings about deeply ambivalent social practices from a democratic perspective. The 'conversationalisation' of institutional including scientific discourse also works as a discursive technology that simulates ordinary life intimacy while masking relations of power (Fairclough 1994). The key point is that these are not just processes of extension 'carrying further' discourses of antiquity or 'plain English', they are processes of recontextualisation, which means that they are shifting articulations – for instance, bureaucratic discourse is not simply scientific discourse in a different range of social practices, it is an articulation of scientific discourse with a range of specialised discourses in different institutional domains, each of which becomes a site of struggle over the appropriation and meaning of recontextualised discourses. This means that in studying the relationship of scientific discourse with structures of power in contemporary societies (as discussed in Martin 1998), we also need to study the specific articulations of discourses of science with 'local' systemic discourses and to pay attention to the relationships of appropriation and colonisation between them. This is one way of assessing the specific ideological functioning of scientific discourse across contexts of social practices as well as assessing the potentials for resistance and change in these contexts (Martin and Veel 1998 move in this direction in discussing the science–education relationship).

The trajectory of scientific English is therefore to be seen in terms of recontextualisations within orders of discourse rather than shifts in the system of language induced by scientific discourse. Both these accounts connect the semiotic with (other moments of) the social, but the former relates shifts in the semiotic to theoretically informed accounts of societal transformation and is therefore more apt to address the co-genetic logic of the semiotic and the social. We need the concepts of inderdiscursivity and order of discourse as, in Halliday's terms, a 'higher order semiotic' in order to be able to relate sociologically Halliday's valuable analysis of the development of grammar with wider social processes of transformation in modern societies

– which might for instance be cast in Habermas's terms within the dialectic of system and lifeworld, seeing the emergence of scientific discourse as a facet of the rationalisation of systems, and the bureaucratic and technocratic recontextualisations of scientific discourse as a facet of the colonisation of the lifeworld by systems. SFL does not itself provide a conceptual and analytical framework for systematically addressing the shifting articulations and recontextualisations of discourse involved, yet its concern with the 'co-genetic logic' of the semiotic and the social (Hasan in press b) does in practice, as in Halliday's work on scientific discourse, push it towards the question of how semiotic variation is socially constructed.

One might argue that the SFL concept of 'grammatical metaphor' provides a way of handling the interdiscursivity of texts (for example, in the presence of the 'nominalising, metaphorical grammar' of science within non-scientific texts combined with different elements or grammars), and that the concept of interdiscursivity is therefore superfluous. Apart from the difficulty we have already referred to of determining what is metaphorical and what is not, this would weaken the account of the co-genetic logic of the semiotic and the social for the reasons we have just given, by reducing the social structuring of the semiotic to its linguistic realisations.

SFL AND BERNSTEIN

SFL has had a long-standing relationship with Bernstein's sociological theory, which has influenced developments within SFL. We believe that the complementary relationship between SFL and CDA that we suggest in Chapter 6 helps to further the link between Bernstein's sociology and linguistics.

The research of Hasan and her collaborators on mother–child interaction has shown that first, there are systematic semantic differences in the ways mothers from different social classes talk to their children – these are differences in coding orientation within the same 'register' of (say) child-control (1986, 1992a) and second, that there is a systematic construction of gendered identity, an ideology of motherhood, that cuts across social class differences (Hasan 1986; Hasan and Cloran 1990). These results are an important contribution to critical sociological work, addressing the relationship between discourse and the reproduction of unequal social relations in the categories of class and gender.

In her work on class differentiation, Hasan has developed Bernstein's analysis of coding orientations in SFL terms through the writing of context-specific semantic networks which specify the meaning potential for a given context (for example, child control). Different class-related coding orientations are systematic selections within this meaning potential, which assemble configurations of options from diverse semantic systems into discrete 'semantic styles' – which however have a degree of permeability, i.e., they can be combined. The research is designed to provide a working combination (a 'dialectic' in Bernstein's terms 1996) of a theoretical language and an analytical language of description – the empirical data are analysed in great detail to delineate semantic variation grounded on and reproducing social differentiation. However, this is achieved at a cost: by focusing on the message ('the smallest [semantic] unit capable of functioning as an element of the structure of a text or a textual strategy' – Hasan 1992a: 262), this research misses out on the dynamic properties of text which only unfold when looking at text as interaction – this is the cost of the bias towards system and away from instance which we discussed above. It does not show how the semiotic works in an integrated fashion together with other moments of a social practice, despite Hasan's consistent theoretical position that they co-evolve; it is not oriented towards capturing instances of tension and hybridity across moments of a practice or within discourse; and it does not demonstrate the possibility for social change, in the form of subtle local disruptions of order or alternative constructions of practice. Despite Hasan's interest in these issues (as for example 1986: 141–2 – see below), the research seems to work towards one side of Bernstein's thesis, the reproductionist side, confirming the correlation between coding orientation and social position. However, the potential for change is there in Bernstein's theory, and that is what makes his theory a powerful tool in sociological research on discourse (see Chapter 6). What Hasan's research design does not operationalise is, in Bernstein's terms, the dialectic between voice and message – the potentially transformative tension between social positioning and particular interactional practice.[2] As we argued in Chapter 6, CDA's orientation to practice and to interdiscursive hybridity allow it to operationalise the dialectic of Bernstein's theory in analysis of discourse.

In terms of her work on ideology, Hasan takes a post-Marxist view of ideology which refuses to see it as 'false consciousness' and recognises gender as well as class ideologies – the focus in the research is on ideologies of motherhood. Although Hasan consistently defines ideology as working hand in hand with other aspects of the social, and as being part of social practice, the SFL analytical apparatus (again) 'forces' her to disconnect the semiotic (in the form of the 'message') from other moments of the practice. One danger in defining ideology primarily as semantic configurations is that it overstates the coherence of ideological constructions of motherhood at the expense of identity tensions and contradictions which are apparent only in practice. Hasan seems in fact to imply that there is a uniform identity of womanhood or motherhood which cuts across social positions ('it doesn't matter which section of the population the mothers belong to, they share similar views about woman's work' 1986: 129). We are not denying that there are dominant patriarchal ideologies of motherhood, but insisting that they operate in complex ways in multiple social practices – for instance, discourses of mothers' professional labour (as opposed to domestic labour) or discourses of professional child-care (rather than mother child-care) are increasingly part of the dominant discursive field of motherhood (which means that they are discourses available and operative across both working and non-working mother groups) and they are bound to create tensions of identity that are not accounted for in Hasan's management and analysis of data. Our view is that the links between particular discourses and social positions, and therefore the ideological effects of discourses, are established and negotiated in the process of articulation within a practice. This takes us closer to a relational view of ideology 'not tied to a specific content' but as 'referring to a function or a mechanism' (Barrett

1991: 167 – see also Chapter 2).[3] We believe that a version of CDA based on the view of social life as practice set out in Chapter 2 provides the conceptual and analytical resources for a better balance between the semiotic and other moments and between system and instance. Focusing on practices directs attention to links and relations of internalisation between all the various moments, so that it is possible to assess the work – including the ideological work – that the semiotic moment does in each particular practice.

Hasan's approach to ideology leaves no space for theorising and analysing tension, hybridity and change. Bernstein's voice-message dialectic (see just above) is crucial here:[4] tension and change arise out of specific articulations that momentarily expose the arbitrariness of social position. Relevant questions include: how is the mother constructed in different discursive articulations across practices? how is sexual difference made a pertinent distinction or a moment of tension in these construction? how are relations of subordination constructed or challenged through such a distinction? (see Mouffe 1992).

SEMOLOGIC AND THE DOUBLE STRUCTURE OF THE SEMIOTIC

We believe that the complementary relationship we are suggesting between SFL and CDA also contributes to a better grasp of the semologic, the generative power of the semiotic. We see two domains of structure as germane to the specification of semologic: the structure of semiotic systems (including language) and the social structuring of semiotic hybridity, i.e., the order of discourse. Language as an open system has unlimited capacity to make meaning through generating syntagmatic and paradigmatic connections, but it is the dynamism of the order of discourse in generating new articulations of discourses and genres which keeps the language system open in that such articulations are realised in (and in a sense open up) new syntagmatic and paradigmatic connections in language and other semiotic systems (gesture, image). Conversely, it is the fixity of the order of discourse that limits the generative power of language by precluding certain connections. Moreover, the order of discourse specifies relations of flow across discursive practices and relations of recontextualisation between discourses and genres which entail specific and differing dispersals of text types and their particular features (for example, the grammatical metaphor of nominalisation) across social practices and therefore across contexts of interpretation. The point is that one aspect of semologic is what Derrida calls 'iterability' – the openness of language to new contexts and therefore new meanings (1977). Like the capacity for meaning-making of semiotic systems, iterability can be understood as without limit, yet both are subject to the social constraints of the order of discourse.

In terms of critical realism, we might be interpreted as saying no more than that the generative power of the semiotic is mediated by the generative powers of other moments of the social. But we are suggesting something rather different: that the semiotic has a double structure (language system, order of discourse) which has emerged through the internalisation of the logic of the social into the semiotic at different levels – in the social structuring of language and other semiotic systems, and in the social structuring of semiotic diversity.

TEXTUAL ANALYSIS IN CDA

What differentiates CDA from some Foucaultian versions of discourse analysis used by social scientists is that it is, in the terms of Fairclough (1992a), a 'textually-oriented' discourse analysis, i.e., it anchors its analytical claims about discourses in close analysis of texts. Convincing social scientists of the value of CDA in social research is very much a matter of convincing them that detailed analysis of text will always enhance discourse analysis (see Fairclough 1992c for an argument along these lines). At the same time, linguists have to be convinced that the social concerns of CDA do not deflect from detailed and careful linguistic (and semiotic) analysis of texts. Much work in CDA so far has been theoretical and programmatic, and CDA has been criticised for not carrying out the sort of systematic analysis of large, representative bodies of texts, including the use of quantitative and computational methods, which could actually give a firmer linguistic grounding to its social claims about discourse (Stubbs 1997; Toolan 1997). It would also allow the comparisons which CDA so often draws to be made in a more systematic way – between different historical periods, different types of discourse, or different language communities. Stubbs (1997: 112, 1996) shows for instance that studying changes in the meaning and grammar of keywords such as *care* (and comparatively for German *Pflegen*) in large diachronic and contemporary corpora can provide valuable documentation for critical discourse analysis – in this case for analysis of the important contemporary discourse of caring, the 'caring society'(see also de Beaugrande 1998).

We agree that CDA could be strengthened in these ways, though we see their value as supporting qualitative analyses of particular texts which can illuminate particular situated forms of the text–system dialectic. Our focus in this final section is on an aspect of qualitative text analysis. We want to draw upon SFL perspectives on the textual meta-function (for example, Martin 1992; Matthiessen 1992) to argue for a methodological principle to be adopted in CDA which we believe would contribute to enhancing textual analysis. The principle is that in CDA one should aim not only to show what interdiscursive resources are drawn upon in a text under analysis and how they are realised semiotically and linguistically, but also to show through an analysis of the texture of the text how these resources are articulated together in the textual process, how they are 'worked' in the development or 'unfolding' of the text in time (spoken texts) or space (written texts).

Matthiessen (1992) sees the textual meta-function as specifying in the semiotic system the dynamic potential of language – the 'dynamic character of textual meaning: what was new becomes given, what was rhematic often becomes thematic, what was non-identifiable becomes identifiable, and so on'. Or again, nominalisation is a dynamic process in texts which allows a clause to be 'summarised' as a nominalised participant which might itself for instance figure as the theme of a clause. Text development is a 'semiotic journey', a '(text) history' in which a particular part of the text has a past and a future (1992). It is a journey in which the ideational and interpersonal metafunctions are woven together as 'carriers' (1992) of the textual meta-function, so that text development is inseparably and simultaneously the development of texture (for example, what was new becomes given) and the development ideational and interpersonal meanings. Putting it differently: no construction of reality without negotiation of social relations and identities, but neither of these without the unfolding of the text. We may say, in the terms of Chapter 2, that one form which the social practice of production takes is a specifically semiotic form, the production of texts, and we may try to specify how semiotic production figures variably within production overall in different social practices. But what we want to argue here is the importance of attending to the specific productive process of semiotic production, which is texturing, the specifically semiotic 'enabling' process which makes it possible to produce socially in a semiotic, textual mode.

However, while SFL has valuably emphasised the importance of attending to texture and textual processes, we find manifested here again the bias towards language system which we discussed earlier, and an overly narrow understanding of what textual processes involve. In particular, what is missing is the weaving together of different texts, discourses and genres. Let us begin with texts. Fairclough (1992a) draws a distinction between 'manifest intertextuality' and 'interdiscursivity' – the former is the mixing together of elements from different specific (real or imagined) texts within a text, the latter is the mixing together of different discourses and genres. The former includes 'reported speech' or 'discourse representation' (Fairclough 1988) – the weaving together of the words of another or others with my words, the weaving together of different 'voices'. Discourse representation does not just bring different voices together, it combines and orders them in a particular way, for instance setting up hierachical relations between them so that one voice is used to frame another or to inflect another. The various forms of representations ('direct speech', 'indirect speech', 'free indirect speech', etc.) are resources for effecting orderings – for instance, while direct speech generally commits you to the words which the other actually used, indirect speech allows you to translate the words of the other into your own words. Fairclough 1995a (79–85) for instance is a detailed analysis of how a BBC radio news report on the attempt to extradite Libyans accused of planting a bomb on an aircraft subordinates Libyan voices to Western voices through such translation and through the way in which Libyan voices are ordered and framed in the report. Weaving different voices together in particular ways is part of the textual process, and the concept of 'texture' can be extended to include it.

The same applies to the weaving together of different discourses and genres. Recall for instance the reanalysis of Dorothy Smith's texts in Chapter 4. We pointed out that in lines 025–044 a considerable range of discourses is drawn upon to construct the police and their actions. Again, the issue is not simply what discourses are assembled here but how they are textually worked together. For example, in line 027 (*Suddenly two policemen, no, two uniformed thugs, were upon her*), the shift between discourses is located within a process of self-correction, and the second of the two discourses (what we referred to as a discourse of political opposition) is constituted through a collocation of lexical items which themselves evoke different discourses – officialdom and criminality (*uniformed* + *thugs*). Such collocations are small instances of logogenesis – the textual creation of new language through the condensation of different and in this case contradictory discourses into a single expression. A similar condensation occurs later in the extract in the collocation *uniformed hoods*. More generally, the analysis of this passage invites a discussion of the rhetorical work which leads to the particular ordering of and movement between the different discourses. Such local, rhetorical articulations and orderings of discourse in specific events cumulatively contribute to changes which can be discerned at the level of conjunctures, though by their nature these cannot easily be illustrated in particular texts. This underlines the need to combine qualitative text analysis with quantitative analysis of large bodies of text. The general point however is that the voice–message dialectic in Bernstein's terms is cumulatively played out in textual processes conceived as one form of social production.

This is not to deny the importance of framing analysis of the dynamics of text in terms of accounts of the potentials which texts draw upon, i.e., of systems, including language systems. However, there is room for debate about the nature of these systems within socially oriented research on language. Van Leeuwen (1993a, 1993b, 1995) for instance has developed systemic networks which specify the representational potential of English – for instance, what choices are available in English for representing social actors in texts – which in comparison with more conventional versions of SFL might be seen as specifying a social potential and its linguistic realisations rather than in a direct way a linguistic potential. We find van Leeuwen's framework extremely valuable in analysing texts within CDA. The more general point however is that if we wish to address the complex issue of the co-genetic logic of the social and the semiotic, we have to be prepared to radically question the linguistic theories currently available (as indeed SFL has itself done).

CONCLUSION

Extending our conversation in this book to include linguistics is crucial to the project of CDA. We have presented CDA as contributing to critical social research systematic accounts of the discourse moment of contemporary social practices. To undertake this successfully, CDA needs to be more clearly and firmly grounded in three directions. First, in a critical social scientific view of the social and of critique. Second, in the field of critical social research on late modernity. And third, in the theory and analysis of language and semiosis. Our hope is that this book has made a contribution in these directions.

NOTES

1. This analytical 'bias' has to do with what Halliday identifies as a difficulty in applied linguistic research, namely that 'the quantitative and gradual' nature of the social effects of language use make it hard to illustrate these effects from text examples, i.e., from the instance side: 'if we represent them *instantially*, we need very large samples of discourse to bring them out. But, by the same token, we can represent them *systemically* – as features of the system rather than of the instance' (Halliday 1993: 14 – original emphasis). Although, as Halliday adds, in SFL the separation is based on the condition that the two are treated 'not [as] distinct but as complementary aspects of the same phenomenon', the effect is that SFL privileges accounts of the system (through systems networks), backgrounding the instance. We believe that the sort of qualitative analysis of instances which CDA carries out plus its orientation to the systemic social ordering of semiotic variation in orders of discourse (see below) can help correct this language–systemic bias.

2. Hasan does seem to be aware of the limitations of this research in addressing Bernstein's sociological agenda, and points to the need to move to the analysis of variation in textual organisation: 'there still remains the question whether semantic variation tells the whole story of variation in coding orientation … codes regulate relevant meanings and their organisation within the context of specialized interactive practices relevant to distinct contexts. This implies that a full-scale linguistic study of variation in coding orientation must analyse not simply the elements of messages but also the deployment of messages in texts, probing into variation in textual organization' (Hasan in press a).

3. See for example the 'silly mummy' argument (Hasan 1986: 131) in which ideological function is glossed in terms of a dominant construction of a woman as 'lacking in intellect'; although Hasan brings the alternative explanation that a play down of the adult's intellect in child–mother talk may be a 'boost' for the 'child's ego', she immediately invalidates this argument as 'simple rationale' – yet a more plausible assessment of the ideological effect of such interactions would need to take into account how different discourses work in the specific context of a practice – what is at stake in that practice at any specific moment (something which is not possible from the way data are managed and presented); in such cases perhaps the question of power and the management of the power relationship between child and mother (the 'boosting') would not have been only a 'simple rationale'. The point again is not that such dominant discourses are not at work – rather that how they function in a particular context, in a chain of other social moments or in a chain of other practices, is what make them assessable as ideological – and that context of practice is not 'fully blown' in Hasan's work.

4. In fact it is implicit – not analytically operationalised – in Hasan's analysis, where she is often pointing to dislocations (gaps) between the consistency of mothers' self-representations and (the analyst's knowledge of) their engagement with a range of other social practices that points to alternative representations.

Bibliography

Althusser, L. (1969), *For Marx*, London: Allen & Unwin.

Althusser, L. (1971), Ideology and ideological state apparatuses. In *Lenin and Philosophy and other Essays*, London: New Left Books.

Althusser, L. and E. Balibar (1970), *Reading 'Capital'*, London: New Left Books.

Arendt, H. (1958), *The Human Condition*, Chicago: The University of Chicago Press.

Atkinson, P. (1955), From structuralism to discourse: Bernstein's structuralism. In A. R. Sadovnik (ed.), *Knowledge and Pedagogy. The Sociology of Basil Bernstein*, Norwood NJ: Ablex Publishing Corporation.

Austin, J. L. (1962), *How to Do Things with Words*, Oxford: OUP.

Bakhtin, M. (1968), *Rabelais and his World*, Cambridge MA: MIT Press.

Bakhtin, M. (1981), *The Dialogic Imagination: Four essays by M. M. Bakhtin*, trans. H. Holoquist (ed.), C. Emerson and M. Holoquist, Austin: Texas University Press.

Bakhtin, M. (1984), *Problems of Dostoevsky's Poetics*, trans. C. Emerson, Manchester: Manchester University Press.

Bakhtin, M. (1986), *Speech Genres and Other Late Essays*, Austin: Texas University Press.

Barát, E. (1998), Women's identities: a tension between discourses and experience. Paper delivered at conference on CDA, Brasilia, May 1998

Barát, E. and N. Fairclough (1997), Globilization of TV news in Hungary. Working paper.

Barrett, M. (1991), *The Politics of Truth*, Cambridge: Polity Press.

Baudrillard, J. (1972), *Pour une critique de l'économie politique du signe*, Paris: Gallimard.

Baudrillard, J. (1983), *Simulations*, trans. P. Foss, P. Patton and P. Beitchman, New York: Semiotext(e).

Baudrillard, J. (1988), *Selected Writings*, M. Poster (ed.), Cambridge: Polity Press.

Baudrillard, J. (1993), *Symbolic Exchange and Death*, London: Sage.

Bauman, Z. (1987), *Legislators and Interpreters*, Cambridge: Polity Press.

Beck, U. (1994), The reinvention of politics: towards a theory of reflexive modernization. In Beck et al. 1994.

Beck, U., A. Giddens and S. Lash (1994), *Reflexive Modernization. Politics, Tradition and Aesthetics in the Modern Social Order*, Cambridge: Polity Press.

Bell, D. (1978), *The Cultural Contradictions of Capitalism*, New York: Free Press.

Benhabib, S. (1990), Epistemologies of postmodernism: a rejoinder to Jean-François Lyotard. In L. Nicholson (ed.), *Feminism/Postmodernism*, London: Routledge.

Benhabib, S. (1992), *Situating the Self: Gender, Community and Postmodernism in Contemporary Ethics*, Cambridge: Polity Press.

Benhabib, S. (ed.) (1996), *Democracy and Difference*, Princeton: Princeton University Press.

Benhabib, S. and F. Dallmayr (eds) (1990), *The Communicative Ethics Controversy*, Cambridge MA: MIT Press.

Benjamin, A. (ed.) (1992), *Judging Lyotard*, London: Routledge.

Bernstein, B. (1971), *Class Codes and Control Vol. 1: Theoretical Studies Towards a Sociology of Language*, London: Routledge.

Bernstein, B. (1981), Codes, modalities and the process of cultural reproduction: a model, *Language & Society* 10 (also in Bernstein 1990).

Bernstein, B. (1990), *The Structuring of Pedagogic Discourse: Class Codes & Control*, vol. IV, London: Routledge.

Bernstein, B. (1996), *Pedagogy, Symbolic Control and Identity*, London: Taylor & Francis

Bernstein, B. (1997), Class and pedagogies: visible and invisible. In A. Halsey, J. Floud and C. Arnold Anderson (eds), *Education, Economy, Society*, Oxford: Oxford University Press.

Bernstein, B. (1998), B. Bernstein, synenteuxi me ton Iosif Solomon. Pegagogiki, tautotites, synora; milontas gia mia theoria symvolikou elenhou (B. Bernstein interview with Joseph Solomon. Pedagogy, identities, boundaries; talking about a theory of symbolic control), *Synchrona Themata* 66.

Bernstein, R. (ed.) (1985), *Habermas and Modernity*, Oxford: Blackwell.

Best, G. and D. Kellner (1991), *Postmodern Theory. Critical Interrogations*, London: Macmillan.

Bhabha, H. (1994), *The Location of Culture*, London: Blackwell.

Bhaskar, R. (1979), *The Possibility of Naturalism*, Hemel Hempstead: Harvester Wheatsheaf.

Bhaskar, R. (1986), *Scientific Realism and Human Emancipation*, London: Verso.

Billig, M. (1991), *Ideology and Opinions*, London: Routledge.

Billig, M. (1992), *Talking of the Royal Family*, London: Sage.

Billig, M. (1994), Sod Baudrillard! or ideology critique in Disney world. In Simons and Billig, 1994.

Billig, M. (1995), *Banal Nationalism*, London: Sage.

Billig, M. (1996), *Arguing and Thinking: A Rhetorical Approach to Social Psychology*, Cambridge: Cambridge University Press.

Bordo, S. (1990), Feminism, postmodernism and gender-scepticism. In L. Nicholson (ed.), *Feminism/Postmodernism*, London: Routledge.

Bourdieu, P. (1977), *Outline of a Theory of Practice*, Cambridge: Cambridge University Press.

Bourdieu, P. (1984), *Distinction: A Social Critique of the Judgement of Taste*, London: Routledge.

Bourdieu, P. (1990), *In Other Words: Essays Toward a Reflexive Sociology*, Cambridge: Polity Press.

Bourdieu, P. (1991), *Language and Symbolic Power*, Cambridge: Polity Press.

Bourdieu, P. (1994), *The Field of Cultural Production. Essays on Art and Literature*, Cambridge: Polity Press.

Bourdieu, P. (1998a), *On Television*, New York: New Press.

Bourdieu, P. (1998b), A reasoned utopia and economic fatalism, *New Left Review* no. 227.

Bourdieu, P. and P. Collier (1988), *Homo Academicus*, Stanford, Stanford University Press.

Bourdieu, P., J.-C. Passeron and M. Saint-Martin (1994), *Academic Discourse. Linguistic Misunderstanding and Professorial Power*, Cambridge: Polity Press.

Bourdieu, P. and L. Wacquant (1992), *An Invitation to Reflexive Sociology*, Cambridge: Polity Press.

Bourne, J. (1992), Unpublished PhD thesis, University of Southampton.

Butler, J. (1990), *Gender Trouble*, London: Routledge.

Butler, J. (1997), *Excitable Speech*. London: Routledge.

Butler, J. (1998), Merely cultural? *New Left Review* no. 227.

Butler, J. and J. Scott (eds) (1992), *Feminists Theorize the Political*, London: Routledge.

Calhoun, C. (1992), *Habermas and the Public Sphere*, Cambridge MA: MIT Press.

Calhoun, C. (1995), *Critical Social Theory*, London: Blackwell.

Calhoun, C., E. LiPuma and M. Postone (eds) (1993), *Bourdieu. Critical Perspectives*, Cambridge: Polity Press.

Callinicos, A. (1985), Anthony Giddens: a contemporary critique, *Theory and Society* 14.

Cameron, D. (1995), *Verbal Hygiene*, London: Routledge.

Castoriades, K. (1987), *The Imaginary Institution of Society*, Cambridge: Polity Press.

Chomsky, N. (1957), *Syntactic Structures*, The Hague: Mouton.

Chomsky, N. (1965), *Aspects of the Theory of Syntax*, Cambridge MA: MIT Press.

Chouliaraki, L. (1995), *Regulation and Heteroglossia in One Institutional Context. The Case of a 'Progressivist' English Classroom*, Unpublished PhD thesis, University of Lancaster.

Chouliaraki, L. (1996), Regulative practices in a 'progressivist' classroom: 'good habits' as a 'disciplinary technology', *Language and Education*, Special Issue on the 'Discursive Construction of Educational Identities', S. Sarangi (ed.), vol. 10, nos 2 and 3.

Chouliaraki, L. (1998a), Regulation in 'progressivist' pedagogic discourse: individualized teacher–pupil talk, *Discourse & Society* 9.1.

Chouliaraki, L. (1998b), *Media Discourse and National Identity Among Greek Youth*, Unpublished research project. Institute of Danish Dialectology, University of Copenhagen.

Chouliaraki, L. (in press), Media discourse and national identity: death and myth in a news broadcast. In R. Wodak et al. (eds), *Challenges in a Changing World*, Vienna.

Chouliaraki, L. (2000), Political discourse in the news: democratizing responsibility or aestheticizing politics, *Discourse and Society* 12.3.

Chouliaraki, L. and Fairclough, N. (1999), A response to Hasan's 'The disempowerment game', *Linguistics and Education* 10.2.

Christie, F. and J. R. Martin (eds) (1997), *Genre and Institutions. Social Processes in the Workplace and School*, London: Cassell.

Cicourel, A. (1992), The interpretation of communicative contexts. The example of medical encounters. In A. Duranti and C. Goodwin (eds), *Rethinking Context*, Cambridge: Cambridge University Press.

Cicourel, A. (1993), Aspects of structural and processual theories of knowledge. In Calhoun et al. 1993.

Cilliers, P. (1998), *Complexity and Postmodernism*, London: Routledge.

Clark, R., N. Fairclough, R. Ivanic and M. Martin-Jones (1990), Critical language awareness part 1: a critical review of three current approaches, *Language and Education* 4.4.

Clark, R., N. Fairclough, R. Ivanic and M. Martin-Jones (1991), Critical language awareness part 2: towards critical alternatives, *Language and Education* 5.1.

Clark, R. and Ivanic, R. (1997), *The Politics of Writing*, London: Routledge.

Clifford, J. (1986), Introduction: partial truths. In J. Clifford and G. Marcus (eds), *Writing Culture: the Poetics and Politics of Ethnography*, Berkeley: University of California Press.

Cohen, I. J. (1989), *Structuration Theory. Anthony Giddens and the Constitution of Social Life*, New York: Macmillan.

Collier, A. (1994), *Critical Realism*, London: Verso.

Collier, A. (1998), Language, practice and realism. In Parker 1998.

Collins, J. (1993), Determination and contradiction: an appreciation and critique of the work of Pierre Bourdieu on language and education. In C. Calhoun et al. 1993.

Coombe, R. (1998), *The Cultural Life of Intellectual Properties*. Durham and London: Duke University Press.

Corsaro, W. A. (1994), Discussion of R. Hasan's 'Situation and the definition of genres'. In *What's Going on Here? Complementary Studies of Professional Talk* vol. 2, in *Advances in Discourse Processes* vol. XLIII, Norwood NJ: Ablex Publishing Corporation.

Davies, M. and I. Ravelli (eds) (1992), *Advances in Systemic Linguistics*, London: Pinter

de Beaugrande, R. (1998), Theory and practice in applied linguistics: disconnection, conflict or dialectic? *Applied Linguistics* 18.3.

Derrida, J. (1977), Signature, event context, *Glyph* I 172–97.

Derrida, J. (1978), Structure sign and play in the discourse of the human sciences. In *Writing and Difference*, Chicago: University of Chicago Press.

de Saussure, F. (1974), *Course in General Linguistics*, trans. W. Baskin, London: Fontana.

di Stefano, Ch. (1990), Dilemmas of difference: feminism, modernity and postmodernism. In L. Nicholson (ed.), *Feminism/Postmodernism*, London: Routledge.

Drew, P. and J. Heritage (eds) (1994), *Talk at Work. Interaction in Institutional Settings*, Cambridge: Cambridge University Press.

Dreyfus, H. and P. Rabinow (1993), Can there be a science of existential structure and social meaning? In C. Calhoun et al. 1993.

Dubiel, H. (1985), *Theory and Politics. Studies in the Development of Critical Theory*, Cambridge MA: MIT Press.

Fairclough, N. (1988), Discourse representation in media discourse, *Sociolinguistics* 17 129–39.

Fairclough, N. (1989), *Language and Power*, London: Longman.

Fairclough, N. (1992a), *Discourse and Social Change*, Cambridge: Polity Press.

Fairclough, N. (ed.) (1992b), *Critical Language Awareness*, London: Longman.

Fairclough, N. (1992c), Discourse and text: linguistic and intertexual analysis within discourse analysis, *Discourse & Society* 3 193–217.

Fairclough, N. (1994), Conversationalisation of public discourse and the authority of the consumer. In R. Keat, N. Whiteley and N. Abercrombie (eds), *The Authority of the Consumer*, London: Routledge.

Fairclough, N. (1995a), *Media Discourse*, London: Edward Arnold.

Fairclough, N. (1995b), *Critical Discourse Analysis. The Critical Study of Language*, London: Longman.

Fairclough, N. (1995c), Critical discourse analysis and the marketization of public discourse: the universities. In Fairclough 1995b.

Fairclough, N. (1995d), Ideology and identity in political television. In Fairclough 1995b.

Fairclough, N. (1996a), Technologisation of discourse. In R. Caldas-Coulthard and M. Coulthard (eds), *Texts and Practices: Readings in Critical Discourse Analysis*, London: Routledge.

Fairclough, N. (1996b), A reply to Henry Widdowson, *Language & Literature* 5 49–56.

Fairclough, N. (1997), Discourse across disciplines: discourse analysis in researching social change, *AILA Review* 12 3–17.

Fairclough, N. (forthcoming a), Global capitalism and critical awareness of language. To appear in a special edition of *Language Awareness* on critical language awareness, R. Clark and R. Ivanic (eds).

Fairclough, N. (forthcoming b), Democracy and the public sphere in critical research on discourse. In R. Wodak et al. (eds), *Challenges in a Changing World*, Vienna.

Fairclough, N. (forthcoming c), The discourse of social exclusion. To appear in M. Reisigl et al. (eds), Vienna.

Fairclough, N. and R. Wodak (1997), Critical discourse analysis. In T. van Dijk (ed.), *Discourse as Social Interaction*, London: Sage.

Farrell, L. (1997), Presentation at 'Texts and Practices Network' conference, London, November 1997.

Featherstone, M. (1991), *Consumer Culture and Postmodernism*, London, Sage.

Featherstone, M. (1995), *Undoing Culture. Globalization, Postmodernism and Identity*, London: Sage.

Firth, J. R. (1957), *Papers on Linguistics, 1934–1945*, Oxford: Oxford University Press.

Flax, J. (1990), Postmodernism and gender relations in feminist theory. In L. Nicholson (ed.), *Feminism/Postmodernism*, London: Routledge.

Forgacs, D. (1988), *A Gramsci Reader*, London: Lawrence & Wishart.

Foucault, M. (1971), *L'ordre du discours*, Paris: Gallimard.

Foucault, M. (1972), *The Order of Things*, London: Tavistock.

Foucault, M. (1977), *Discipline & Punish*, London, Allen Lane.

Foucault, M. (1981), *The History of Sexuality vol. 1, An Introduction*, Harmondsworth: Penguin.

Fowler, B. (1997), *Pierre Bourdieu and Cultural Theory. Critical Investigations*, London: Sage.

Fowler, R., B. Hodge, G. Kress and T. Trew (1979), *Language and Control*, London: Routledge.

Fowler, R. (1996), On critical linguistics. In R. Caldas-Coulthard and M. Coulthard (eds), *Texts and Practices: Readings in CDA*, London: Routledge.

Fraser, N. (1989), *Unruly Practices: Power, Discourse and Gender in Contemporary Social Theory*, Minneapolis: University of Minnesota Press.

Fraser, N. (1992), Rethinking the public sphere: a contribution to the critique of actually existing democracy. In C. Calhoun (ed.), *Habermas and the Public Sphere*, Cambridge MA: MIT Press.

Fraser, N. (1997), *Justice Interruptus: Critical Reflections on the 'Postsocialist' Condition*, New York: Routledge.

Fraser, N. and L. Nicholson (1990), Social criticism without philosophy: an encounter between feminism and postmodernism. In L. Nicholson (ed.), *Feminism/Postmodernism*, London: Routledge.

Garfinkel, H. (1967), *Studies in Ethnomethodology*, Englewood Cliffs NJ: Prentice Hall.

Gee, J. P., G. Hull and C. Lankshear (1996), *The New Work Order. Behind the Language of the New Capitalism*, Sydney: Allen and Unwin.

Geras, N. (1987), Post-Marxism? *New Left Review* no. 163, May–June 1987.

Gibson, R. (1984), *Structuralism and Education*, London: Methuen.

Giddens, A. (1965), *A Contemporary Critique of Historical Materialism*, 2nd edn, London: Macmillan.

Giddens, A. (1984), *The Constitution of Society. Outline of the Theory of Structuration*, Cambridge: Polity Press.

Giddens, A. (1985), *The Nation-state and Violence*, Cambridge: Polity Press.

Giddens, A. (1990), *The Consequences of Modernity*, Cambridge, Polity Press.

Giddens, A. (1991), *Modernity and Self-Identity*, Cambridge, Polity Press.

Giddens, A. (1992), *The Transformation of Intimacy*, Cambridge, Polity Press.

Giddens, A. (1993), *New Rules of Sociological Method: A Positive Critique of Interpretative Sociologies*, Cambridge: Polity Press.

Giddens, A. (1994a), *Beyond Left and Right*, Cambridge, Polity Press.

Giddens, A. (1994b), Living in a post-traditional society. In Beck et al. 1994.

Giglioli, P. (ed.) (1972), *Language and Social Context*, Harmondsworth, Penguin.

Giroux, H. (1997), *Pedagogy and the Politics of Hope*, Boulder CO: Westview Press.

Gouveia, C. (1997), Review of R. Caldas-Coulthard and M. Coulthard 1955 in *Discourse & Society* 8.1

Gramsci, A. (1971), *Selections from the Prison Notebooks*, London: Lawrence & Wishart.

Habermas, J. (1972), *Knowledge and Human Interest*, London: Heinemann.

Habermas, J. (1976), *Zur Rekonstruktion des Historischen Materialismus*, Frankfurt, Suhrkamp.

Habermas, J. (1979), *Communication and the Evolution of Society*, Boston: Beacon Press.

Habermas, J. (1984), *The Theory of Communicative Action vol. 1, Reason and the Rationalization of Society*, London: Heinemann.

Habermas, J. (1987a), *The Theory of Communicative Action vol. 2, Lifeworld and System: A Critique of Functionalist Reason*, London: Heinemann.

Habermas, J. (1987b), *The Philosophical Discourse of Modernity*, Cambridge MA: MIT Press.

Habermas, J. (1988), *On the Logic of Social Sciences*, London: Heinemann.

Habermas, J. (1989), *The Structural Transformation of the Public Sphere*, Cambridge: Polity Press.

Habermas, J. (1990), *Moral Consciousness and Communicative Action*, Cambridge: Polity Press.

Hall, S. (1996a), Signification, representation, ideology: Althusser and the Post-Structuralist debates. In J. Curran, D. Morley and V. Walkerdine (eds), *Cultural Studies and Communications*, London: Edward Arnold.

Hall, S. (1996b), Who needs identity? In Hall and du Gay 1996.

Hall, S. and du Gay, P. (eds) (1996), *Questions of Cultural Identity*, London: Sage.

Halliday, M. (1961), Categories of the theory of grammar, *Word* 17.

Halliday, M. A. K. (1978), *Language as Social Semiotic. The Social Interpretation of Language and Meaning*, London: Edward Arnold.

Halliday, M. (1992), How do you mean? In Davies and Ravelli 1992.

Halliday, M. (1993), *Language in a Changing World. Occasional Papers 13*, Sydney: Applied Linguistics Association of Australia.

Halliday, M. A. K. (1994a), *Introduction to Functional Grammar*, 2nd edn, London: Edward Arnold.

Halliday, M. A. K. (1994b), So you say 'pass' … thank you three muchly. In *What's Going on Here? Complementary Studies of Professional Talk* vol. 2. In *Advances in Discourse Processes* vol. XLIII, Norwood NJ: Ablex Publishing Corporation.

Halliday, M. A. K. (1995), On language in relation to the evolution of human consciousness. In *The Relation Between Language and Mind*, Nobel Symposium 1992 Proceedings, Stockholm.

Halliday, M. and R. Hasan (1989), *Language, Context and Text. Aspects of Language in a Social Semiotic Perspective*, Oxford: OUP.

Hammersley, M. (1996), On the foundations of critical discourse analysis, *Occasional Papers 42*, Centre for Language and Education, University of Southampton.

Haraway, D. (1990), A manifesto for cyborgs: science, technology, and socialist feminism in the 1980s. In L. Nicholson (ed.), *Feminism/Postmodernism*, London: Routledge.

Haraway, D. (1988), 'Situated Knowledge', *Feminist Studies* 14.

Harding, S. (1990), Feminism, science and the anti-enlightenment critiques. In L. Nicholson (ed.), *Feminism/Postmodernism*, London: Routledge.

Harker, R. and S. A. May (1993), Code and habitus: comparing the accounts of Bernstein and Bourdieu, *British Journal of Sociology of Education* 14.2, pp. 164–78.

Hartsock, N. (1990), Foucault on power: a theory for women? In L. Nicholson (ed.), *Feminism/Postmodernism*, London: Routledge.

Harvey, D. (1989), *The Condition of Postmodernity: An Enquiry into the Origins of Cultural Change*, Oxford: Blackwell.

Harvey, D. (1996), *Justice, Nature and the Geography of Difference*, London: Blackwell.

Hasan, R. (1973), Code register and social dialect. In B. Bernstein (ed.), *Class Codes and Control* vol. 2, London: Routledge.

Hasan, R. (1986), The ontogenesis of ideology: an interpretation of mother–child talk. In T. Threadgold, E. Grosz, G. Kress and M. A. K. Halliday (eds), *Semiotics, Ideology, Language*, Sydney: Sydney Association for Studies in Society and Culture.

Hasan, R. (1987), The grammarian's dream: lexis as most delicate grammar. In M. Halliday and R. Fawcett (eds), *New Developments in Systemic Linguistics* vol. 1, London: Pinter.

Hasan, R. (1992a), Rationality in everyday talk: from process to system. In J. Svartvik (ed.), *Directions in Corpus Linguistics*, Proceedings of the Nobel Symposium 92, Berlin, Mouton de Gruyter.

Hasan, R. (1992b), Meaning in sociolinguistic theory. In K. Bolton and H. Kwok (eds), *Sociolinguistics Today: International Perspectives*, London: Routledge.

Hasan, R. (1993), Speech genre, semiotic mediation and the development of higher mental functions, *Language Sciences* 14.4.

Hasan, R. (1994), Situation and the definition of genres. In *What's Going on Here? Complementary Studies of Professional Talk* vol. 2. In *Advances in Discourse Processes* vol. XLIII, Norwood NJ: Ablex Publishing Corporation.

Hasan, R. (1995), The conception of context in text. In P. Fries and M. Gregory (eds),

Discourse in Society: Systemic Functional Perspectives, Norwood NJ: Ablex Publishing Corporation.

Hasan, R. (1996), *Ways of Saying: Ways of Meaning. Selected Papers,* London: Cassell.

Hasan, R. (in press a), Society, language and the mind: the meta-dialogism of Basil Bernstein's theory. In F. Christie (ed.), *Pedagogy and the Shaping of Consciousness: Linguistic and Social Processes,* London: Cassell.

Hasan, R. (in press b), The disempowerment game: a critique of Bourdieu's view of language, *Linguistics and Education.*

Hasan, R. and C. Cloran (1990), A sociolinguistic interpretation of everyday talk between mothers and children. In M. Halliday, J. Gibbons and H. Nicholas (eds), *Learning, Keeping and Using Language* vol. 1, Selected Papers of the 8th World Congress of Applied Linguists, Amsterdam: Benjamins.

Held, D. (1980), *Introduction to Critical Theory. From Horkheimer to Habermas,* London: Hutchinson.

Held D. and J. B. Thomson (eds) (1990), *Social Theory of Modern Societies. Anthony Giddens and his Critics,* Cambridge: Cambridge University Press.

Hennessy, R. (1993), *Materialist Feminism and the Politics of Discourse,* London: Routledge.

Heritage, J. (1984), *Garfinkel and Ethnomethodology,* Cambridge: Polity Press.

Hodge, R. and G. Kress (1988), *Social Semiotics,* Cambridge: Polity Press.

Hodge, R. and G. Kress (1993), *Language as Ideology,* 2nd edn, London: Routledge.

Iedema, R. (1997), The language of administration: organizing human activity in formal institutions. In F. Christie and J. R. Martin (eds), *Genre and Institutions. Social Processes in the Workplace and School,* London: Cassell.

Iedema, R. (1998), Institutional responsibility and hidden meanings, *Discourse and Society* 9.4.

Iedema, R. and R. Wodak (1999), Introduction: organisational discourses and practices, *Discourse and Society* 10.1.

Ivanic, R. (1990), Critical language awareness in practice. In R. Carter (ed.), *Knowledge about Language: the LINC Reader,* London: Hodder & Stoughton.

Jameson, F. (1984), Foreword to Lyotard 1984.

Jameson, F. (1988), Postmodernism and consumer society. In A. E. Kaplan (ed.), *Postmodernism and its Discontents: Theories, Practices,* London: Verso.

Jameson, F. (1991), *Postmodernism, or, The Cultural Logic of Late Capitalism,* London: Verso.

Jenkins, R. (1996), *Social Identity,* London: Routledge.

Jørgensen, W. and L. Phillips (1998). *Diskursanalyse som Teori og Metode,* Roskilde: Samfunds Litteratur.

Kellner, D. (1988), Postmodernism as social theory: some challenges and problems in theory, *Culture and Society* 5.

Kellner, D. (1989), *Critical Theory, Marxism, Modernity,* Baltimore: John Hopkins University Press.

King, R. (1981), Bernstein's sociology of the school. A further testing, *British Journal of Sociology* 32, pp. 259–65.

Kress, G. (1985), *Linguistic Processes in Sociocultural Practice,* Oxford: OUP.

Kress, G. (1998), *A satellite view of language. Some lessons of a science classroom,* Institute of Education Working Paper, United Kingdom.

Kress, G. and T. Threadgold (1988), Towards a social theory of genre, *Southern Review* 21.

Kress, G. and T. van Leeuwen (1996), *Reading Images,* London: Routledge.

Kristeva, J. (1986), *The Kristeva Reader,* T. Moi (ed.), Oxford: Blackwell.

Labov, W. (1972), The logic of non-standard English. In Giglioli 1972.

Laclau, E. (1983), The impossibility of society, *Canadian Journal of Political and Social Theory* 7.

Laclau, E. (1996), *Emancipation(s),* London: Verso.

Laclau, E. and Mouffe, C. (1985), *Hegemony and Socialist Strategy*, London: Verso.

Larrain, J. (1979), *The Concept of Ideology*, London: Hutchinson.

Larrain, J. (1983), *Marxism and Ideology*, London: Macmillan.

Larrain, J. (1994), *Ideology and Cultural Identity. Modernity and the Third World Presence*, Cambridge: Polity Press.

Lash, S. (1988), Discourse or figure? Postmodernism as a regime of signification theory, *Culture & Society* 5.

Lash, S. (1993), Cultural Economy and Social Change. In Calhoun et al. 1993.

Lash, S. (1994), Reflexivity and its doubles: structures, aesthetics, community. In Beck et al. 1994.

Lash, S. and J. Urry (1988), *The End of Organized Capitalism*. London: Sage.

Lash, S. and J. Urry (1994), *Economics of Signs and Spaces*, London: Sage.

Lemke, J. (1984), *Semiotics and Education*, Toronto, Victoria University.

Lemke, J. (1995), *Textual Politics. Discourse and Social Dynamics*, London: Taylor & Francis.

Lemke, J. (1998), Multiplying meaning: Visual and verbal semiotics in scientific text. In Martin and Veel 1998.

Levi-Strauss, C. (1993), *Structural Anthropology*, New York: Basic Books.

LiPuma, E. (1993), Culture and the concept of culture in a theory of practice. In Calhoun et al. 1993.

Luria, A. R. (1981), *Language and Cognition*, J. V. Wertsch (ed.), New York: Wiley Intersciences.

Lury, C. (1996), *Consumer Culture*, Cambridge: Polity Press.

Lyotard, F. (1971), *Discours, figure*, Paris: Klicksieck.

Lyotard, F. (1984), *The Postmodern Condition: A Report on Knowledge*, Manchester: Manchester University Press.

Lyotard, F. (1990), *The Differend*, Manchester: Manchester University Press.

Mandel, E. (1972), *Late Capitalism*, London: Verso.

Marcuse, H. (1964), *One Dimensional Man*, London: Routledge and Kegan Paul.

Martin, J. (1985), Process and text: two aspects of human semiosis. In J. Bendon and W. Greaves (eds), *Systemic Perspectives on Discourse* vol. 1 Norwood NJ: Ablex Publishing Corporation.

Martin, J. (1992), *English Text: System and Structure*, Amsterdam: Benjamins.

Martin, J. (1997), Analysing genre: functional parameters. In Christie and Martin 1997.

Martin, J. & Veel, R. (eds) (1998), *Reading Science: Critical and Functional Perspectives on the Discourse of Science*, London: Routledge.

Matthiessen, C. M. I. M. (1992), Interpreting the textual metafunction. In Davies and Ravelli 1992.

Meehan, J. (1995), *Feminists Read Habermas*, London: Routledge.

Melucci, A. (1996), *Challenging Codes: Collective Action in the Information Age*, Cambridge: CUP.

Melucci, A., J. Keane and P. Mier (eds) (1992), *Nomads of the Present: Social Movements and Individual Needs in Contemporary Societies*, Philadelphia: Temple University Press.

Morrow, R. with D. Brown (1994), *Critical Theory and Methodolgy*, London: Sage.

Mouffe, C. (1992), Feminism, citizenship and radical democratic politics. In Butler and Scott 1992.

Mouzelis, N. (1990), *Post-Marxist Alternatives. The Construction of Social Orders*, London: Macmillan.

Mouzelis, N. (1998), On the privatization of Greek universities, *To Vima Tis Kyriakis*, 28 June 1998.

National Committee of Inquiry into Higher Education, The (1997), *Higher Education in the Learning Society*, London: The Stationery Office.

Norris, C. (1994), *Truth and the Ethics of Criticism*, Manchester: Manchester Unviersity Press.

Olin-Wright, K. (1990), Models of historical trajectory. In Held and Thompson 1990.

Outhwaite, W. (1987), *New Philosophies of Social Science: Realism, Hermeneutics and Critical Theory*, London: Macmillan.

Outhwaite, W. (1994), *Habermas*, Cambridge: Polity Press.

Parker, I. (1992), (ed.), *Discourse Dynamics. Critical Analysis for Social and Individual Psychology*, London: Routledge.

Parker, I. (1988), *Social Constructivism, Discourse and Realism*, London: Sage.

Pennycook, A. (1994), Incommensurable discourses, *Applied Linguistics* 15.2 115–38.

Peters, T. (1994), *The Tom Peters Seminar. Crazy Times Call for Crazy Organizations*, New York: Vintage Books.

Phillips, L. (1999), Mediated publicness in Danish television, *Media Culture and Society* 15.

Phillipson, R. (1992), *Linguistic Imperialism*, Oxford: Oxford University Press.

Poster, M. (1990), *The Mode of Information. Postructuralism and Social Context*, Cambridge: Polity Press.

Potter, J. (1996), *Representing Reality: Discourse, Rhetoric and Social Construction*, London: Sage.

Poulantzas, N. (1978), *State, Power, Socialism*, London: New Left Books.

Pujolar, J. (1997), *De Que vas Tio? Genere I Llengua en la Cultura Juvenil*, Barcelona: Editorial Empuries.

Readings, B. (1992), Pagans, perverts or primitives? Experimental justice in the empire of capital. In Benjamin 1992.

Ricoeur, P. (1977), *Interpretation Theory: Discourse and Surplus of Meaning*, Austin TX: Christian University Press.

Ricoeur, P. (1986), *Lectures on Ideology and Utopia*, New York: Columbia University Press.

Rorty, R. (1985), Habermas and Lyotard on postmodernity. In Bernstein 1985.

Rorty, R. (1989), *Contingency, Irony and Solidarity*, Cambridge: Cambridge University Press.

Said, E. (1978), *Orientalism*, New York: Vintage Press.

Sarangi, S. and S. Slembrouck (1996), *Language, Bureaucracy and Social Control*, London: Longman.

Sayer, A. (1997), Critical realism and the limits to critical social science, *Theory of Social Behaviour* 27.4.

Schegloff, E. (1997), Whose text? Whose Context? *Discourse and Society* 8.2

Scollon, R. (1998), *Mediated Discourse as Social Interaction. A Study of News Discourse*, London: Longman.

Scollon, R. and S. Scollon (1981), *Narrative, Literacy and Face in Interethnic Communication*, Norwood NJ: Ablex Publishing Corporation.

Scollon, R. and S. Scollon (1995), Somatic communication: How useful is orality for the characterization of speech events and cultures? In U. M. Quasthoff (ed.), *Aspects of Oral Communication*, Berlin: de Gruyter.

Searle, J. (1969), *Speech Acts*, Cambridge: Cambridge University Press.

Shotter, J. (1993), *Conversational Realities*, London: Sage.

Simons, H. and M. Billig (eds) (1994), *After Postmodernism. Reconstructing Ideology Critique*, London: Sage.

Skutnab-Kangas, T. (1990), *Language, Literacy and Minorities*, London: The Minority Rights Group.

Smith, D. (1990), *Texts, Facts and Femininity. Exploring Relations of Ruling*, London: Routledge.

Stubbs, M. (1993), *Language, Schools and Classrooms*, London: Methuen.

Stubbs, M. (1996), *Text and Corpus Analysis*, Oxford: Blackwell.

Stubbs, M. (1997), Whorf's Children: Critical Comments on CDA. In A. Ryan and A. Wray (eds), *Evolving Models of Language*, Papers from the 1996 Annual Meeting of BAAL, Milton Keynes: Multilingual Matters.

Stubbs, M. and Delamont, S. (eds) (1976), *Explorations in Classroom Observation*, London: Wiley.

Swales, I. and Rogers, D. (1998), Discourse and the projection of corporate culture: the mission statement, *Discourse & Society* 6.2.

Taylor, C. (1986), Foucault on freedom and truth. In D. C. Hoy (ed.), *Foucault: a Critical Reader*, Oxford: Blackwell.

Taylor, C. (1989), *Sources of the Self*, Cambridge MA: Harvard University Press.

Thibault, P. (1989), Semantic variation, social heteroglossia, intertextuality: thematic and axiological meaning in spoken discourse, *Critical Studies* 1.2.

Thibault, P. (1991), *Social Semiotics as Praxis*, Minneapolis: University of Minessota Press.

Thompson, J. (1984), *Studies in the Theory of Ideology*, Cambridge: Polity Press.

Thompson, J. (1960), The theory of structuration. In Held and Thompson 1990.

Thompson, J. (1995), *The Media and Modernity*, Cambridge: Polity Press.

Threadgold, T. (1989), Talking about genre: ideologies and incompatible discourses. *Journal of Cultural Studies* 3.1.

Threadgold, T., E. Grosz, G. Kress and M. Halliday (eds), *Semiotics, Ideology, Language*, Sydney: Sydney Association for Studies of Society and Culture.

Thrift, N. (1996), *Spatial Formations*, London: Sage.

Toolan, M. (1997), What is critical discourse analysis and why are people saying such terrible things about it? *Language and Literature* 6.

Torfing, J. (1998), *New Theories of Discourse: Laclau and Mouffe and Zizek*, London: Blackwell.

Touraine, A. (1997), *What is Democracy?* Boulder CO: Westview Press.

van Dijk, T. (1987), *Communicating Racism*, London: Sage.

van Dijk, T. (1991), *Racism and the Press*, London: Routledge.

van Dijk, T. (1993), *Discourse and Elite Racism*, London: Sage.

van Dijk, T. (1995a), Esoteric Discourse Analysis (Editorial), *Discourse and Society* 5.1.

van Dijk, T. (1995b), A Rejoinder (Esoteric Discourse Analysis), *Discourse and Society* 5.4.

van Dijk, T. (1998), Discourse and Ideology (Editorial), *Discourse and Society* 9.3.

van Leeuwen, T. (1993), Genre and field in critical discourse analysis: a synopsis, *Discourse and Society* 4.2.

Volosinov, V. (1973), *Marxism and the Philosophy of Language*, Cambridge MA: Harvard University Press.

Vygotsky, L. S. (1962), *Thought and Language*, Cambridge MA: MIT Press.

Watts, R. (1992), *Family Discourse*, Amsterdam: Mouton de Gruyter.

Wertsch, J. (1991), *Voices of The Mind: A Sociocultural Approach to Mediated Action*, London: Harvester Wheatsheaf.

Wetherell, M. (1998), Positioning and interpretative repertoires: CA and post-structuralism in dialogue, *Discourse and Society* 9.3.

Whorf, B. L. (1956), *Language, Thought and Reality: Selected Writings of Benjamin Lee Whorf*, J. B. Carroll (ed.), Cambridge MA: MIT Press.

Widdowson, H. (1995), Discourse analysis. A critical view. In *Language and Literature* 4.3.

Widdowson, H. (1996), Discourse and interpretation. Refutations and conjectures (Reply to Fairclough). In *Language and Literature* 5.1.

Williams, R. (1977), *Marxism and Literature*, Oxford: Oxford University Press.

Wittgenstein, L. (1972), *Philosophical Investigations*, Oxford: Blackwell.

Wodak, R. (1996), *Disorders of Discourse*, London: Longman.

Wodak, R., P. Nowak and J. Pelikan (1990), *'Wir sind alle unschuldige Täter': Diskurshistorische Studien zum Nachkriegsantisemitismus*, Frankfurt: Suhrkamp.

Zimmerman, D. and D. Boden (eds) (1991), *Talk and Social Structure*, Cambridge: Polity Press.

Zizec, S. (1994), *Mapping Ideology*, London: Verso.

Index